Literacy Tutoring in the Community

Literacy Tutoring in the Community presents best practices in literacy tutoring through a guidebook of high-impact and systematic instruction toward successful tutoring. With a grounding in pedagogical philosophies, this book includes structured approaches to tutoring aligned to the five pillars set forth by the National Reading Panel, and it focuses on a variety of proven tutoring models (e.g., supplemental instruction, cross-age tutoring, parents as tutors).

This book emphasizes the importance of leveraging literature to enrich tutoring practices, while also making connections between tutoring and schoolwork from the elementary level up to college entry. Through an intentional culturally responsive lens, the authors build on funds of knowledge and use a language experience approach along with culturally and linguistically diverse texts to enhance instruction for diverse learners. The book ends with a series of case studies highlighting specific literacy challenges, as well as tools for tutors, such as a tutoring session lesson plan, literacy lesson log, reading skills checklist, tutor report form, and more.

This book will be a beneficial resource to tutors working with learners across all ages and school levels. It can serve as a desk reference for literacy-focused tutoring programs in libraries, community centers, colleges, service-learning classes, philanthropic organizations, and more.

Laurie A. Henry is Dean of the Seidel School of Education and Professor of Literacy Studies at Salisbury University.

Norman A. Stahl is Professor Emeritus of Literacy Education at Northern Illinois University.

Literacy Tutoring in the Community

A Guidebook for High Impact Practices

EDITED BY LAURIE A. HENRY AND NORMAN A. STAHL

Routledge
Taylor & Francis Group

NEW YORK AND LONDON

Designed cover image: © Getty Images

First published 2026
by Routledge
605 Third Avenue, New York, NY 10158

and by Routledge
4 Park Square, Milton Park, Abingdon, Oxon, OX14 4RN

Routledge is an imprint of the Taylor & Francis Group, an informa business

© 2026 selection and editorial matter, Laurie A. Henry and Norman A. Stahl; individual chapters, the contributors.

The right of Laurie A. Henry and Norman A. Stahl to be identified as the authors of the editorial material, and of the authors for their individual chapters, has been asserted in accordance with sections 77 and 78 of the Copyright, Designs and Patents Act 1988.

All rights reserved. No part of this book may be reprinted or reproduced or utilized in any form or by any electronic, mechanical, or other means, now known or hereafter invented, including photocopying and recording, or in any information storage or retrieval system, without permission in writing from the publishers.

For Product Safety Concerns and Information please contact our EU representative GPSR@taylorandfrancis.com. Taylor & Francis Verlag GmbH, Kaufingerstraße 24, 80331 München, Germany.

Trademark notice: Product or corporate names may be trademarks or registered trademarks and are used only for identification and explanation without intent to infringe.

ISBN: 978-1-032-68857-2 (hbk)
ISBN: 978-1-032-68637-0 (pbk)
ISBN: 978-1-032-68858-9 (ebk)

DOI: 10.4324/9781032688589

Typeset in Bembo and Gill Sans
by codeMantra

Contents

List of Figures	viii
List of Tables	ix
List of Contributors	x
Acknowledgments	xii
Introduction	xiv

Chapters

1 Philosophical Considerations That Frame Successful Tutoring Programs 1
Laurie A. Henry and Norman A. Stahl

2 The Tutorial Program 17
Laurie A. Henry and Norman A. Stahl

3 Foundations of Literacy 35
Laurie A. Henry and Norman A. Stahl

4 Naturalistic Authoring Approaches 55
Laurie A. Henry, Norman A. Stahl, and James R. King

5 Culturally Intentional Tutoring with Multilingual Learners 74
Laurie A. Henry and Norman A. Stahl

6 Assessing Literacy Interests, Attitudes, and Competencies 88
Laurie A. Henry and Norman A. Stahl

7 Connecting Tutoring to Schoolwork and High-Stakes Assessments 102
James R. King, with Carson Binder and Denise Perez Binder

Case Studies

Case A. Home and Community Literacy 116
Norman A. Stahl

Case B. The Story of Jake: Who Was "Never Going to Become a Reader" 124
MaryEllen Vogt

Case C. Connecting through Reading: Tutoring Incarcerated Youth 136
Olivia M. Gore and Mary E. Styslinger

Case D. Tutoring Diverse Student Populations 149
Katherine Marsh and Elizabeth Dinelli

Case E. Shifting Ideologies: Teacher as Learner 157
Gemma Cooper-Novack

Case F. Upward and Onward: Supporting First-Generation College-Bound Students 163
Annette Teasdell and Erin Harden Lewis

Appendices 171

A. Brain Break Resources 173

B. Reading Interest Inventory 175

C. K-W-L Chart 177

D. Alliteration Book List 178

E. Tutors' Friends: Strategies, Learning Games, and Instructional Books 179

F.	Tutee Writing Evaluation Checklist	183
G.	The Poor Scholar's Soliloquy	185
H.	San Diego Quick Assessment Record Form	188
I.	Reading Attitude Scale	190
J.	Teacher Referral Form	193
K.	Parent Permission Form	195
L.	Tutor Application	196
M.	Tutor Interview Guide	199
N.	Tutee Attendance Record	202
O.	Tutor Self-Evaluation	204
P.	Annual Tutor Evaluation	206
Q.	Tutor Training Course Outline	208
R.	Tutoring Manual and Training Topics	210
S.	Program Administration Resources	211

References

1. References for Tutoring Program Administrators and Coordinators	212
2. References	216
Tutoring References Across the Years	228

Author Index   231
Subject Index   234

List of Figures

1.1	Key Elements of High-Impact Tutoring	4
1.2	Image of a rubric used to evaluate instructional materials developed by INFOhio.org.	8
3.1	Example of an Elkonin Box	40
3.2	Image of cookie sheet with magnetic letters attached	41
3.3	Phonics skills mastered by grade band	42
3.4	Five-finger method to determine text reading level	45
4.1	Authorship Cycle	56
5.1	Cultural Relevance Rubric	84
B.1	Photograph of young author holding first published book	125
B.2	Photograph of boy in ball cap writing his first sentence on a whiteboard	128
B.3	Photograph of boy standing with the author celebrating his 100th reading lesson	129
B.4	Photograph of boy standing with the author celebrating his reading progress	134
C.1	Miscue analysis markup from first reading session	143
C.2	Miscue analysis markup from second reading session	145
C.3	Miscue analysis coding sheet with documented miscues from oral readings	146

List of Tables

2.1	Outline of a tutorial lesson plan	27
2.2	Example of a reading log used to document genres of text	33
3.1	Example chart to document literacy skill areas addressed over time	37
3.2	Elements of phonetic decoding	41
3.3	Target words per minute reading rate by grade level	47
3.4	Designing an inductive outline	51
5.1	Funds of Knowledge inventory matrix	77
5.2	Overview of the Sheltered Instruction Observation Protocol for tutoring	85
6.1	Tutee attitude toward reading scale	97
C.1	Anticipation Guide example	139

List of Contributors

Carson Binder is currently a senior in high school and a varsity athlete. He started working with his uncle in third grade, learning he *was* a good reader and a good writer, despite not being able to engage with in-class instruction. He did not stop, passing third grade and becoming a straight-A student in middle school.

Denise Perez Binder has a master's degree in Special Education and a bachelor's degree in Speech-Language Pathology. She had respected teachers' approaches and worked at home when her boys struggled. That stance changed when her younger son assumed "bubble kid" status in reading instruction, tanking his self-esteem.

Gemma Cooper-Novack is a writer, writing coach, and literacy education scholar. She received Syracuse University's 2022 All University Doctoral Prize for her hybrid poetic dissertation exploring affective experiences of queer teenage writers. Her academic and creative work has appeared in more than 50 journals and books, including *English Journal, LR:TMP*, and *Lambda Literary*.

Elizabeth Dinelli is the Director of a learning center for students with learning disabilities in the northeast United States. She is certified by the Orton-Gillingham Academy. She has over 30 years of teaching experience. She is a diagnostic and prescriptive practitioner who enjoys meeting the individual needs of her students.

Olivia Gore holds a Bachelor of Arts in English and a Master of Teaching in Secondary Education from the University of South Carolina. She earned endorsements in Read to Succeed and Adverse Childhood Experiences (ACE). She is currently teaching at Catawba Ridge High School in Fort Mill.

James R. King is an Emeritus Professor of Literacy Studies at the University of South Florida – Tampa. After three years of retirement and fear of pickleball, he has returned to his formative labyrinth at USF as an Assistant Professor of Instruction. He hopes to get it right(er) this time.

Erin Harden Lewis, with a decade of experience in education, leverages her deep understanding of curriculum development and instructional strategies to foster significant improvements in teaching and learning across diverse educational settings. She is a senior program manager at an organization dedicated to enhancing teacher professional learning and advancing educational equity.

Katherine Marsh is a tutor and school consultant in the northeast United States. She received a doctoral degree in reading education in 2022. She has worked as a teacher and a tutor in diverse learning and enjoys adapting her teaching strategies to fulfill individualized student needs at all age levels.

Mary E. Styslinger is a Professor of English and Literacy Education at the University of South Carolina. She is passionate about interweaving literacy into the English curriculum and serving at-risk youth. She is the author of *Workshopping the Canon for Democracy and Justice*, *Workshopping the Canon*, and *Literacy Behind Bars*.

Annette Teasdell is a curriculum consultant and an Assistant Professor of Curriculum and Instruction at Clark Atlanta University. Her research centers on the belief that culturally responsive pedagogy, combined with a curriculum that is accurate, relevant, and appropriate, can yield improved student outcomes.

MaryEllen Vogt, Professor Emerita at California State University, Long Beach, with a doctorate from UC Berkeley, is a literacy expert and prolific author. She co-developed the SIOP Model and has provided professional development worldwide. A Reading Hall of Fame member, she served as President of the International Literacy Association.

Acknowledgments

Let us begin by acknowledging all the individuals, whether highly trained literacy specialists, community organizers, or dedicated volunteers, who provide hour upon hour of literacy tutoring to children, adolescents, or adults who find reading and the associated language arts to be a challenge. As the editors of this tutoring guidebook, we cannot thank you enough for your endeavors.

While it might be viewed as an unusual acknowledgment, we would be remiss if we did not acknowledge the thousands of tutees from across the land who receive the services of community-based tutorial services. Personal experience tells us that being directed to and then receiving tutorial instruction can be at times the very last activity in which a tutee desires to partake. In borrowing from a renowned tutor, Mary Poppins, we hope that the methods, techniques, and cases in this guidebook provide the sugar that helps the medicine go down.

Of course, we would like to acknowledge the talented contributing authors, some of whom have been with us in the earlier editions published in this community literacy series. Without them sharing their scholarly knowledge and practical experiences, this tutoring resource would not be possible. In every possible way, they are master tutors who share of their minds and from their hearts in their respective chapters and cases.

Additionally, we are most grateful for Megha Patel, who has served as our editor with this text. We are equally grateful for her colleagues at the Routledge/Taylor & Francis Group for support with the two earlier texts in this series – *Literacy Across the Community: Research, Praxis, and Trends* (Henry &

Stahl, 2021) and *A Field Guide to Community Literacy: Case Studies and Tools for Praxis, Evaluation, and Research* (Henry & Stahl, 2022).

Last but certainly not least, we are ever so grateful for our spouses, Bill and Carolyn, for their encouragement of our scholarly endeavors. We understand that undertaking such requires a focus and time commitment that so often requires hours of solitary work. We thank them both for their understanding and unwavering support. Our appreciation is ever so deep!

Introduction

Throughout the history of pedagogy, numerous innovations, reforms, and rediscoveries have been heralded as miracle cures for the malaises plaguing varied categories of learners. In far too many cases, the clarion calls for improvements from politicians, policy makers, pedagogues, and publishers, all representing a multitude of positions, have led to faddish and often short-lived panaceas that have provided little in the way of constructive change in the betterment of children's literacy achievement. Yet, one time-tested process that has routinely demonstrated successful results has been the varied types of tutoring. The proof for such a statement is based on sound theory and found within a sizable body of research.

Most tutorial projects, particularly in this post-pandemic environment, are closely aligned if not a direct extension of the local education authority. Hence, the tutor, whether a volunteer or a professional employed by the school system (public, charter, religious) or a contractual entity, adopts the pedagogical philosophy and practice orientation not unlike that delivered by a classroom teacher, special educator, or reading specialist serving in one of the institutions. As such, in this current era, they are likely to utilize a prepackaged, hierarchically sequenced, and uniform approach to literacy instruction. In other words, one size fits all. Furthermore, learners receiving such tutorial services may receive a form of instruction that has already failed them over time. In other words, more of the same.

On the other hand, a tutorial service that is delivered by a community agency or an individual community-oriented volunteer has options that can go beyond a rigidly structured system that is designed and implemented to serve the overall population within a particular school site or district. A community center tutorial program can reach out beyond the confines of the school to benefit from the total community as a learning laboratory with its unique neighborhood characteristics. Tutoring lessons can and should draw from local cultural, recreational, religious, and youth services. A goal then is to develop a sense of community belonging as the tutee extends literacy competencies through a life-centered curriculum built on the local environment. While it must be acknowledged that every tutor should work in partnership with a tutee's teachers, the tutorial experience should build upon the learner's past experiences and knowledge as well as interests.

This text serves as a guidebook for those who provide literacy tutoring services or for someone who is interested in launching a tutoring initiative in their community. Community-based tutoring is independent of the formal school setting but is oftentimes complementary to the curricula. Through a complementary approach, tutors can supplement traditional learning techniques with more diverse experiential activities suited for individual and small groups of learners. Tutoring programs provide a wide array of offerings, from one-to-one daily tutoring sessions in one's household to formalized online tutoring offered by a for-profit company. For the purpose of this book, we are focusing on individual and small-group community-based literacy tutoring designed to address learning gaps in literacy, oftentimes described as below-grade-level reading skills.

Given such a premise, the position taken throughout much of this guidebook is that instruction should be both flexible and geared towards the unique needs and interests of the respective tutee. Hence, whenever possible, the tutoring sessions should focus on experience-based learning that has a reality-based orientation promoting learning by doing. The emphasis of tutoring should not simply employ a skills or factual orientation that impacts the cognitive outcomes but should equally promote affective outcomes to lead the tutee to be a committed lifelong learner.

Across the Centuries

Throughout recorded history, there have been numerous references to tutoring as an educational practice. In fact, across the centuries, tutoring was the main method of imparting knowledge from one generation to the next. The wealthy and elite classes have consistently utilized tutors to educate their offspring. Hence, as Arendale (2010) pointed out, there was little or no stigma associated with tutoring. As it is well beyond the purpose of this guidebook to delve deeply into the history of tutoring, particularly since Gordon and Gordon (1990) in their text *Centuries of Tutoring: A History of Alternative Education in America and Western Europe* cover the methods and philosophies of tutoring across nine historical eras beginning with the ancient Greeks in 400 BC up through the 1980s, interested scholars will wish to peruse that text as well as Gordon, Morgan, O'Malley, and Ponticell (2007).

From 1900 to 1960, there was limited mention of tutoring in the schools and little in the way of research. In the 1960s and 1970s, research began to emerge, although much of the focus was on peer tutoring. With the reforms generated by the report "A Nation at Risk" (National Commission on Excellence in Education, 1983), school-wide programs such as Success for All and Reading Recovery promised positive outcomes for students identified as being at-risk for literacy failure. Yet these types of school-based programs required extensive professional development for teachers who were to serve in a tutorial role. With the turn of the century, the *America Reads Challenge* (United States Department of Education, 1997) and the *No Child Left Behind Act* (United States Congress, 2001) opened the doors for additional forms of tutorial programming. With the latter legislation, federal funding could be used such that struggling students might receive Supplemental Educational Services, often outside of the local education authorities.

A Perfect Storm

Today, there is an even greater emphasis on tutoring for students enrolled in public schools as a result of what might be considered a "Perfect Storm" in the public education system. In his 1997 book titled *The Perfect Storm*, author Sebastian Junger describes the fiercest storm in modern history that resulted from three massive weather fronts that collided in the Atlantic Ocean in 1991. One might argue that we are in a similar position in education today with three fronts colliding that include (1) severe shortages of qualified teachers, (2) decreasing reading scores, and (3) learning loss from the COVID-19 pandemic school shutdowns.

Teacher Shortages

Public schools in America are facing the greatest teacher shortage of all time. In 2022, researchers at the Annenberg Institute reported 36,000 vacant teaching positions and 136,000 positions filled by underqualified teachers (Nguyen et al., 2022). The National Center for Education Statistics (NCES, 2023) reported 86 percent of public schools were experiencing hiring challenges in the 2023–2024 school year with "the most frequently cited teaching positions with vacancies that needed to be filled were general elementary (cited by 71 percent of public schools) and special education teachers (cited by 70 percent)." The greatest barrier was identified as the "lack of qualified candidates" available to enter the classroom.

Decreasing Reading Scores

The National Center for Education Statistics (NCES, 2023) long-term trend analysis of reading scores on the National Assessment for Educational Progress (NAEP) shows a continuing downward trend in reading scores among 13-year-old students. The 2024 national average of 258 was five points lower than the 2019 administration of NAEP, two points lower than 2022, and only three points higher than the initial 1971 administration documenting an average reading score of 255 (NCES, 2024). This downward trend of decreasing reading scores has occurred over the last decade since an all-time high score of 263 was realized in 2012. Perhaps more concerning is the widening reading gap along socioeconomic lines and when comparing Black and Multiracial students to the performance of White students.

Learning Loss Due to School Closures

In today's preK–12 classrooms, more and more students are experiencing learning gaps because of the school closures caused by the COVID-19 global pandemic. Research conducted by the Center for School and Student Progress examined test scores of nearly 6.7 million third through eighth-grade students and discovered "the average student will need the equivalent of 4.1 additional months of schooling to catch up in reading" (Lewis & Kuhfeld, 2023, p. 2). This phenomenon has resulted in many state and federal programs with direct support of tutoring services that seek to address and ultimately close these gaps. The Partnership for Student Success (formerly known as the National Partnership for Student success) led by the Department of Education, AmeriCorps, and the Everyone Graduates Center at Johns Hopkins University is one such initiative. The Partnership for Student Succes established a coalition of institutions of higher education, and educator preparation programs in particular, in partnership with nonprofit organizations to leverage Federal Work Study (FWS) students as a national tutoring corps (Partnership for Student Succes, 2022).

Through this partnership, more low-income college students who qualify for FWS can work as tutors for children enrolled in preK-9th grade classrooms.

Legislative Landscape

While tutoring has deep historical roots, tutoring demands in the United States have increased over time as a result of educational policies that strive to ensure all students in preK-12 schools have equitable educational outcomes. In recent years, many states have adopted the Science of Reading approach to teaching foundational reading skills through the legislative process (Schwartz, 2022/2025). These legislative actions have created a politically charged education environment in our public schools. Rather than step into this potential resurgence of what has been coined historically as the *Reading Wars* (DeJulio, et al., 2023), in this text we put forward tried and true literacy methods that draw from several pedagogical philosophies proven to lead to successful cognitive (academic) and affective outcomes. While a multitude of books and guidebooks focusing on varied populations, for-profit concerns, and educational providers have been released across the past decades, this text uniquely focuses on programming and pedagogy that is to be delivered in out-of-school confines and hours that draw upon the richness of the tutee's personal funds of knowledge.

Text Overview

In Chapter 1, we set the stage for this text with a focus on philosophical considerations that frame successful tutoring programs. First, we provide a brief summary of learning theories that help ground effective tutoring programs. We then introduce a framework for high-impact tutoring practices. We also spend time describing the importance of contextual factors that enhance learner engagement and end with an overview of programmatic decision making.

Chapter 2 provides greater detail about the programmatic aspects of successful tutoring programs with a focus on systematic instruction. Considerations for program design and instructional frameworks based on the target audience, program contextual factors, and learning integrations are presented. As we move into Chapter 3, we open with a brief definition of literacy from the professional field. Then, we describe the essential functions of literacy learning based on the five pillars of literacy development. We provide proven instructional strategies for each of the essential functions for a variety of learners across multiple communities.

Chapter 4 describes how tutors can use reading and writing connections to leverage different age-appropriate texts to enhance and enrich the literacy learning experience for readers at all learning levels. Then, Chapter 5 focuses on the use of culturally and linguistically diverse texts and intentional instructional practices to build upon a learner's funds of knowledge and lived experiences to activate prior knowledge as a foundation for learning. We also map out the benefits of integrating listening, speaking, reading, and writing through the personal experiences of the reader.

In Chapter 6, we emphasize the importance of assessments for learning. These include formative assessments that can be used for instructional planning and summative assessments that document learning growth over time. A variety of assessment techniques are shared to assist the tutor in documenting learning growth through ongoing assessment cycles and applied data usage. As we move into Chapter 7, we present a tutoring memoir based on the tutorial experiences of an elementary-age learner who was in danger of failing a gateway test to advance to the fourth grade. This narrative includes perspectives from the tutor, tutee, and caregiver, as well as interactions with the school site professionals.

The final portion of the text presents a variety of case studies with learners of different age groups set in a variety of contexts. These cases include community-sourced tutorial practices that evolved from a junior high school tutorial experience, tutoring strategies for a neurodiverse elementary-age boy, an overachieving LGBTQ+ adolescent, incarcerated youth, high school to college transitional programs, and individuals with dyslexia. Our text closes with a practical toolbox of appendices to support program planning, operation, instruction, and evaluation, including a robust reference list of additional resources.

Chapter 1

Philosophical Considerations That Frame Successful Tutoring Programs

Laurie A. Henry and Norman A. Stahl

When one is considering the development of a literacy tutoring program, whether for a single individual or a more formalized and structured approach, there are philosophical considerations one needs to contemplate. In other words, one must be aware of the beliefs and assumptions they are making in relation to how students learn. Dewey (1997) describes these considerations as ethical decisions that help promote positive learning environments. We posit the need to first identify your own programmatic philosophies that will provide the framework for your tutoring program. Then, design your program so it is grounded in high-impact tutoring practices to ensure positive learning outcomes. Finally, determine your programmatic elements that will drive your instructional practices and support your desired learning goals.

Theories of Learning

The purpose here is not to provide an overview of learning theories but to contextualize a tutoring approach with sound grounding within certain theories of learning shown to be effective for tutoring. Our philosophical position blends together sociocultural and strength-based cognitive approaches to learning with an emphasis on contextual factors to be considered by the tutor to best meet the needs of the individual learner.

Vygotsky's Zone of Proximal Development

One such sociocultural theory is Vygotsky's Zone of Proximal Development (1978), which emphasizes the importance of guidance by someone who is more skilled in the concepts to be learned. Vygotsky describes the Zone of Proximal Development (ZPD) as "the distance between the actual developmental level as determined by independent problem solving and the level of potential development as determined through problem solving under adult guidance or in collaboration with more capable peers" (p. 86). Using this theoretical model to ground tutoring helps guide the learner while an expert provides modeling and scaffolding with the goal of the learner becoming independent as they develop the skills themselves. Thus, the ZPD continually shifts as the learner eventually gains mastery of the concepts being taught.

To illustrate this point, we look to an emergent literacy skill, the identification of the alphabetic sign system. Within the child's ZPD, a parent or caregiver might initially introduce the alphabet through song, letter play with blocks, and reading ABC books. Once the child has grasped the concept of letter identification without assistance, the ZPD may shift to phonemic awareness by helping the child match letters of the alphabet to their distinct sounds. In this example, what the learner can do only with guidance (naming letters) shifts to what the learner knows and can perform independently, thus creating a new ZPD in which a new skill is introduced that is too difficult for the learner to master on their own without guidance.

Strength-Based Approach

Similarly, a strength-based (or asset-based) approach to learning focuses on "teachers identifying what a child can or could achieve when provided with educational support and motivation" (State of Victoria Department of Education and Early Childhood Development, 2012, p. 7), thus emphasizing what a learner can do rather than a deficit approach that focuses on what a learner cannot do. Strength-based instruction centers the student and builds upon their strengths to attain the desired outcomes. This approach promotes intellectual growth by leveraging known strengths and differentiating (or modifying) instruction based on the individual student's needs. Hence, "the tutor recognize[s] the pupils' natural talents at an early age, and, by learning about his possibilities, propose[s] the most appropriate path of development" (Szuba, 2020, p. 58). Building upon a learner's strengths helps promote motivation to learn, as positive interactions can help drive instruction at the outset and increase learner confidence and independence.

One way to learn about a student's strengths is by using an interest inventory and self-assessment tools to gauge a learner's motivation to read. (See examples of these informal assessments in Chapter 6). An interest inventory will help determine an individual's likes and dislikes. When you know the interests of your tutee, you can leverage your instructional materials to increase motivation and engagement by selecting topics the student identifies as interesting to them. By using a self-assessment tool, you can gain valuable insight about the learner's self-efficacy and feelings related to their ability to read. When learners consider themselves *bad readers*, it is important to celebrate even the smallest areas of growth to increase engagement and combat the learner's self-doubts about being successful in the literacy classroom.

Contextual Factors

It is also important to recognize that learning does not occur within a vacuum. Using a sociocultural lens, the importance of contextual factors also needs to be considered. Contextual factors are factors "that originate from outside the student" (Lee & Shute, 2010, p. 186) and influence the learning environment. These factors include the learner's funds of knowledge (Moll & Arnot-Hopffer, 2005) or lived experiences they bring to the learning environment as well as the tutor's efficacy and ability to motivate the learner. A sociocultural approach "aims to make learning a process of self-improvement that explicitly recognizes the self and the social context of learning and teaching and recognizes the needs of the individual learner in the interaction" (Patel, 2003, p. 272). When a learner's background, likes and dislikes, lived experiences, and language development are taken into consideration, the tutor can more easily build upon a student's strengths to ensure perseverance and motivation for learning while minimizing any stigma that may be associated with the need for additional instruction.

High-Impact Tutoring

Before designing a tutoring program, knowledge of research-based, high-impact tutoring practices should ground your programmatic decisions. What is meant by high-impact practices? The National Student Support Accelerator (n.d.) has developed a framework for high-impact tutoring (see Figure 1.1) that contains four key elements: (1) well-supported tutors who are reliable and consistent with knowledge of equitable practices; (2) high-quality instruction implemented frequently in small groups with high-quality materials; (3) learning integration with ongoing communication between

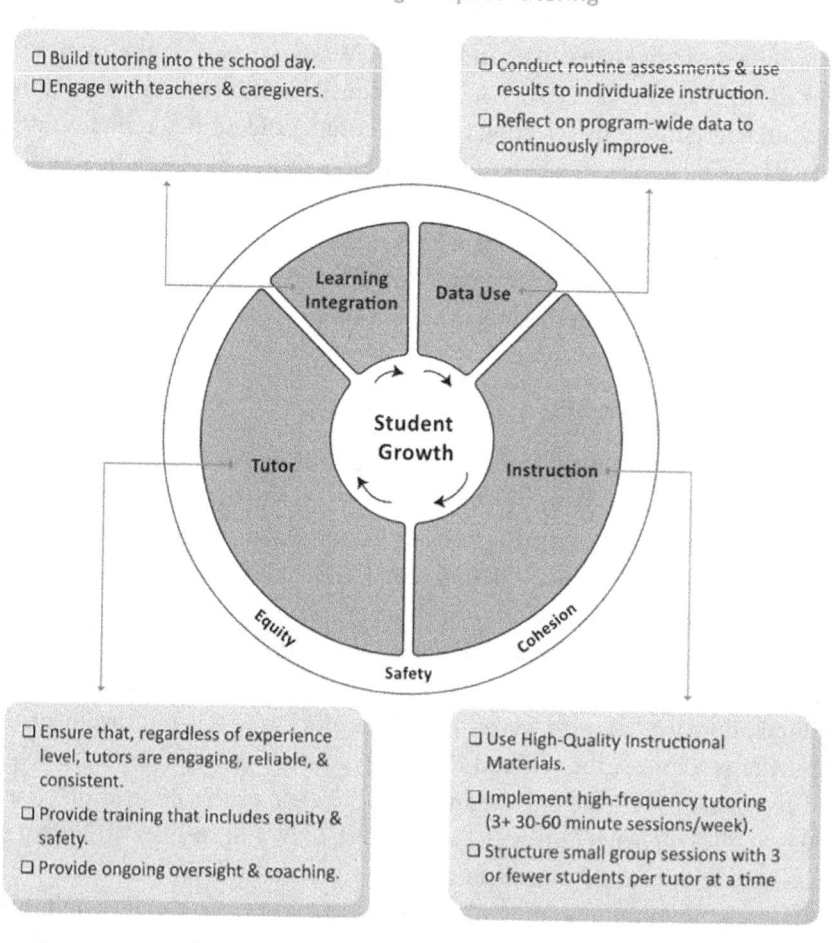

Figure 1.1 Image depicting key elements of high-impact tutoring provided by the National Student Support Accelerator.

tutors, teachers, and caregivers; and (4) use of regularly administered assessments to drive instruction and inform program improvements. Together, these elements support student growth by providing a safe and nurturing learning space.

High-Impact Practices

Research shows the most effective tutoring programs use high-impact practices to best reach the desired learning outcomes, including:

- Creating high-dosage opportunities
- Offering one-to-one or small group sessions
- Providing structure to support learning
- Building strong tutor-tutee relationships
- Using high-quality instructional materials
- Targeting learners with the greatest needs

High-Dosage Tutoring

Tutoring dosage is determined by the amount of time that is spent during direct tutoring sessions as well as the frequency of those sessions. High-dosage tutoring ensures a sufficient amount of tutoring occurs (quantity and frequency) to provide the greatest impact on learning outcomes. Robinson et al. found, "tutoring is most likely to be effective when delivered in high doses through tutoring programs with three or more sessions per week or intensive, week-long, small group programs" (2021, p. 1). High-dosage tutoring should provide multiple sessions per week for 30–45 minutes per session for at least ten weeks to show significant growth (Robinson et al., 2021). The youngest students may benefit from shorter sessions (20–30 minutes) with greater frequency (five times per week) to address the reduced attention span and ensure success. However, quantity without quality may result in diminished outcomes.

Regardless of the age of the learner, it's important for the tutor to pay attention to the stamina of the tutee during the tutoring session. This is especially important if tutoring sessions are scheduled at the end of the school day. One way to combat mental fatigue is to provide short brain breaks to break up longer tutoring sessions (see Appendix A). The use of a kitchen timer can be helpful in keeping the learner on task by knowing how long each instructional segment will last. Many tutors will build in a snack break or a movement break to help the tutee regain focus after a period of concentration.

Group Size

One of the most salient characteristics of tutoring programs is group size. Oftentimes, community-based tutoring programs focus on one-to-one tutoring that pairs volunteers with individual learners. While this is the most ideal option for high-impact practice, it can be challenging to recruit enough volunteers to address the needs of the local community. Small groups of no more than three or four students per tutor can also be an effective tutoring model but should be reserved for the more experienced tutors. Guided Reading (Fountas & Pinnell, 2016) may be the most well-known model for working with a small group of students that leverages Vygotsky's ZPD to support learners. In this approach, students are grouped based on similar reading ability. The teacher skillfully models and scaffolds reading strategies to help the learners decode and comprehend the text based on their individual needs. For example, one student may need word attack strategies while another student summarizes a story to demonstrate comprehension. By maintaining a small group, the skilled tutor can still personalize instruction for each individual learner. However, research shows one-on-one, high-quality tutoring to be the most effective.

Providing Structured Tutoring Sessions

A review of tutoring programs by Wasik (1998) not only emphasized the quality of the tutoring sessions for learner success but also indicated the importance of structure in the tutoring sessions. Successful literacy tutoring programs contained four common structural elements, including:

> (a) reading of new material by the student, (b) reading books in which either the words or the entire story were familiar to the student, (c) an activity that emphasized word analysis and letter-sound relationships, and (d) a writing activity that emphasized composing.
>
> (p. 282)

Providing structure that is repeated each week helps establish learning expectations from session to session.

Some tutors might post each segment of a lesson where the tutee can see it in order to track their progression through a tutoring session. This can be established with time blocks showing how much time will be spent on each segment, which can help the learner stay focused on the task at hand. If a time block strategy is used for motivational purposes and to limit distractions, it's important to include an indication of any planned breaks. However, as previously mentioned, the tutor needs to be cognizant of mental fatigue and flexible enough to take a break "off schedule" when warranted.

Building Strong Relationships

Building strong relationships is the key to tutoring success, "tutoring programs that have choice, control, flexibility, and an emphasis on building relationships can help adolescents develop an awareness of their own literacy learning and foster persistence and commitment in learning more" (Friedland & Truscott, 2005, p. 560). The importance of building strong relationships between the tutor and learner cannot be overemphasized. This is especially crucial for students with low self-efficacy regarding their reading ability and those with a lack of motivation to read. Research shows that tutors learned "building positive learning partnerships" with their learners was as important as "being able to teach a student how to use context to decode an unfamiliar word" (Friedland & Truscott, 2005, p. 557). We emphasize the word "partnership" here as the tutor-tutee relationship should be decisively different than a teacher-student relationship, which is typically a more formal bond. Szuba (2020) discovered that the tutor-tutee relationship was "most often based on friendship and mutual trust, that facilitated honest and bold exchange" (p. 58), thus enhancing the learning experience. The tutor should view her/his role as a coach or facilitator of the learning, providing ample opportunity for learner choice.

Relationship building begins with the very first tutoring session. The tutor should greet the learner with a positive and friendly hello. Then, using a reading interest inventory (see Appendix B), you will discover more about the learner's likes and dislikes. Use this as an opportunity to engage in some follow-up informal conversation about your tutee's interests: *I see here you like to read fantasy books. Tell me more about that.* This will help you select texts that are of interest to the learner. Another strategy for building relationships leverages brain breaks to go on a short "walk and talk" session in which you ask the learner about non-academic interests: *Do you play any sports? Do you have a favorite video game? Do you have any plans for the weekend?* By engaging in non-academic talk, the learner will begin to view you as someone who is interested in more than their academic success. However, it is also important to note that relationship building takes time and the learner may not be willing to share very much until they become more comfortable with you through positive tutoring interactions.

High-Quality Instructional Materials

The use of high-quality instructional materials (HQIM) is the hallmark of any tutoring program. It is critically important that instructional materials align with subject-specific, grade-level standards (EdReports, 2021) and appeal to the learner. Instructional materials may include texts, visual and audio materials, flashcards and other hands-on manipulatives, as well

INFOhio
Instructional Materials Rubric

Use this abbreviated version of the Instructional Materials Rubric to evaluate supplemental resources for your classroom. The complete rubric with indicators for criteria follows this version.

#	Standard	Y/N
Standards Alignment		
A	Explicitly aligned to Ohio's Learning Standards or one or more national standards which would allow for crosswalking to Ohio standards.	
Research-Based Strategies		
B	Content builds on prior learning.	
C	Content supports learning by gradually removing supports, requiring advanced skills and concepts, and application of literacy skills.	
D	Content provides for authentic learning, student-directed inquiry, analysis, evaluation, and/or reflection.	
E	Uses technology and media to deepen learning and engage students.	
F	Content includes options for differentiation to meet the needs of all learners.	
G	Content is presented with an objective view on the topic and is free of bias.	
H	Content creates student experiences that enable all children to reach empowering and rigorous learning outcomes.	
Usability		
I	Materials follow Web Content Accessibility Guidelines (WCAG 2.1).	
J	Materials would not require consistent high-speed internet access for content such as large video files or high-resolution photos.	
K	The visual design of materials is clean and coherent, lending itself to ease of learning.	
Flexibility		
L	Materials are flexible to allow students to access and complete work online or offline as needed.	
M	Materials can support and facilitate learning in hybrid or online delivery methods.	
N	Content includes support, documentation, and guides for effective use.	

Figure 1.2 Image of a rubric used to evaluate instructional materials developed by INFOhio.org.

as interactive media such as mobile devices with literacy Apps installed. HQIM are shown to engage learners and promote a positive learning experience. HQIM should be standards-aligned, research-based, and culturally responsive while also being flexible, adaptable, and ensuring ease of use (EdReports, 2021). INFOhio (2022), a division of the Management Council of the Ohio Education Computer Network, provides a checklist and rubric for pK-12 teachers to evaluate traditional and digital instructional materials (see Figure 1.2).

Serving Students Most in Need

By putting learners' needs first, tutors can provide highly personalized instruction that can result in higher academic gains for the learner. Need-driven and targeted instruction for students who perform below particular thresholds can lead to more positive outcomes. In fact, the America Reads Challenge Act of 1997 called for reading programs that would serve "a high number or percentage of children from low-income families or with the greatest need for reading assistance" (United States Department of Education, 1997, p. 11). These learners are often those who are reading below grade level, are English Learners, or have significant learning gaps.

Below Grade Level Students

Below grade level students oftentimes struggle to learn new concepts as their energy is focused on trying to decode and comprehend texts that are beyond their reading ability. This is an area that tutoring programs can further support by making connections to the school curriculum through the integration of the tutoring and classroom experiences. Tutors can select instructional materials that focus on upcoming content from the classroom at the appropriate reading level to help bolster a learner's background knowledge. This can be accomplished by using a basic K-W-L chart (see Appendix C) to engage learners in active reading of expository texts.

The K-W-L chart (Ogle, 1986) first activates a student's background knowledge by identifying what they *already (K)now* about a given topic. At this step, the student brainstorms a list of things they know or believe to be true. Next, the student generates a list of things they *(W)ant to know* about the topic. This strategy helps develop a purpose for reading as the student seeks to discover the answers to their questions in the text. Lastly, the student completes the *(L)earned* column to summarize what they learned about the topic from the reading. By completing this activity ahead of the concepts being introduced in the classroom, the student can better make connections to the content from their background knowledge of the topic, thus enhancing their success in the classroom. See Chapter 3 of this text for additional ways to use the K-W-L strategy.

Multilingual Learners

There is a wealth of research that shows Multilingual Learners can benefit greatly from additional instructional time outside the regular classroom. An important area of focus for Multilingual Learners is content area vocabulary development as well as learning the meanings of commonly used English phrases and expressions (Gersten et al., 2007). Instruction should also focus on developing academic language (or the language of schools) and how word meanings can differ from conversational English. For example, "some words used in everyday conversation, such as *fault, power,* or *force* take on special meanings when used in science" (Gersten et al., p. 16). Also, some words can have different meanings based on the context, baseball *pitcher* versus a water *pitcher*.

Creating a welcoming environment and building supportive, trusting relationships are key when working with Multilingual Learners. It is important to determine whether your ML student was born in the United States or immigrated from another country. This information will help you understand what cultural norms have been established and whether your tutee is trying to adjust to an unfamiliar cultural setting in addition to learning a new language. The Colorín Colorado website (2023) provides a wealth of information for working with MLs, including the award-winning video, *You Are Welcome Here: Supporting Newcomer Students in Dearborn, MI,* that highlights how a Michigan public school district is supporting its immigrant student population for success. Chapter 5 provides additional guidance on working with this unique population.

Addressing Learning Gaps

In today's classrooms, more and more students are experiencing learning gaps in large part because of the school closures caused by the COVID-19 global pandemic (2019–2020) and the passive participation of remote learning. Targeted tutoring sessions can help close these learning gaps by focusing on missed concepts and the development of foundational reading skills to help learners become more confident with their literacy skills. When we talk about learning gaps, there are two main areas to consider: (1) skills gaps in which the learner has not yet attained specific skills with proficiency, and (2) knowledge gaps in which the learner has not been exposed to key concepts or has not yet reached mastery of the content. The ongoing collection and review of a variety of data points becomes important to address specific gaps. Formative assessments and communication with the student's teacher or caregiver can provide essential information to help drive instruction.

But, more importantly, you can work directly with the student to identify their areas of struggle or their understanding of key concepts to determine how to address any challenges. The tutor can garner a wealth of information directly from the learner by talking about the struggles and discovering specifically where the breakdown occurs. First, it is important for the tutor to help the tutee understand that making mistakes is part of the learning process. Then, the use of encouragement and praise can keep the learner engaged with the activity at hand. Providing opportunities for repetitive practice of skills tailored to their needs and ensuring they have a firm understanding of concepts will help the learner be successful. Even the smallest successes can help the learner become more confident as they celebrate their progress.

Regardless of the learner's background, documenting their progress can also result in increased motivation. This can be in the form of a reading log that records the number of pages of independent reading, a list of books completed, or a vocabulary word cloud. Even the most reluctant reader will enjoy a visual representation of the progress made as a result of their tutoring experience.

Programmatic Decision Making

An emphasis on high-impact tutoring practices leads to additional programmatic decisions to consider. First, you need to determine the target audience (grade level and learning needs) for the tutoring services. How will tutees be selected? Is there a referral process? Once you know your target audience, then basic structural decisions need to be made that include the following:

- Delivery mode (face-to-face, online, hybrid)
- Dosage (frequency and consistency over time)
- Group Size (ratio of tutors to students)
- Location (public library, community center, school, private home)
- Tutor Selection (background and experience)
- Learning Environment (space and structure)
- Instructional Elements (content focus, activities, assessment)
- Curricular Connections (standards alignment)
- Program Evaluation (ongoing improvements)

Delivery Mode

Identifying your targeted learners will help you select the most appropriate delivery mode. Determining the complexity of the learner's needs, potential engagement level, and comfort with technology will guide your decisions about your instructional delivery. The most complex learning needs are best supported with face-to-face tutoring sessions, which offer the greatest impact. Virtual tutoring may provide more equitable access by eliminating transportation challenges as long as issues related to the digital divide (i.e., high-speed internet access) are not at play. A hybrid approach that rotates face-to-face and virtual sessions can support learner growth by providing higher dosage and greater consistency over time, especially if the virtual sessions focus on the practice of skills introduced during the face-to-face session.

Dosage

Dosage focuses on the quantity and frequency of the tutoring sessions. As previously stated, 30–45 minutes multiple times per week is ideal to ensure consistent growth. However, there are several factors that need to be considered. First, the age of the learner may determine if you need shorter instructional sprints or if longer periods of focused instruction are plausible. Next, your schedule and the learner's schedule will establish parameters that need to be met. It is important to coordinate schedules to identify the best time slots that will minimize potential disruptions to a regular meeting pattern. Finally, a predetermined goal and estimated end point help bound the tutoring with a point of closure. Similar to instructional pacing within individual tutoring sessions, a set number of tutoring sessions or a period of time (e.g., ten weeks) can help motivate the learner when they can see an end in sight.

Group Size

There are both advantages and disadvantages to small group tutoring. Tutoring in small groups can reduce the cost of tutoring for individual students if the tutoring services are calculated by an hourly rate. Small group tutoring can provide socialization for students with similar academic goals and support collaborative learning and problem-solving that often leads to enhanced engagement. However, small groups also result in less individualized instruction, feedback might not be as specific, and the scope of topics may be diminished. Small group sessions can be more challenging for students to stay focused, or they may feel more self-conscious of their performance in front of their peers. Ideally, one-on-one tutoring is preferred as it provides the most tailored personal learning experience and yields the most positive impact on learning outcomes.

Location

Whether a public or private space, there are several factors that need to be considered when selecting a tutoring location. First and foremost, the tutoring space should be as free from distractions as possible. This includes background noise that might interfere with the learner's concentration or visual stimulation from a nearby window or passerby that momentarily diverts the learner's attention. When distractions are unavoidable, you may need to repeat key information or provide additional skills practice to gain mastery of the lesson content. Other physical characteristics should also be addressed, including temperature, lighting, accessibility, and seating, to ensure a high level of comfort is present to best support the learner.

Tutor Selection

If you are establishing a program that will utilize multiple tutors, then you should create an application and selection strategy to ensure the tutors' values align with your own and will meet the needs of your tutees. You should begin by developing a profile of an ideal tutor that illustrates the qualities you seek. Then determine which qualities, skills, and knowledge are essential for the position and which qualities, skills, and knowledge you can develop through training. Once you have determined the essential qualifications, these become the basis for your selection criteria. After you establish your tutoring corps, it is important to have a feedback loop that provides the opportunity for tutees to evaluate their tutors on a regular basis. This will help you identify tutor strengths to make better matches between tutors and tutees in the future as well as any areas of weakness that can be addressed through additional training.

Learning Environment

We view the importance of establishing a positive learning environment in a variety of ways. First and foremost, it is critical to establish an environment that is welcoming and viewed as a safe space for authentic learning to occur. The environment should be filled with appropriate instructional materials to maximize learning potential, spur student interest, and motivate the learner to succeed. The learning environment should be free from outside distractions yet provide a space for unstructured activity and informal dialogue that promotes trust and enhances the tutor-learner relationship. The learning environment should be literacy-rich, stocked with a variety of texts, and provide opportunities for problem-solving and creativity through hands-on experiences. Finally, the learning environment should provide the right amount of structure to maximize engagement and fully support the learner based on their needs and interests.

Instructional Elements

When determining the instructional elements you will use during your tutoring sessions, you'll first need to decide on your content focus. Will you include word attack strategies, vocabulary development, reading and listening comprehension, writing, or a combination of these? Which are areas of strength for your tutee? You'll want to make certain to include an area of strength, so the tutee is sure to experience success.

Two of the most common instructional strategies for tutoring (modeling and scaffolding) are grounded in Vygotsky's ZPD theory. Modeling provides the tutor the opportunity to explicitly demonstrate a reading strategy for the tutee. Scaffolding by the tutor is a practice in which guidance is slowly taken away as the learner gains more and more competence to complete the literacy task independently. A common practice is to begin with modeling a strategy to show the learner what to do, then assist the learner until the assistance or scaffolding is no longer needed. This cycle is repeated with the introduction of each new strategy.

Ongoing assessment helps determine when learning has occurred. Initially, assessments can be used to establish a baseline of knowledge and skills. The baseline can be used to help determine the end goal for the tutoring service (e.g., increase reading level by 100 Lexile points). Formative assessments are used as informal learning checks during each tutoring session. Data from formative assessments helps drive instruction by determining the instructional focus for the next tutoring session. Summative assessments are often used as a pre/post measure during the first and final tutoring sessions to document learning gains. See Chapter 6 for more information about using assessments in your tutoring program.

Curricular Connections

The most successful tutoring will leverage HQIM that are connected to the school curriculum. These connections can make learning more meaningful for the student as they are able to draw similarities between school learning and their tutoring sessions. One way to make curricular connections is to use nonfiction texts focused on topics the learner is experiencing at school. For example, a fifth grader might be learning about biomes and ecosystems at school. Knowing this is a topic of focus lets you match texts to the topic of study. While you can get this information directly from your tutee or their caregiver, having a direct line of communication with the school can help you plan for upcoming topics of study in advance.

Program Evaluation

An important aspect of providing tutoring services is to engage in continuous program evaluation to make improvements to the programming. As a program director, you can accomplish this through surveys completed by tutees or using direct observation of tutoring sessions. If you offer individual tutoring services that are not part of a formal program, then self-reflection becomes key. Following each tutoring session, you should jot down what went well, what strategies appealed to the learner, and any growth you noted from your formative assessment. You should also note if something did not go as well as you hoped or if there was a book the tutee did not like. This self-reflection will help you plan your instruction for the next tutoring session as well as guide continuous program improvements overall.

As you can see, there are many programmatic considerations and program design elements that need to be determined as you embark on the development of a successful tutoring service. From understanding your own philosophical stance about learning to creating a reflective feedback loop for continuous improvement, it is most important to remember to center your learner when making your programmatic decisions.

Programmatic Guidelines

When embarking on a new tutoring service venture, there are many decisions that require your attention. Within the appendices, we have provided a collection of documents that can serve as useful draft tutorial guidelines and administrative forms. These resources may be used as presented or can serve as useful examples (prototypes) that can be customized to meet the immediate needs of a specific community tutoring program. These example documents are included in the appendices and include the following:

Teacher Referral Form (Appendix J)
Parent Permission Form (Appendix K)
Tutor Application (Appendix L)
Tutor Interview Guide (Appendix M)
Tutee Attendance Record (Appendix N)
Tutor Self-Evaluation Form (Appendix O)
Annual Tutor Evaluation (Appendix P)
Tutor Training Course Outline (Appendix Q)
Tutoring Manual and Training Topics (Appendix R)
Program Administration Resources (Appendix S)

Chapter 2

The Tutorial Program

Laurie A. Henry and Norman A. Stahl

In any one community there may be any number of tutorial programs. There are equally as many types of tutors and tutees to also be found. The commonality is that there is an individual stepping forward to help another individual meet an educational or life goal. Let us begin by providing a picture of the types of programs you might find in your community, or any community for that matter.

Types of Tutoring

Private tutoring is one of the more common types of tutoring found across the land. In this case, a tutor could be a concerned and caring citizen wishing to serve as a community volunteer, a retired teacher looking to stay in the profession, a college student in a campus-based America Reads or AmeriCorps program, or a church member assisting a fellow parishioner to read the Bible. A tutor provides literacy or educational services for an individual at any stage of the lifespan who has educational desires and needs that cross multiple personal and pedagogical boundaries. Individualized instruction is tailored to meet the needs of the tutee. Individualized one-to-one tutoring can be in-person or, nowadays, frequently offered online. Tutors may be serving as volunteers, as paid tutors, or as college tutors receiving academic credit, meeting internship requirements, or tutoring as part of the federal work-study program.

Online tutoring features virtual tutors who make their homes anywhere in the world. Such services are thus available around the clock and available for tutees who may have limited options based on home geography. Such services, particularly since the pandemic, have become the product of numerous online companies. The topics covered range from basic and traditional school subjects to the most advanced subjects found in postsecondary education.

Group tutoring is designed to serve several tutees in a clustered setting. Generally, tutees served in such a manner are closely matched in their needs with similar instructional goals. This approach allows for group activities to be undertaken while still permitting individualized instruction. Fountas and Pinnell (1996) introduced the Guided Reading Framework (built off the work of Marie Clay), which is an instructional approach for small groups of students with similar reading levels and skills to help them develop targeted reading strategies like word recognition, fluency, and comprehension (see also Morgan et al., 2023). Still, we do mention a caveat. Not until a tutor has been successful in the one-to-one (individualized) experience should that individual assume the role of a small group tutor.

Peer tutoring and cross-age tutoring programs focus on students helping students. Peer tutoring is generally found in a school setting when a student who is achieving in an academic area takes on the role of tutor to assist a student (the tutee) who is struggling with the topic. With peer tutoring, the tutor and the tutee are both of similar age (i.e., same grade level). Cross-age tutoring matches an older student with a younger student. Here, the example might be the middle school tutor who has mastered the content spending fifth period tutoring a third grader in reading at the neighboring elementary school. The idea is that a peer tutor or a cross-age tutor has what might be called "insider knowledge" of the tutee's needs so as to promote the tutee's academic performance, attitude about school and learning, and self-confidence.

Who Is the Tutee?

Look in any number of dictionaries and you will find that the definition of a tutee is an individual who is tutored. That definition is right to the point, but it is not all that helpful given the vast categories of tutees that can be identified. So, exactly who are they? Within any community there exists any number of tutorial programs serving individuals in the literacy arena. There are primary grade tutees benefitting from tutorial services focused on basic reading instruction that includes instruction in phonemic awareness, phonics, or other forms of word attack mastery. There are middle-grade students who are receiving targeted instruction to promote vocabulary development and new comprehension strategies. Secondary school-aged tutees may receive tutoring associated with disciplinary literacy. At the community college, tutors might work with tutees who have yet to master "learning to learn" strategies and tactics or applications within specialized content areas. Tutees can also be found receiving instruction in Adult Basic Education programs and G.E.D. preparation programs as well. A tutee may be found at a local church receiving literacy tutoring so that the Bible can be read in services or at home. Tutees wishing to master the English language can also be found in state-funded programs at community centers and community colleges. Across so many of these skill- and competency-oriented services, a common goal for instruction is to expand the tutee's literacy interests and promote the individual's positive attitudes about reading in general or as specific to a particular content area.

All this said, it is clear that the simple definition of a tutee, as provided initially, serves a purpose as it does provide a basic understanding of a person receiving literacy services from a tutor, but it also falls short of explicating the range of individuals receiving these tutoring services. Depending upon the type of program in which one serves, a tutor may work with a tutee from any one of a number of demographic or academic backgrounds with a range of literacy needs. Given the great need for literacy tutors across the globe, a prospective tutor should have a degree of choice in the program where one might choose to serve. Hence, let us now turn to programs sponsoring tutorial programming.

Locations for Tutoring Services

The beauty of the tutorial experience is that it can take place practically anywhere two individuals can come together. Determining the appropriate locale for a tutoring session will depend upon what both the tutee and the tutor bring to the experience. For younger or academically struggling tutees, it is suggested that the location be conducive to focused instruction, thus being free of any tangential environmental or personal distractions. This likely means the location may be a bit more formal in nature as opposed to the local Starbucks.

There are private tutors who are often receiving a stipend either directly from the tutee's family, a governmental agency, or a private tutoring business who will go directly to the tutee's home. In this case, it is imperative that the location for tutoring be free of distractions, which includes family members (particularly siblings), television programs, telephone conversations, etc. Other private tutors may have a space for tutoring neighborhood children in their own family room or home office.

Volunteer tutors can serve in programs sponsored by an area's public library, a local church, or a neighborhood community center. In each of these cases, there is often a room set aside for the tutoring program to operate. It might be found anywhere on the premises of the respective site's building(s), and it can be available at all times or just when it coincides with the site's planned schedule of activities. The layout will certainly be different from one location to the other, and the material and technological supports will vary based on a range of factors. Tutors may be recruited by a local Volunteer Bureau, United Way, or other non-profit agency.

Tutors may also serve in a school setting through a local school-site program or district-wide volunteer tutoring program. With the former situation, the tutor and tutee will be matched by either the school's learning specialist or a tutorial program coordinator. With the latter situation, a member of the school staff has submitted a request to the centralized school volunteer program, and a volunteer tutor has been assigned to the school. In either case, tutoring may take place in a classroom, school library, dedicated tutoring center, or in some other quiet corner of the school. Generally, unless the tutor holds a teaching certificate, the sessions must be supervised by a certified member of the school staff.

Tutoring centers structured on the franchise business model do exist throughout the nation. Huntington Learning Centers, Sylvan Learning, Gradepower Learning, or Kumon Centers are found in many communities. These centers provide a range of tutoring services for tutees across the lifespan. As these are for-profit businesses, the tutoring services require a financial commitment by the tutee or the tutee's family. Tutors generally hold a teaching certificate and are paid for their services.

Finally, institutions of postsecondary education often provide tutorial services to the general public. In some cases, these services are provided by a literacy clinic staffed by a professor and drawing upon the services of students seeking initial teacher certification or an advanced reading specialist's endorsement. Some institutions offer Techniques of Tutoring classes as electives for undergraduates undertaking a service-learning requirement (see Appendix Q). Other schools will have an America Reads, AmeriCorps, or federal work-study program where undergraduates receive a work-study stipend for tutoring youth in the community. The PATHS to Tutor Act of 2024 (spearheaded by Deans for Impact, 2021) was introduced in the House of Representatives during the 118th Congress "to establish a grant program for innovative partnerships among teacher preparaton programs, local educational agencies, and community-based organizations to expand access to high-quality tutoring in hard-to-staff schools and high-need schools" (United States Congress, 2024). This type of legislation would further support community-based tutoring programs staffed by aspiring teachers.

Tutoring as a Helping Relationship

How might one describe the tutorial experience? First and foremost, it is built upon what might be called a helping relationship. Within such, there are two participants: the tutor and the tutee, with both individuals bringing to the relationship a unique set of backgrounds, experiences, and needs. Both the tutor and tutee hope to gain something from the relationship. Indeed, for the tutorial experience to be successful, both the tutor and the tutee must have certain respective needs being met.

Both the tutor and the tutee will bring to the interactions a perception of oneself, expectations or goals for the tutoring, beliefs about the respective roles to be played, opinions of the standards to be met, and anticipations about the other participant in the tutorial situation. Hence, there should be little surprise that the tutoring relationship from session to session and week to week will be both dynamic and complex.

One of the most important factors to understand from the onset of tutoring a learner is that it is not easy to offer help to another person, nor is it easy for many tutees to receive help from another person. As the tutoring begins, the tutee is put in the position of having to admit to having learning difficulties with basic literacy skills or academic content at a time when trust between the two is yet to be earned. Indeed, the tutee may have a personal history of failed academic achievement intertwined with deeply held attitudes that have led to negative dispositions about literacy, content matter, or school-based instruction of any sort.

As such may be the case, the tutorial relationship must be built upon a firm foundation of mutual trust along with joint assessment, identification, and exploration of the tutee's needs. To achieve this level of rapport, all communication must be open and supportive, particularly with the tutor being an attentive listener. Furthermore, the tutor must demonstrate warm and caring behaviors that make it easy for the tutee to participate fully in each of the tutoring sessions. Finally, while the tutor should not avoid the academic problems or negative learning experiences that the tutee may bring to the tutoring table, it is imperative that the instruction focuses on the tutee's strengths and successes both past and recent.

Given these facets of a positive helping relationship, there should be a clear understanding and acceptance of the importance of positive communication between the tutor and tutee. As the tutor provides initial instruction or feedback to the tutee during lessons, the following actions are paramount. Feedback should focus on being:

1. Descriptive with explanations rather than giving evaluative feedback found in formal testing;
2. Specific to the tutee's performance, not ambiguous or overly general in nature;
3. Considerate and supportive of the tutee's needs;
4. Focused on behaviors and performance that lead to desired competencies being achieved;
5. Delivered at the time of need and readiness; and
6. Solicited either directly by the tutee's actions or based on manifested actions.

Mastery of these communicative skills will not happen overnight. Such tutorial competencies for promoting a tutorial bond built on trust will come with attention to established guidelines, along with ongoing practice and self-reflection after every tutoring session.

Guidelines for Tutors

As noted previously, the tutorial experience is first and foremost about caring and empathy. The tutor enters the experience of tutoring with the power of a one-to-one relationship, which is quite likely different from what the tutee receives in the traditional school setting. The most important rationale for the tutoring activity is for the tutor to give the tutee individualized attention. It is imperative that the tutor value the tutee as an individual who is unique with both personal needs and educational competencies. Effective tutoring for a striving literacy learner is most often based on building a close rapport rather than a tutor's expertise in a specific content area.

To that point, a tutor should not try to be the tutee's teacher (nor parent or guardian). The tutor not only supports the tutee's formal education but also provides a degree of enrichment and interaction that comes with an effective tutoring experience. The personal concern for the tutee will be one's greatest asset in building the tutorial relationship. That means a tutor must understand that the tutee will share both similarities and differences with any particular tutor. Both must be accepted and valued.

However, a most important ethical caveat is that all the information that is learned about the tutee must remain confidential. The center, school, or clinic will have guidelines for ethical behavior. It is important to review them and follow them at all times. If serving as a private tutor or if the tutorial program does not have a written code of ethical behaviors, a tutor should review the Code of Ethics for the National Tutoring Association (https://www.ntatutor.com/code-of-ethics.html).

The key to building rapport with the tutee is by presenting oneself in a natural manner that says, "We are here to learn together." Consider beginning the first tutoring session by sharing with the tutee some information about yourself that the learner would find of interest. Of course, as a component of the initial tutorial session, the tutee should be given an opportunity to tell you something interesting about themselves. Still do not pry. In moving from tutorial session to tutorial session, there will be opportunities to share much more with each other.

From the very first tutorial session throughout the entire time working together, there are some fundamental guidelines that should always be followed. The first point almost needs not be said. Arrive for the session promptly and check in with the office or supervisor. Remember that this is one of the behaviors that are modeled for the tutee. The point here is that positive behaviors and dispositions displayed by a tutor are at least as important as any instruction that is delivered. Secondly, in beginning the tutoring in earnest, start instruction where the tutee has been successful with the subject area for which tutoring has been recommended. Then move into new material slowly. Do not overwhelm the tutee, particularly during the first few sessions. Please be patient. But, with that said, every tutor should hold high expectations for the tutee's learning potential. Let the tutee know what is expected for each lesson and then do all that can be done in promoting the learner to meet those expectations successfully. With time, it is hoped that the tutee will internalize the same high expectations.

When meeting the tutee for the first time, ask how this learner desires to be addressed, including their use of pronouns as appropriate. Then, whether it is the tutee's actual name or chosen nickname, call the tutee by name at every opportunity possible and be intentional about using the appropriate pronouns. The University of Illinois Chicago has resources related to inclusive and equity-minded teaching practices that can be reviewed for more information about appropriate pronoun usage (Bartlett, 2022).

Begin your tutoring session with an activity that ensures success for the learner. Then proceed in a direct and steady manner into the content that the tutee is to master. Be sure to give clear instructions. Asking questions will help to clear up any misconceptions or difficulties the tutee might be having with the lesson. Every session should end with an activity with which the tutee has a successful experience. It goes without saying that speaking in a positive and consistent manner and providing praise to the learner for every activity where there is great effort (and hopefully success) are essential tutorial traits. Make sure that the tutee understands how and why success was achieved in every instructional activity.

A fundamental goal for any tutorial session is for the tutor to promote a positive mindset where the tutee is led to believe that success is more than fleeting and is actually something that can be achieved regularly. It is important to point out that learning from one's failures is also a positive trait. And yes, mastery of literacy or content competencies is of clear importance, but so too is the goal of boosting the tutee's self-confidence and self-esteem. One of the key measures of success for the tutoring experience is that the tutee develops a positive attitude toward learning and, thus, hopefully, to school itself.

Finding Assistance

On a more procedural note, do not be afraid to ask questions of the tutorial coordinator about program policies and procedures associated with tutoring activities, the physical space, and the materials available for instructional use. The program coordinator can likely point out the tutee's educational challenges and perhaps make suggestions for viable solutions. When serving as a private tutor with no institutional association or when volunteering as a tutor in a school setting, communicate regularly with the tutee's teacher or school learning specialist to seek guidance in developing a plan for tutoring.

It is likely that the new tutor at a center or school will be expected to undertake an orientation session to learn of important procedural information. Programs also often provide training sessions for basic tutor training before a learner is assigned a tutor, and later there may be professional development activities to support the tutor's ongoing service. In either case, regular participation will be of great benefit. Furthermore, in the appendices for this guidebook, there are several helpful materials that can be reviewed, copied, and used in support of your tutorial endeavors.

A Tutorial Lesson

Let us now talk about what goes on in a tutorial lesson. A fundamental premise is that each lesson must be planned out before the scheduled tutoring session. That means the tutor not only plans for the session, but must also be fully prepared to deliver the content for the session. This may call for any tutor to rehearse the session beforehand and to be the master of all content and competencies to be taught. Another goal for every tutoring session is leading the tutee to learn how to learn. This means the tutor is an instructional mentor who does not get into the trap of doing the work for the tutee.

Success is far more likely to be the outcome if there is a carefully developed lesson plan that provides guidance throughout the session and provides for evaluation after the meeting. The length of the tutoring session will be dependent upon the competency to be developed or the content to be covered, but this in and of itself requires careful consideration of the academic achievement levels and emotional maturity of the tutee. If the session is too short, the learning objective(s) for the session may not be adequately achieved. If the session goes for too long, the tutee's attention and interest may wander before the session is over. If tutoring at a community center or at a school site, ask the coordinator if there is any set policy pertaining to the time usually allotted for a tutorial session. Many resources released over the years suggest that a session with multiple activities be capped at no longer than 45 minutes in length, with short breaks between instructional activities.

With each session, plan for time intervals that allow for varied activities. Remember that tutees' attention spans will differ, and for some learners, it will be short. Here is an example of how a tutorial session for a younger learner might be structured. First, there is the activity of revisiting and reinforcing the content of the previous session. This is done not only to promote a seamless progression of tutorial instruction across time but also to provide for undertaking an evaluation of the successes achieved in previous tutoring sessions.

As the new session is based on predetermined learning objectives, the stage needs to be set using a motivational activity to engage the learner at the outset. Perhaps the tutee might first read a high-interest story. Be sure to pre-teach any new vocabulary words and help the tutee activate any prior knowledge or prior experiences that could be foundational to comprehending the selected text. This reading activity would be followed by a discussion about the content. Ask questions at the literal (exactly what the text states), inferential (what the text means, but is not directly stated), or evaluative (what the text says about the world outside the story) levels. The tutee should also be given opportunities to voice opinions on the text and even ask for clarifications or further information about the content. If the answer to a question is not known, be honest about it and promise to find the answer to the question for the next session or schedule time to find the answer together using appropriate research activities including the use of programs featuring artificial intelligence.

Finally, the tutee might be permitted to play a reading game that promotes word attack, vocabulary, or comprehension competencies. This activity, in many cases, will be to reinforce the current tutorial session's content or learnings from previous sessions. Be sure to end the session with a recap of what the tutee mastered and inform the tutee what will be the focus of the next meeting. The key point is that the tutorial meeting should be broken into multiple segments with varied activities.

Let Your Lesson Plan Be the Guide

Now all this may sound simple, but you need to be organized for every session. Such organization calls for the creation of a lesson plan. Logically, one may ask, what is the design or format of a lesson plan? The answer is simple…it all depends. Each community program, private tutoring session, or techniques of tutoring class can have its preferred lesson plan format. Nevertheless, let us share a format that has been designed based on lesson plans used by tutors across the country. In this case, the lesson plan in Table 2.1 promotes a structured and systematic lesson that can be used for multiple tutorial sessions with one or more tutees.

This prototypic lesson plan format has nine sections. The first section comprises four components that identify the who, what, when, and where of the tutoring session. This information will be the same for each tutorial session as it focuses on the learner. The instructional guide section of the tutorial lesson plan is comprised of the following sections: Review, Learning Objectives, Materials and Technology, Motivation, Procedure, Reinforcement, Content Mastery, and Evaluation/Reflections. Each section will now be described in turn.

Review

This section of the lesson plan focuses on review of the material covered in the previous lesson or lessons. The reason for this activity is that it is necessary to determine if the content of previous tutorial sessions has been retained by the tutee before moving into new territory. The review step also provides

Table 2.1 An outline for a tutorial lesson plan

Date/Time	
Tutee's name	
Tutor's name	
Tutoring space	Location of tutoring session
Tutorial subject	General topic to be covered
Review	What topics or competencies covered previously in tutoring will you revisit?
Learning objectives	What are you going to teach your tutee? What will the tutee know or be able to do as an outcome of the lesson?
Instructional materials	What will you need to have on hand to teach your lesson? Include technology and/or digital resources.
Motivation	How will you build interest and elicit the tutee's prior knowledge?
Procedure	Outline each of the specific steps you will follow in teaching the lesson.
Reinforcement	What forms of practice (reinforcement) will you provide?
Content mastery	How will you assess whether the tutee achieved the objective?
Evaluation and reflection	Did you achieve your goal for the lesson? How might you improve your tutoring? What skills or topics will you cover in the next session?

for the retrieval of and practice with skills and content across time. A tutor should always be evaluating past instructional endeavors, and the review step clearly allows for such to be undertaken on a regular basis. Taking careful notes as to whether your tutee has been able to retain the competencies and skills from previous lessons will aid in designing reteaching or reinforcement activities. If the tutee is not successful with any review activities, revisit that skill or material once again, perhaps through another approach. Finally, if the lessons delivered are part of a systematic, structured instructional sequence of skills or competencies, the review step serves as the foundation for moving into the next set of skills in the program's hierarchy.

Learning Objectives

The next section requires the inclusion of the learning objective(s) of each session. Some programs may use the generalized term lesson goal. Others might use the term student learning outcome or learning target. Each has a different level of specificity, but this lesson plan format uses the term objective as it serves as a statement of what the tutee will know, understand, or be able to do as an outcome of the tutorial lesson. Hence, the objective(s) for the lesson provides the tutor with a focus and clarity for the entire session. It also provides the desired outcome from the lesson for the tutee, and it provides the criterion by which you can assess the success of the tutorial session.

Here are several examples of learning objectives for different literacy skills that might be found in a lesson plan:

- Phonics focus: After completing page 62 of *Fun with Phonics,* my tutee will be able to recognize the "ai" grapheme, say the "ai" phoneme, recognize the "ai" phoneme in words, and segment and blend "ai" words.
- Comprehension focus: After reading the section pertaining to the Missouri Compromise in *Expansion of Our Nation: Slavery and the Missouri Compromise* (Herschbach, 2018), my tutee will be able to synthesize the main ideas into a coherent written summary.
- Vocabulary focus: After looking up the meanings of confusing word pairs (chews, choose; through, threw; flower, flour; rein, rain) and then explaining the meaning of each, my tutee will state the denotation of each and use each in a written sentence.

These prototypical objectives provide examples for the description of this section of a lesson plan. One important thing to remember is that objectives should be few, direct, clear, and measurable.

Materials and/or Technology

The materials or technology section contains information to which a tutor will refer to during the preplanning stage and then throughout the lesson itself. In planning the lesson and gathering the materials that will be central to the activities to be undertaken in the lesson, it is important to list them in order of use within this section. Before your tutee arrives, review this section of the lesson plan to make sure everything that is required to deliver the lesson is at hand. There is nothing more disastrous for a session than discovering that a necessary instructional component of the lesson is sitting on the dining room table. Past practice by tutors suggests that having a linen or fiber grocery bag filled with tutorial supplies (e.g., pencils, paper, crayons, glue) along with materials for the upcoming lesson (e.g., story book, phonics game) should become a tutor's personal instructional "to go" bag.

There was a time when the materials would simply be comprised of items such as books, instructional games, writing materials, art supplies, etc. The ever-expanding role of technology for instruction will likely play an important role in your tutoring. Technology tools (e.g., tablet or laptop) along with any digital resources (websites, interactive word games, etc.), either for initial instruction or reinforcement, should be included in this section. Internet-based resources should be thoroughly reviewed and bookmarked ahead of time for a seamless transition from the physical to the digital tools. It goes without saying that a tutor must be the master of all technology that is planned for use during the lesson. That may require you to receive a form of tutoring yourself from the program coordinator, teacher, center technology specialist, or fellow tutor to ensure personal mastery of the technology available to you.

Motivation

Think back to high school or the first year of college to a class where the instructor walked into the classroom, slammed his lecture notes down on the podium, and began to lecture immediately. In all too many cases, within a short time of the lecture's start, many of the students' minds were 1,000 miles away from that classroom. A tutor does not want this to be the case with the tutoring experience, as it is likely that the learner may have had a few similar experiences regardless of grade level. The key here is motivating the tutee to want to be an active participant in the tutorial lesson.

We will delve more deeply into the importance of motivation throughout this guidebook, but now let us think about how a tutor can approach the motivation stage of a lesson plan. First, consider what has gone before. In this case, we refer to what is known about the tutee's interests, prior experiences, and prior knowledge. A tutor should also consider the content of the tutorial lessons that have been delivered previously. Next, carefully consider the purpose of the learning objective(s) for the current lesson. Then decide upon what type of short activity would get the tutee motivated to participate fully in the lesson to follow.

There are so many options. For instance, read a short story on a topic of the lesson or of high interest to the tutee; share a photograph, a web page, or a YouTube video; or engage in a conversation to elicit prior knowledge or activate memories of relevant prior experiences. The list goes on. The point is that a tutor should have a specific motivational activity that draws a tutee into the session and focuses on what is to come in the lesson as you strive to promote mastery of new knowledge or competencies with the learner. Hence, fully develop a plan to promote the tutee's interest in and positive attitude about the upcoming lesson in this section of the lesson plan.

Procedure

The section of the lesson plan entitled Procedure requires determining each and every step of the lesson that will be delivered throughout the tutoring session. The steps associated with the method or strategy incorporated into the lesson would be listed here along with the specific instructional steps to be followed in conducting the lesson. In listing these steps, be most explicit. This will be the instructional game plan. Nothing should be left to chance. In fact, as one first undertakes the process of designing lesson plans, it is suggested that a friend or supervisor review the lesson plan and explain each step to be undertaken during the lesson. If this individual has any difficulties explaining the steps, the lesson plan likely needs to be fleshed out to a greater degree.

In the chapters and case studies that follow, there is a range of activities pertaining to phonemic awareness, word attack, vocabulary instruction, reading fluency, comprehension, and writing instruction. There can also be found several useful reference sources both from traditional texts and digital sources that can serve as instructional resources.

Reinforcement

The reinforcement stage of the session may be delivered in either of two variations (or when time permits or need requires both options). First, the knowledge or skills associated with the current session should be reinforced to promote mastery. In a sense, this activity might simply be called practice. Secondly, research over the decades shows us that there is a need to promote long-term recall of the knowledge and competencies taught in previous sessions. Such is the role of reinforcement activities.

Regardless of the direction followed in undertaking a reinforcement activity, this should be an enjoyable part of the lesson. Whenever possible relate what has been taught in this lesson to the tutee's interest areas, prior knowledge, past experiences, and certainly previous instruction. Many tutors find that playing an educational game promoting the learning objective is a viable yet enjoyable reinforcement activity. In some cases, the program will have a tutorial resource center with games that fit the bill, or it will have technology with appropriate preloaded educational software. In other cases, the tutee's teacher may have appropriate games or materials that can be borrowed, or you can design a learning game or adapt one from a source found on the Internet. The ReadWriteThink.org website has a collection of interactive tools that can be used online to support literacy learning.

Across the period of multiple tutoring sessions, reinforcement can take on a project approach, such as writing a book, producing a podcast, developing a photo essay, or organizing an exhibit. The idea is for the tutee to develop a greater knowledge base as well as the ability to see the culmination of tasks through time. One of the key points for any tutor is to make sure that the learning goals from each tutorial session have been integrated into the reinforcement activity for each session and then also across the span of the entire project.

Content Mastery

This section lays out the process for measuring whether the tutee achieved the learning objective that was the focus of the lesson. Such a measure may be based on either a formal or informal assessment. Formal assessments are often thought of as demonstrating mastery via instrumentation of some variation (e.g., standardized test, published diagnostic measure). Informal assessment may be based upon the observation of a tutee's successful undertaking of an activity that requires mastery of the objective for the lesson. For instance, completing a worksheet, playing a game, or reading a text excerpt is considered an informal measure. The key is for the tutor to determine whether there was mastery and to then be prepared to revisit the objective in the future via a different or revised lesson if mastery was not achieved. See Chapter 6 for more in-depth information on assessments.

Evaluation/Reflections

The tutor does not simply measure the tutee's accomplishments but must fully evaluate what aspects of the session went well and what aspects might need revision for the future. This activity will focus on the tutee's performance, but it also examines the effectiveness of the tutorial experience for that day, which requires a degree of honest self-reflection on the tutor's part.

This evaluative reflection should be undertaken shortly after the session has been completed so that all the events, responses, and interactions are fresh in one's mind. Again, let us stress that honesty must be foundational to any evaluation, yet it is fair to both understand and accept that not every session will be 100 percent successful. Whenever a new objective or a new instructional approach is introduced, there is a possibility that there may not be smooth sailing as was hoped as the outcome. An instructional clunk happens to even the most practiced tutor.

Every tutor is learning how to be more effective at one's craft, all the while the tutee is learning new skills and content, and hopefully developing more positive dispositions about literacy. The topics or competencies may be different, but it is important to have the mindset that every tutor is always a learner.

Experienced tutors use the self-reflective evaluation step for self-growth, leading to even more instructional success in the future.

This step of self-reflection also has a planning component, as it is where the initial plans for the next session are formulated. This is another action that needs to be undertaken when the events of the current session are fresh in one's mind. Yes, the design of the next instructional sequence will be fleshed out in the days leading up to the next session, but having a basic game plan for the next session in mind shortly after a session ends allows for more directed planning to be undertaken.

While each lesson plan might be laid out on a single sheet of paper, it will be useful to keep these daily plans in a binder, notebook, or digital file to be referenced on a regular basis. Across time, the experienced tutor comes to understand that, as important as it is to have a lesson plan at the ready, one should be flexible enough to veer away from the lesson plan if warranted. There will be times when there is a need to change plans during a lesson. Such can be called a teachable moment, and the instructional freedom to engage in such is one of the great benefits of the tutorial relationship. Take advantage of each teachable moment or impromptu conversation, especially if the tutee is motivated to learn more.

Some tutors find that it is useful to keep a daily diary or journal on one's personal thoughts about the ongoing sessions. Such a diary needs to be kept on a regular basis, and it will likely include aspects of self-reflection. Through such a writerly approach, any tutor will often find that ideas evolve, problems are solved, and future directions are determined. A now classic book that began as a diary of a tutor's relationship and experience with a young man is entitled *Benjamin: Reading and Beyond* by Thom Hawkins (1972). Throughout the chronological coverage across a year, Hawkins provides a picture of the ups and downs and then downs and ups of the tutorial experience. So too can you by keeping a diary or daily journal.

Instructional Texts

As there is the opportunity to integrate alternative ways to meet learning objectives, such can also be said about providing a tutee with variety in the genre of texts to be read as part of the tutorial experience. Whether these are traditional print texts or digital versions of text, tutees should be encouraged to cross discourse borders. Within each category, the tutee may tackle articles, sections of texts, or book-length works. Topics may change or stay the same, but it is the classification of text that should reflect variety.

Finding such sources may be from the community center library, the public library, donations you might obtain, or something the tutee is reading for school. Table 2.2 provides a prototypic chart that allows a tutor to keep track of the varied forms of texts that a tutee might read across a set of tutoring experiences.

Bishop (1990) shared an important metaphor comparing the reading of books to mirrors, windows, and sliding glass doors to expand the world of learning through texts. Books as mirrors reflect our own culture, texts as windows provide a look inside another culture, and those that represent sliding glass doors provide the reader with a step into and becoming part of a culture different from your own. Therefore, it is important to select a variety of instructional texts that help your tutee see the world beyond their immediate environment. See Chapter 5 for more details about the intentional selection of culturally relevant texts.

Table 2.2 An example of a reading log used to document genres of text

Text Genre	Title	Completed	Abandoned
Biography			
Fantasy			
Science fiction			
History			
Historical fiction			
Science/STEM			
Classics			
Romance			
Poetry			
Sports			
Humor			
Mystery			
Short stories			
Drama			
Horror			
Screenplay			
Autobiography			
Fables/Folklore			
Urban legend			
Other			

Conclusion

It has been the goal of this chapter to present the basic foundations for the tutorial mission as well as the fundamentals of best practice for the tutorial process. While this content sets the stage for tutorial program coordinators and neophyte tutors alike, the information included, particularly that which is focused on praxis, should be viewed and reviewed on an ongoing basis by every tutor. The recommendations provided here will likely be adapted over time as an individual becomes skilled in the art of tutoring. A list of additional books, guidebooks, and manuals on tutorial programs and tutoring activities as published across multiple decades can be found in the appendix of this volume. Many of these sources would make useful additions to a program's resource collection, and many of them can also be found in collections of public and postsecondary libraries.

Chapter 3

Foundations of Literacy

Laurie A. Henry and Norman A. Stahl

As outlined in the introduction, as a nation we are facing diminished reading acumen among pK-12 students, which has reached an all-time low since the 1970s. We are also in the midst of a national movement to adopt a Science of Reading approach to teaching reading in the pK-12 setting to address what some might identify as a "Nation at Risk – Round 2" (see National Commission on Excellence in Education, 1983). Within what has become a politically charged decision for many states, we choose to refrain from any discussion regarding which approach to reading instruction is preferable. Rather, we focus on instructional strategies grounded in the research and demonstrated as successful in enhancing literacy learning. Wasik and Slavin (1993) proclaim that "reading success in the early grades is an essential basis for success in the later grades" (p. 179). Therefore, we look to the foundational reading skills required for literacy achievement that converge as competent readers apply these skills in multiple contexts for learning.

The National Reading Panel Report (2000) identified five pillars of reading, including (1) phonemic awareness, (2) phonics, (3) oral reading fluency, (4) vocabulary, and (5) comprehension. While these pillars of reading are often taught in isolation or through strategy instruction, the ultimate goal is to integrate these skills to develop competent readers and enhance student learning. Therefore, literacy tutoring sessions should also include opportunities

DOI: 10.4324/9781032688589-3

for integrating and applying these foundational skills through reading, writing, and communicating in a variety of contexts.

While literacy researchers don't necessarily agree on the best instructional approach for students to develop these foundational skills (see references to the *reading wars* used in scholarly articles and popular media, DeJulio et al., 2024), it is undeniable that "reading requires that we identify words in print and make meaning through them" (Cacicio et al., 2023, p. 8). Development of foundational reading skills does not occur in isolation from one another. Rather, "reading is an active process that integrates different components such as background knowledge, phonemic awareness, comprehension, and vocabulary" (p. 8). These skills are developed or enhanced through the tutoring process based on the individual learner's strengths and identified needs as determined by assessments of knowledge and skill.

In Chapter 1, we introduced modeling and scaffolding as the most common instructional approaches used in tutoring sessions. What follows are tried and true instructional strategies for each of the foundational reading skills that rely heavily on the tutor first modeling a strategy and then supporting the learner through a gradual release of support until independence of the task is achieved (Vygotsky, 1978). The tutor's role is to make sure progress is being made on specific skills and concepts, which can be monitored through formative assessments (see Chapter 6).

Research shows the most comprehensive tutoring programs that incorporate all aspects of the reading process are the most impactful on student learning (Wasik & Slavin, 1993). Experienced tutors fully understand that there are generally multiple ways to reach any learning objective. This means that over time, the tutor is developing a bag of tricks (i.e., alternative learning experiences) to engage the tutee by providing some level of autonomy. As long as the tutor employs a long-term game plan for a set of tutoring sessions, there is nothing wrong (and indeed just the opposite is true) with allowing the tutee to select at least one activity based on their interests to be undertaken as part of every lesson. Providing the tutee with a degree of choice and autonomy in the learning activity can enhance motivation to learn and overall engagement.

To ensure all foundational skills are consistently addressed, the tutor should create a systematic log of instructional activities. The prototype chart shown in Table 3.1 is one way the instructional activities can be documented to ensure all literacy skill areas are addressed and developed over time.

It is unlikely that a specific session will be comprised of but a single instructional focus area, as keeping a tutee's attention and engagement more than likely will require a variety of instructional activities. The chart employed by

Table 3.1 An example chart to document literacy skill areas addressed over time

Tutee's Name:	Session 1	Session 2	Session 3	Session 4
Phonological awareness	X	X	X	
Phonics		X	X	X
Vocabulary			X	X
Fluency	X	X		
Comprehension				
Writing	X	X	X	X
Digital	X			X

any tutor is quite likely to include multiple tick marks for a range of skills covered in each session. This type of chart can be used solely by the tutor for tracking purposes, or it can be shared with the tutee to mark off as each skill is addressed to track their progress throughout the tutoring sessions.

Instructional Strategies to Develop Foundational Skills

It is important for the tutor to use a systematic approach that follows a developmentally appropriate scope and sequence (order in which content and skills will be taught) to introduce each skill, which includes explicit instruction and modeling, followed by practice of that skill in a variety of applied contexts to ensure transferability. The tutor should provide immediate corrective feedback through scaffolding until the learner can demonstrate the skill with independence. An appropriate 30-minute tutoring session might be structured in the following manner:

1. Word Work: Phonemic Awareness, Phonics, or Vocabulary Practice (two to three minutes)
2. Review: Previous Skill or Concept (three to four minutes)
3. Skill Development: Introduce New Skill or Concept that builds on #2 (four to five minutes)
4. Applied Practice: Practice New Skill or Concept in Different Contexts (four to five minutes)
5. Integrating Skills: Fluency or Comprehension Development (seven to eight minutes)
6. Learner's Choice: End with a Fun Learning Game Selected by Tutee (four to five minutes)

What follows is a brief explanation of each of the foundational skills for reading development, followed by a sampling of teaching strategies derived from best practices for literacy instruction.

Phonological Awareness

Phonological awareness focuses on the sound structure of spoken words, which includes the ability to recognize, identify, and manipulate the sounds in spoken language at the word, syllable, and phoneme levels. Phonological awareness is broken into two types of skills, *phonological sensitivity* and *phonemic awareness* (Indiana Department of Education, 2021). Phonological sensitivity focuses on whole words, syllables, and onset/rhyme patterns. Phonemic awareness focuses on individual phonemes or sounds in words. Young learners develop phonological sensitivity first, as phonemic awareness is a more complex skill to master.

Phonological Sensitivity

The most basic level of phonological sensitivity is the ability to hear individual words within a phrase or sentence (e.g., understanding "my ball" has two words). Next, at the syllable level, learners can identify parts of a single word (syllabification) by dividing the word into syllables that each contain a vowel phoneme/sound. Finally, learners begin to manipulate word patterns through onset-rime (division of a syllable into two parts, the initial consonant/c/or consonant blend/ch/followed by the vowel and any additional consonant sounds/at/, which form *cat* and *chat*) as well as rhyming (repetition of word endings that sound similar, *small, tall, ball*) and alliteration (the same letter sound at the beginning of words, such as *dainty delightful dragon*).

Word Level Identification

Use a hopscotch board for the learner to identify individual words in a phrase. Say a silly phrase or sentence (e.g., The dragon eats cookies). Have the learner hop on a different hopscotch square for each word in the sentence. As the learner develops, move toward more complex sentences (e.g., The dragon eats cookies before bed). For more advanced learners, you can include compound words that correspond with two feet landing on the hopscotch board at the same time (e.g., *The* – Hop on 1, *cat* – 2, *eats* – 3, *cookies* – jump on 4 and 5 together). In place of hopscotch, you can substitute a game board with squares, building blocks, or other types of manipulatives.

Syllabification

Clap It Out: Help learners identify syllables in a word by clapping them out. For each syllable in a word, the learner claps their hands (e.g., *cat* – 1 clap, *kitten* – 2 claps, *piano* – 3 claps). The tutor and tutee can take turns selecting words to clap out. This strategy can also be used to review vocabulary words the tutee is learning.

On-Set/Rime with Word Families

The concept of onset and rime can first be introduced by reading children's books that contain words that rhyme (e.g., *The Cat in the Hat* by Dr. Seuss). Then use letter blocks or word tiles (*Scrabble* tiles work well) to create word families, such as *at: cat, hat, bat, splat*, or *ack: back, hack, tack, slack*. For older learners, you can use the popular web-based game *Wordle* to see how many word families can be created.

Alliteration

Alliteration is the repetition of words with the same beginning sound. Use picture books that emphasize alliteration to introduce the concept to your learner, such as *Alligators All Around* by Maurice Sendak (see Appendix D for more alliteration book suggestions). You can also use common tongue twisters (e.g., Sally Sells Seashells by the Seashore) or make up your own using found objects around you.

Phonemic Awareness

At the most basic level, learners first develop phonemic awareness as they begin to identify, isolate, and manipulate sounds and corresponding letters and letter blends. Phonemes are the smallest part of spoken language. In the American English language, there are 26 letters and 44 phonemes. As an example, c/a/t has three letters and three distinct phonemes/sounds, whereas h/igh contains four letters yet only two phonemes/sounds. Advanced ability in phonological awareness shows skill in manipulating phonemes by isolating, deleting, adding, blending, segmenting, and reversing phonemes. Phonemic awareness is essential for sight-word learning and developing skilled reading strategies. Most young learners master phonemic awareness by the end of first grade.

Elkonin Boxes

Use Elkonin Boxes to help learners segment words into phonemes. Draw one box for each phoneme in the word or words. Younger learners can place

Figure 3.1 An example of an Elkonin box.

a token (e.g., colored chip or cube) in a box for each sound they hear in the word, as shown in Figure 3.1. Older learners can write the corresponding phonemes/letters in the boxes instead of using tokens.

Phoneme Manipulation

Phoneme manipulation focuses on the learner's ability to change the phonemes or sounds in a word by deleting, adding, or substituting the phonemes to create a new word. Phoneme manipulation should be taught in isolation and follow the order below:

1. Deleting phonemes: Removing a phoneme from a word to make a new word. Deleting phonemes includes the beginning sound (name/aim), the middle sound (time/tie), or the ending sound (goat/go).
2. Adding phonemes: Adding a phoneme to a word to make a new word. Adding phonemes includes the beginning sound (ice/mice), the middle sound (cap/clap), or the ending sound (key/keep).
3. Substituting phonemes: Changing a phoneme in a word to make a new word. Phoneme substitution includes trading the beginning sound for a new sound (bat/cat), the middle sound (sit/sat), or the ending sound (top/tot).

You can model phoneme manipulation using colored magnetic letters on a cookie sheet, whiteboard, refrigerator, or other metal surface. Use one color for the initial, middle, or last letter sound to be manipulated, and a different color for the other letters that make up the word, as shown in the example of phoneme substitution in Figure 3.2.

Foundations of Literacy 41

Figure 3.2 An image of a metal cookie sheet with magnetic letters attached.

This strategy helps the learner visualize the letter/sound correlation as the phonemes are manipulated, which leads them toward phonics development as well. As the learner becomes competent with this activity, more advanced strategies can be introduced.

Phonics Instruction

Phonics instruction focuses on the relationship between letters and sounds and is often referred to as a "code-based approach" to reading through phonetic decoding. When learners can understand the sound/letter relationships and identify graphemes, morphemes, and distinct syllables, they have cracked the code to reading. See Table 3.2 for further explanation of the elements of phonetic decoding.

Table 3.2 Elements of phonetic decoding

Phonetic Code	Explanation	Examples
Phoneme	Smallest unit of spoken language	d/o/g = 3 letters, 3 phonemes sh/i/p = 4 letters, 3 phonemes w/eigh/t = 6 letters, 3 phonemes
Grapheme	Letter or group of letters that represent a single phoneme	c/a/t = 3 graphemes h/igh = 2 graphemes w/eigh/t = 3 graphemes
Morpheme	Smallest unit of meaning that cannot be further divided	play = 1 morpheme re/play = 2 morphemes (root word "play" meaning enjoyable activity and prefix "re" meaning again)
Syllables	Part of a word containing a single vowel sound that is pronounced as a unit	high = 1 syllable high/er = 2 syllables high/light/ed = 3 syllables

Phonics instruction should begin with learning sound-letter correspondence, which is the identification of the sounds associated with individual letters /c/ and letter blends /ch/. Then, basic CVC (consonant-vowel-consonant) words can be introduced (e.g., bat/cat, map/mop, rub/rug). As these foundational skills are developed, more complex concepts can be introduced along the phonics continuum as shown in Figure 3.3.

Letter-Sound Correspondence

Initially, you would begin with the youngest learner by teaching sound-letter correspondence to identify letter names in upper- and lower-case form (Mm) and the corresponding letter sound /m/. Letter-sound correspondence should be taught one at a time. A new letter-sound correspondence is introduced once the learner can identify previously introduced letter-sounds with automaticity. It is important to separate letters that look and sound similar (e.g., b and d) in the instructional sequence to avoid simple confusion. High-frequency letters (e.g., m, t, p, s) and short vowel sounds should be introduced first. The tutor can use phonics flashcards (Edmentum, 2021, offers a free set of printable flashcards), or digital flashcards can easily

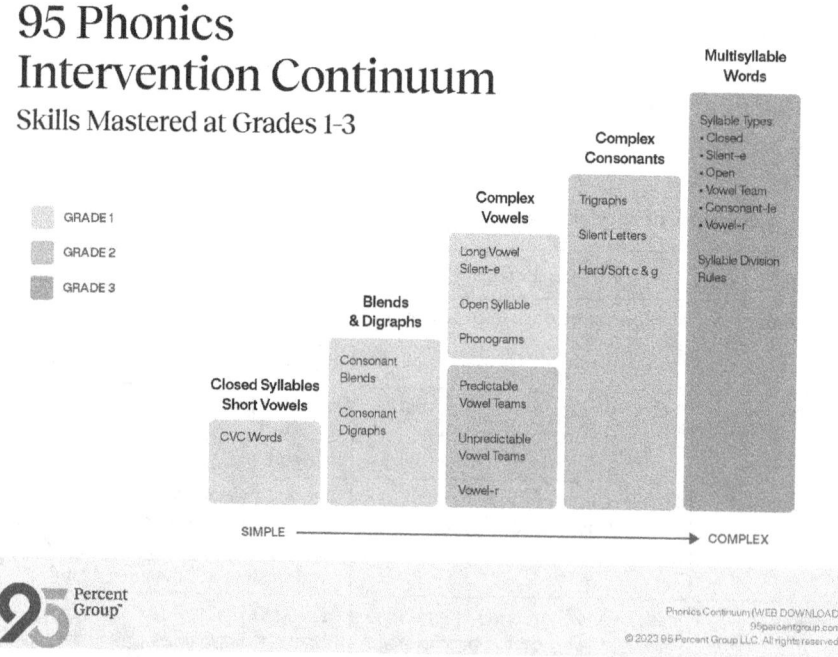

Figure 3.3 Phonics skills mastered by grade band.

be created using slide presentation software in which each slide contains images of the letter (Bb) and a picture that begins with the letter sound (bat). Creating your own flashcards provides the opportunity to personalize the flashcards based on the tutee's interests.

Teaching CVC Words

CVC words follow the consonant-vowel-consonant spelling pattern (e.g., cat, rug, tag, his). The word always begins and ends with a consonant, and the vowel is a single short vowel sound. CVC words are most often the first words introduced to beginning readers and help build foundational phonics knowledge into the development of early reading skills. You can use CVC words for a variety of early literacy development activities, such as word building, vocabulary expansion, informal reading assessments, and emerging writing skills. A fun way to practice CVC word identification is with Word Bingo. Create a bingo card with CVC words that have been introduced to your tutee. Then, as you say different words, the tutee places a chip on the word. You can give points or prizes for each "bingo" that is made or for filling the entire card. Bingo cards can be laminated, then using a dry erase marker to "X" out each word on the card, allowing you to reuse cards for continued practice.

Moving through the Phonics Continuum

As your learner masters the simple CVC word pattern, you can then begin to introduce more complex letter patterns, moving through each stage of the continuum shown in Figure 3.3. Most importantly, the tutor must ensure the tutee has the prerequisite foundational skills before adding a level of complexity. It is also essential to continue to practice and review the foundational skills related to grapheme-phoneme correspondence and vowel patterns to ensure the learner can apply these skills with automaticity to develop reading fluency.

Sight-Word Vocabulary

Part of phonics instruction also focuses on the development of sight-word vocabulary. These are irregularly spelled high-frequency words that do not follow the traditional sound/letter decoding strategy, but are words that are identified through instant recognition. Sight words are some of the most frequently used words in the English language and can improve reading fluency and comprehension when the reader can recognize these words quickly with little effort. There are many sight word lists available on the internet. LakeshoreLearning.com (Lakeshore, 2025) offers a printable list of the 300 most common sight words (additional lists can be found with a quick internet search). One fun way to practice sight words is using a flashcard matching memory activity. Create a set of 20 flashcards in which there are ten pairs of sight words. Mix up the cards and place them face down on a table. Then have your tutee turn over pairs of cards, matching the two cards with the same sight word on them.

Fluency

Fluency focuses on reading quickly with high accuracy and expression. Developing as a fluent reader is dependent on decoding with accuracy, automaticity with sight words, vocabulary knowledge, and reading practice of familiar texts. Fluency is often seen as the bridge between decoding words and understanding text because fluent readers can shift their energy from decoding to comprehension. Fluent readers can also interact with the text on a higher level, developing critical thinking skills that help them make connections.

One key aspect of fluent reading is to ensure the text that is used is appropriately matched to the learner's reading skill level. Texts can be categorized at three levels: frustration, instructional, and independent (Gickling & Armstrong, 1978). The independent level matches a text to the learner with the expectation that they can read the text independently with little to no support. At the instructional level, scaffolding will be necessary, and the text may contain a few new vocabulary words or a different text structure that has not yet been encountered by the reader. A text at the frustration level should be abandoned or used solely by the tutor as a read-aloud or mentor text to demonstrate a particular reading skill. One quick way to determine the text level is using the five-finger method, as shown in Figure 3.4.

If the learner encounters five words that are unknown on one page or section of text, then the text is too difficult for the learner's reading level. However, it is important to match text selection with the purpose of the instructional activity. If a scaffolded reading engagement is planned, then a text at the instructional level is appropriate. But if a lesson on fluency is at hand, then a text at the independent level is key for the learner to experience reading success.

5 Finger Method

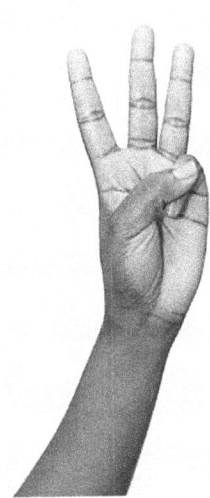

1. Student self-selects a text to read
2. Student turns to a full page of text in the middle of the book
3. Student begins reading page holding up one finger for each word they do not know
4. If five fingers are held up by the end of the first page, the book is too difficult for independent reading.
5. 0-1 fingers, the text is too easy
6. 2-3 fingers, the text is just right
7. 3-4 fingers, the reader will need some support

Figure 3.4 An image of a hand with five fingers and instructions to determine text level.

Modeling Fluent Reading

Research suggests that learners of all ages enjoy listening to a fluent reader share an interesting and captivating article, short story, or chapter from a book. In the realm of tutoring, the tutee not only has the opportunity to enjoy the content of the work being shared but also to observe the tutor modeling fluent reading. Furthermore, the tutee can follow along with a copy of the text as the tutor is reading orally. While the procedure may be as simple as the tutor reading to the tutee at a given point during every tutoring session, the activity will pay greater dividends if it includes a discussion about the content once the oral reading has been completed. To ensure the success of such a discussion, the tutor should prepare a set of questions or discussion points to share with the tutee. These should focus not only on the literal content of the reading but also ask the tutee to make inferences and critically evaluate the message being delivered.

Still, it is important to be flexible with pre-selected questions, as the discussion can branch out in other valuable directions as driven by the text or the tutee's curiosity. If the modeling focuses on a single text (i.e., a book) or a single topic across multiple texts (e.g., skiing, cooking, animal care) as an ongoing component of each tutoring session, it is beneficial to have the tutee and tutor recap the important aspects of the text that were covered during the previous session(s) before the next reading episode is undertaken.

Neurological Impress Method

The neurological impress process has been used in one-to-one tutoring for over 50 years in the promotion of fluent reading instruction. In employing neurological impress (Heckelman, 1969), the tutor sits slightly behind and to the side of the tutee, and together they simultaneously read a selected passage orally. The process calls for the tutor to read the passage such that the tutee hears the text directly as he or she is attempting to read. Admittedly, this arrangement might be a bit awkward for either the tutor or tutee. If so, a tutor and tutee can be sitting side by side. The rate of reading is determined by the tutor, yet it is necessary to be sure that the tutee can move along at a natural and comfortable pace. This is determined in part by selecting reading passages that are at an instructional or independent level.

A key consideration is for the tutee to be able to focus on each word as the tutor voices it. The tutor and tutee will undertake multiple shared readings of the passage until that point when the tutee can read the text in a fluent manner. This method may be used with tutees of varying ages and reading achievement levels, so care should be taken in selecting a particular passage from the perspectives of length, readability, and interest level.

Echo Reading

Echo reading is an approach that can promote reading fluency while using a wealth of texts that build upon a tutee's past knowledge, prior experiences, and personal interests. Whether the texts are drawn from biographies, fictional narratives, poetry passages, popular magazines, or digital sources, the echo reading process is the same. With echo reading, the tutor will orally read a selection of text either at the phrase, sentence, or paragraph length, depending upon the complexity of the text and the ability level of the tutee. Once the tutor reads the text selection, the tutee follows up by reading the same passage...hence, the term echo reading. During the reading of each text, as both the tutor and the tutee read the passage, the tutor moves their finger or a pointer under each word as it is vocalized to assist with word tracking. This is particularly important when using a text at the instructional level to help the reader with newly introduced vocabulary words.

Repeated Reading

Repeated reading is another technique for promoting reading fluency that can be used with a range of texts, whether school-based or selected from

Table 3.3 Target words per minute reading rate by grade level (Rasinski & Padak, 2005)

Grade	Fall	Winter	Spring
1	0–10	10–50	30–90
2	30–80	50–100	70–130
3	50–110	70–120	80–140
4	70–120	80–130	90–140
5	80–130	90–140	100–150
6	90–140	100–150	110–160

beyond the walls of the school. Texts from the latter category can be drawn from the community or might focus on a tutee's areas of extracurricular interest (e.g., sports, music, pets). As the process begins, the tutee selects a text to read or is presented with a set of appropriate options by the tutor. Once the text is selected, the tutor will parse the overall piece into sections of a length that are appropriate for the tutee's reading competency. This could be anywhere from 10 to 25 words for younger students and 50 to 200 words in length for older students. Then the tutee will read and reread the first passage orally until a target reading rate (words per minute) with fluency is achieved. Timed reading assessments can help determine if the reader is making progress on oral reading fluency. Fluency target rates by grade level (Rasinski & Padak, 2005) can help determine if your tutee is on track, as shown in Table 3.3. However, care must be taken to limit the number of repeated readings, so the tutee does not become frustrated or lose interest in the piece.

Vocabulary Development

Vocabulary development focuses on an individual's knowledge of words and their meanings. Connecting meaning to certain spelling patterns helps learners expand vocabulary (e.g., pitcher and picture; there, their, and they're) and to better understand that word meanings can change based on the context. Content-specific vocabulary has greater meaning when used within a subject-specific context. For example, *mass, force,* and *acceleration* within a unit of study on Newton's second law of motion in a science classroom have greater meaning than introducing these words in isolation. Vocabulary knowledge helps hold together ideas, concepts, and stories to help make meaning from texts, which leads to increased levels of comprehension.

Personal or Community Photo Guide

The tutor will first obtain up to a half dozen nine-inch by twelve-inch mailing envelopes. Then, together with tutee input, along with using the interest inventory completed with the tutee or a list of community resources/events, the tutor will write a label on each envelope corresponding to each of the tutee's preferred interest areas. Next, the tutee will cut out photographs and drawings of community resources (e.g., movie theaters, skateboard parks, basketball courts, libraries) or high-interest topics (e.g., music artists, movie stars, video games, sports teams) from varied printed media sources. Should technology be available, downloading and printing images or creating slide decks of images from the internet is appropriate too. If the tutee has an artistic flair, personal drawings or sketches might be included as well. Photographs taken by the tutee with a digital camera or mobile phone would be an extension of this activity.

The tutee will sort and classify the images into the respective envelopes. Once there is a robust collection of visual images or printed content for each interest area, the tutee will use the contents from a respective envelope to develop a photo essay booklet (pasted documents) or slide show on the computer in which definitions of target vocabulary and descriptions of the photos are provided. The guide can also be used as a resource for writing activities that help the learner make direct connections between reading and writing (see Chapter 4).

Savvy Shopper

The tutee will analyze advertisements, whether print or digital, to discern how word choice and descriptive language are employed to target consumers in the community. The tutee should be taught to scrutinize the language and words utilized by the advertiser, the colors found within the advertisement, the formatting of the message(s), and any eye-catching imagery that has been embedded. After evaluating several advertisements, the tutee will use the concepts learned and the linguistic constructs observed to develop an advertisement for a favorite product, community resource, or organization.

Words Where I Live

For the younger tutee or a "New to English" learner, the tutor will print out cards with words associated with items that might be found within the tutee's place of residence (paying close attention to the tutee's cultural background and the preferences of the members of the community). Each word card might also include a photograph or drawing of the item (either front or back) with a simple definition and pronunciation guide as an option. After examining each card, the tutee will categorize the words into predetermined classifications: appliances, furniture, lighting, floor coverings, food products, etc.

An extension activity would be to categorize each item by the room where the object might normally be found, the type or name of store that might sell the item, or the cost of the item. A variation of this activity might have a focus on locations or resources in the community (e.g., playgrounds, neighborhood schools, community centers, grocery stores, automotive repair shops, churches). Important to the success of this activity is for the tutor to learn as much as possible about the learner and their community first. Therefore, this activity should only be used once a trusting relationship has been established.

Reading Comprehension

Reading comprehension is the ability to interpret and gain meaning from text. Experts from the field of reading research (Shanahan et al., 2010) define reading comprehension as "a readers' ability to use their background knowledge and thinking ability to make sense of what they read…to understand what an author has stated, explicitly or implicitly" (p. 5). For a learner to successfully comprehend text, the foundational reading skills (phonological awareness, phonics, fluency, and vocabulary) must be taught and practiced. Then, these skills are brought together and integrated to develop proficiency in reading comprehension.

One of the most used reading comprehension strategies may very well be the K-W-L chart (Ogle, 1986) that was introduced in Chapter 1 of this text as an example for scaffolded instruction (see Appendix C). The K-W-L process supports strategies for before reading (what do you already Know about the topic), during reading (what do you Want to know more about), and after reading (what have you Learned). There have been many variations developed that extend beyond the original K-W-L chart. One extension is to add a fourth column focused on "Further Wonderings" that encourages students to continue their learning about a particular topic (Hill et al., 1998). Hershberger and colleagues (2006) modified K-W-L to K-L-E-W (a play on words for the science classroom) to reflect what students Know (before reading), what is being Learned (during reading), what Evidence supports the learning (during or after reading), and Wondering (supporting after reading classroom dialogue). There are other variations that have been developed. The clever tutor could also modify the K-W-L process based on the content area of focus or the learner's background by creating additional columns based on the lesson objective.

Identifying Key Points in a Text

Tutees of all ages eventually come to a session in which they are asked to read a text passage and respond to the query, "What is the main point?" or "What is the controlling idea?" which are essentially getting at the same thing, a superordinate idea (most general or abstract idea presented). Yet, many tutees will focus on a catchy detail or what might be a subordinate idea (less important than the overall main idea of the piece). Many lessons will then try to teach deductively the construct of the main idea by teaching the tutee where to most likely find it in a passage. Of course, there are three primary locations: (1) as the first or second sentence, (2) in the middle of the passage, or (3) at the very end of the piece, depending upon how the author has crafted the argument. Or, as if the author is playing a trick on the reader, it does not even appear and must be inferred (determined by reasoning without specific evidence present in the text selection). Many aspiring readers will have a basic understanding of the relationship between the superordinate controlling idea (main idea of the passage) and the subordinate ideas (less important details), as well as the process of inferring the meaning from a text. But what should a tutor do if a learner struggles with such deductive reasoning? One option is to approach the task in an inductive manner as described below.

Inductive Outline

One such instructional approach, which also provides a study guide of sorts, is called the Inductive Outline (Bird & Bird, 1945). The idea is that for some learners it makes more sense to move from the parts to the whole in making meaning. This technique is useful when the text covers specific details and examples that support an overall conclusion. To begin the process, while using a large piece of paper, the tutee will write down the title of the chapter or text across the top of the page. Next, the sheet of paper is separated into three vertical columns with the following headings: (1) What are the facts, (2) What is their immediate significance, and (3) What is the overall significance? While this terminology is Bird's, it can be revised in language to fit more directly the sophistication of the tutee (e.g., What is the evidence? Why is it important? Is there a counter-narrative?).

The tutee will then read the first section of text, paragraph by paragraph if it is of sufficient length. Then, in column one, the tutee will number and record in brief statements for each specific fact that is encountered. In many informational texts, features such as italicized or bolded words, figures, and images will likely point out an important fact. Once the tutee has completed this step for the entire text, the next step is to review the notes together on the chart paper.

A second step calls for a second reading. As this is done, the process of the second read, along with a perusal of the notes in column one, should lead to the tutee being able to inductively integrate information to answer the second question by writing out brief integrative statements. Once this process is complete, the tutee reviews the information in the outline once again.

A third step leads the tutee to write a general statement about the significance of the entire work as it pulls together the points in column two. Then the tutee undertakes a metacognitive review by looking at the introduction, a topic statement, a summary statement, etc., to determine if the primary statement as listed in column three captures the superordinate or main idea of the piece.

The procedure is not one that can be completed in a matter of minutes. It will be time-consuming to focus on a piece of text in this form of close reading. Still, for the tutee who has difficulty mastering text, it should provide

Table 3.4 Designing an inductive outline

Purpose: The inductive outline is a step-by-step reading strategy that moves from a parts-to-whole analysis of the passage. It is useful for notetaking where facts lead to a conclusion and for sorting superordinate points from subordinate facts.		
Process: Follow the steps below to create an inductive outline focused on the integration of facts and their significance to determine hierarchical structure to enhance meaning.		
Step 1: Read each passage paragraph by paragraph recording the facts in column one.	Step 2: Review the passage to determine the significance and the relationship to the facts and record in column two.	Step 3: While reskimming the text, review the integrative statements within column two to determine their significance and record this in column three.
What are the facts?	**What is their immediate significance?**	**What is the overall significance?**

practice in a process of identification of main ideas and the relationship to facts, details, examples, etc., as well as a product that can be used in studying or text preparation. Table 3.4 provides an example of an Inductive Outline designed to explicate the process.

Summarization

For nearly 100 years, literacy scholars have been recommending that the act of summarization be taught so learners improve both their reading and writing competencies. A particularly powerful instructional sequence for promoting reading and writing skills was developed by Jeanne Day (1980) as a component of her dissertation research. The ten steps of the procedure for training learners to summarize text as adapted for a tutorial lesson follow. But before instruction begins, the tutor must make a copy of a short article of high interest for the tutee (e.g., *Custom Cars* in Hot Rod Magazine or *What's Climate Change?* in National Geographic). Furthermore, the instructional sequence will require that the tutee use two colored pencils or highlighters.

Initially when employing this technique, it is recommended that the text be written such that it can be read independently by the learner. As the procedure is revisited in the weeks ahead, the text may vary in content, length, and difficulty. Still, it is recommended for the tutoring process that an overarching theme integrate all the articles to be employed in the instructional sequence.

Before the instruction begins, the tutor must be sure that the tutee understands the concept of a summary and its ultimate purpose as the outcome of this work. Furthermore, with the first summarization cycle, the tutor will likely need to both model Day's (1980) ten steps for the summarization process and to scaffold the activity for the tutee:

- Step one: The tutee is asked to undertake an initial reading of the selected text, and the learner is then requested to answer the following: What is this text about? What did the author say? The answers should lead to the identification of the passage's main theme/topic. The tutor and the tutee might next briefly discuss the theme to tap into the tutee's prior knowledge and past experiences.
- Step two: The tutee will next reread the selected text to validate the proposed theme. Important points that are presented throughout the text are identified with each one being noted by the placement of a star or check mark in the margin next to it. The tutee will revisit the identified points in later steps.

- Step three: The next activity provides a degree of focus on the text. Here the tutee will reduce any list of terms into a superordinate category. As an example, the tutee in reading the passage with the exemplary title of *Custom Cars* might encounter a list (at the word level or sentence level) with terms such as manifold, water pump, radiator, fan belt, timing chain, etc., which could be reduced to "parts of the engine." This action is a process of summarization that should be pointed out to the tutee.
- Step four: The tutor will next explain or review the use of a topic sentence (controlling idea). If a topic sentence was provided by the author, the tutee will underline it. It will be transferred directly into the summary as it is prepared. It will be of necessity that the tutee come to understand that an author may explicitly provide a topic sentence at any point in an article. It is a myth that a topic sentence is always the first sentence.
- Step five: Since not every paragraph or section contains an explicit topic sentence, should such be the case, the tutee will need to compose one to integrate into the summary. The tutee's development of a topic sentence is a higher-level comprehension activity that may require initial guidance by the tutor.
- Step six: The tutee is likely to find a degree of enjoyment in this step. At this point the tutee will use a red leaded pencil (or highlighter) to cross out any "repeated stuff" found in the article.
- Step seven: This step continues in the process from the previous step, as the tutee will now use a green leaded pencil (or highlighter) to cross out any "unimportant stuff" found throughout the passage.

Upon the completion of step seven, the tutee's copy of the text will likely show all the components of text to be kept for a summary. In fact, the tutee should be able to read over orally the components that are to be kept in a manner that sounds rather like a draft summary. At this stage, a draft summary can be written using the identified components of value and leaving out components that do not support the summarization activity.

The next three steps lead the tutee through a metacognitive review of the summarization process and the product which has evolved.

- Step eight: Now the tutee will reread the text and state the theme of the work. In doing so, the tutee will ask the following questions: Is the theme a topic sentence? Did I underline it? If a topic sentence was not presented in the text, did I develop one and write it in the margin?

- Step nine: Next, the tutee needs to determine whether any lists or unimportant content might have been left in the summary. If found, it is removed. The tutee will also look for any repetition in the summary, and if anything is found, it should be removed.
- Step ten: The final step requires the tutee to double-check the completed summary as it reads at that moment. Questions might include: Did I skip any important themes? Is all the important information from the text found in my summary? Are there any paragraphs that I neglected to summarize?

Throughout the sequence of tutoring sessions, articles might be selected that build upon or expand an area of interest. Using our example of *Custom Cars,* some related texts might focus on hot rods, low riders, body work, car shows, driver licensing, etc. A set of summaries developed across time can be organized into a book authored by the tutee. Photographs that are taken by the tutee as well as digital images from the internet can be integrated into this text as well.

Conclusion

As can be determined by the above instructional strategies, the five pillars of foundational literacy build upon each other until all skills can be integrated into a successful reading event for the learner. Through modeling and scaffolded instruction, the learner becomes more and more independent in their reading so long as the appropriate text selection is used. As learners experience reading success, they become more engaged in the reading activities and can find enjoyment from reading rather than frustration.

Appendix E provides a reference list entitled *Tutors' Friends: Strategies, Learning Games, and Instructional Books* that lists multiple sources that provide instructional methods and techniques for tutoring each of the five pillars. Many of these texts are available in public and postsecondary institutional libraries and tutorial resource rooms.

Chapter 4

Naturalistic Authoring Approaches

Laurie A. Henry, Norman A. Stahl, and James R. King

There is sound reasoning and research supporting teaching activities that permit students to undertake authorship experiences that integrate reading, writing, and the associated language arts. Such an approach fosters positive attitudes toward printed materials by allowing the students to experience the pride of authorship. One limitation with this approach is the amount of preparation time required of tutors. Because of the large time commitment needed to foster experience-based authorship, the creative talents of volunteer tutors can assist in this area. More than this, volunteer tutors with a minimum of training can conduct the entire range of authorship activities for an individual tutee and/or group of tutees. The following chapter outlines three approaches that promote a tutee's authorship and provides suggestions to enhance their writing skills.

Every Tutee an Author

Every tutee, from preschool to college, is an author at heart. This assumption serves as an underlying rationale for the reading/language cycle used in the stages of the "Every Tutee an Author" as it is apparent that any tutee, as well as all adults, read and write more effectively when they possess a personal interest and background experience about the subject matter.

The cycle presented here leads a tutee to be interested, involved, and invested in the reading-writing-sharing process. The student enters the six-stage cycle through a real or vicarious experience with a subject of interest, and this is followed by additional forms of research that encourage writing activities. The outcome of this composing process is submitted for peer review in a tutee's (editor's) workshop. The reviewed manuscript is developed into a finished product that is published in one of several forms by the tutee. The final step calls for sharing the tutee's work with members of the school or local community. Figure 4.1 shows the cyclical nature of the authorship program, which is further explained in the rest of this chapter.

Experience Stage

An important aspect of this cycle hinges on the belief that emotionally charged, real or vicarious experiences generate a strong desire to read about the interest

Figure 4.1 The authorship cycle that includes six stages of the writing process.

area as well as a need to share the newly learned information with others, in this case through the full range of authorship activities. The pride associated with the authorship activities generates higher quality writing products. Tutees of all ages, even adults, are motivated when given autonomy over their writing. This motivation is understandable as we all tend to extend our efforts and competence on projects of high interest in which we have personally invested our thoughts, energy, and time. The effectiveness of a real or vicarious experience can be maximized by following five basic steps:

1. Determine the tutee's interest areas through a guided interview and the use of an interest inventory (see Appendix B). A tutor should assist a tutee in selecting an interest area (school-related, a hobby, etc.) that can serve as the basis for the authorship cycle. Be sure that the topic is not one that will only be of fleeting interest as the entire authorship process takes time to complete.
2. Determine a real experience (community field trip, on-site visitation, interview, experiment) or a vicarious experience (video, movie, television program, social media) that can be used to motivate the student to undertake authorship activities. In most cases, a real experience will be of greater impact than a vicarious experience. Once again, be sure that the selected experience reflects the learner's interest areas.
3. Preplan and either "pre-take" or preview the experience. When either a real or a vicarious experience is poorly planned, there is a great likelihood that the concept being focused upon will be lost to one or more of the outside stimuli that are present. Proper planning begins when the tutor "pre-takes" the field trip or other experience. This activity will ensure that all the preliminary arrangements can be made. When undertaking this preplanning step, such things as the possible costs, the location of the restroom facilities, the arrangements for eating lunches, the rules and regulations to follow, the sights to point out, and the route to follow should be noted. If it is possible, bring back some postcards, pictures, posters, or video of the visitation site to share with the tutee. If a vicarious experience is the basis for the cycle, the virtual fieldtrip, WebQuest, or videos should be previewed ahead of time. The tutee might be given a study guide (questions or guidelines) to facilitate the learning process.
4. Readiness activities are the next step. At this time, the tutor prepares the tutee to look for things that might otherwise be overlooked during the experience. Preparation may be accomplished through cooperative stories,

dramatic play, general discussion, art activities, viewing YouTube clips or photographs, or internet/AI explorations. Questions posed by the leader should address the reasons for the experience, the connections with the school curriculum and related personal background, as well as rules of proper conduct and safety. The question sequence serves diagnostically to assess what readiness activities should be undertaken, as well as a pre-assessment for later evaluation of what knowledge was gained from the experience.

5. On the day of the experience, the tutor reviews the information noted during step three. In real experiences, the tutee may bring a camera (smartphone), art materials, or notepads to document the activities. If the tutee asks questions that cannot be answered on the spot, encourage the tutee to record the questions so that these can be investigated during the following research stage. Since vicarious experiences often last for a shorter amount of time and may often be repeated or expanded upon, the tutee's attention should be directed with the use of a study guide.

A smooth transition from the experience stage to the next stage of authorship (conducting the background research) is facilitated by a post-experience debriefing session. The tutee and the tutor involved need an opportunity to express and synthesize their feelings, understandings, and questions about the experience. These routinely lead to a further desire to learn more about one or more aspects of the experience through further research.

Background Research

During the debriefing activities, the tutor should guide their learners to write down lists of concepts, questions, or ideas that surfaced during the experience. From these lists, the most central focus areas are identified for further research. The most readily available source of material is the internet and AI programs, but don't overlook the school or local public library. While most tutees have used a library, there is a point at which their library usage skills may become inadequate, depending upon the task at hand. This leads to a second subordinate learning experience centered on the use of a library, but it should not overshadow the basic task of finding information about the previously identified areas of interest.

Numerous other sources of information may also be at the hands of the researchers. Matching the appropriate source to the age of the learner is an important task for the tutor. Some sources of information may include public affairs pamphlets, interviews, letters of inquiry, periodicals, podcasts, television programs, student-prepared books, YouTube videos, and field notes from additional visitation experiences. Tutees may wish to collect various visuals such as pictures, diagrams, and photographs at this point as well.

In assisting the tutee to use background materials, the tutor should strive to (a) make sure that the tutee can find and use the resources, (b) help the tutee summarize the important information, and (c) assist the tutee with organizing the information so that writing activities can proceed. Useful ways to summarize and organize information include audio recordings and transcriptions, note card systems, study guides, and annotated summary notes. Once the tutee organizes the information, they should be guided into the writing stage of the authorship cycle.

Writing

With the writing phase of the cycle, the authors-to-be weave the information from their background research together with their ideas, impressions, or anecdotes formed during their previous experiences. The crucial aspect of this writing stage is the somewhat solitary process of organizing and putting one's thoughts in a readable form. While the writing process remains one of individual discovery and even mysterious interaction between the writer and the discourse, the tutor can assist the process by using facilitative activities. First and foremost, tutees need to be taught that once a word or sentence touches a piece of paper, it does not become sacred. Encourage the tutee to first get one's ideas down on paper, but let the tutee know that revisions can and should be made with the passage later. Once this general idea has been shared, specific activities can be undertaken. For instance, a tutor can suggest that the tutee generate a list of specific details before writing or request that they ponder the task before undertaking it by doing a "brain dump" or brainstorming activity. Also, as any good author does, each tutee should define the nature of his or her audience before writing. Overall, there are few options that tutors can use to directly facilitate the writing stage of authorship. Through encouragement and the previous suggestions, the tutee will be assisted in recording one's ideas for later revision.

Editor's Workshop

When a manuscript is accepted for publication, it is placed under the benevolent scrutiny of an editor. In this stage of the cycle, other tutees or classmates can serve as peer editors to help evaluate the writing of other authors in the class, school, or tutoring center. In general, peer editors read other tutees' papers with the specific purpose of providing supportive feedback in the form of questions and comments for the writer. The workshop steps are based on several assumptions, the foremost of which is that the content of the manuscript is of primary importance. Since communication of ideas is the goal, the overall message, organization, and clarification of thoughts must receive the first emphasis. Mechanics such as accuracy of spelling, correct grammar, and accurate punctuation certainly influence the clarity of the writing; however, their importance is secondary, as premature attention to mechanics can be a deflating influence on the author's desire to write.

Another assumption is that the workshop participants must be taught how to give and receive constructive criticism. Although this calls for guidance from the tutor in the early stages, effective peer feedback will be the endpoint. A final assumption once again pertains to the tutee's investment in the process. Editing and rewriting works best when the tutee is actively involved and can see that the manuscript is moving toward a production stage. The following steps outline the editor's workshop:

1. Peer editors read each other's papers for understanding, clarity of ideas, organization of thoughts, and presentation form.
2. Readers praise specific details, ask clarifying questions, and suggest specific changes for the tutee through verbal and written feedback.
3. During a second reading, peer editors comment on punctuation, spelling, and other errors of writing mechanics. Again, the tutee is given feedback about the overall composition.
4. The tutee reworks the manuscript based on accepted feedback from their peer editors.
5. If desired, the manuscript may be read at another time. This can be to repeat the entire workshop cycle or for a progress check by the tutor.

The tutor should remember and remind the tutee that instances of feedback are opinions. Feedback is tentative until it is acknowledged and accepted by the author. This means that even the tutor's comments should be open to questioning and should be supported by underlying rationale. Further, tutees learn how to give feedback through modeling as well as practice. It is important that the tutor's comments or those by peer editors about the tutee's writing be specific, constructive, and supportive. A "Tutee Writing

Evaluation Checklist" can be found in Appendix F. Motivating the tutee to revise their writing through multiple cycles of review may be difficult. One way to promote revising and rewriting is by only publishing the most polished pieces of writing.

Bookmaking

From the tutee's point of view, this may be the most important step in the authorship cycle. Making books and illustrating their stories are the big payoffs for the entire cycle. However, for most tutees, particularly those experienced with the authorship cycle, there is a building sense of excitement that is realized in all steps that lead to producing books. The actual bookmaking remains an essential aspect of the cycle. There also appears to be some relationship between the intricacy of the books, the quality of the endeavors, and their meaning to the authors.

There are many types of book formats the tutee can independently construct to hold their completed manuscripts. These books may be as simple as fold-and-staple books or as complex as sewn magazines in dry-mount covers. Shaped books, accordion pages, and oversized books are also fun adaptations. Digital texts can support learners who are visually impaired or feel they lack an artistic ability to self-illustrate their text. Of course, the main point in bookmaking is to publish the tutee's writing in a semi-permanent form. Bookmaking can be successful with preschool through adult-age learners. Naturally, the degree of independent work increases with developmental levels. By the middle grades, tutees can independently design and construct their own simple books after only a brief demonstration. If tutorial center supplies allow and tutee work habits warrant, an easy system is to let tutees construct books when they are ready or as a creative break during a more intensive instructional activity.

As with most planning, it is essential to have the materials necessary for the bookmaking on hand. The exact materials depend on the type of book. A good way to determine whether all materials have been gathered is to "pre-make" a book before the tutee begins the process that can be used as a model. This also gives the tutor some notion of where the tutee might experience any challenges. Collections of light cardboard, wallpaper books, art materials, needles, thread, yarn, glue, rulers, lined and unlined paper, and magazines are some of the necessary materials for physical bookmaking. A computer with word processing software and access to the Internet to find images is essential for creating a digital text.

Book Sharing

All too often, the endpoint of any writing assignment is at best a brief exhibition of the finished product. While this may provide a moment of pride for the author, it not only limits the amount of exposure the completed work may receive, but it also does not mirror the actual uses of written materials in business, industry, or publishing. The purpose of authorship is to communicate ideas, and this all too often is not fully undertaken at the end of a bookmaking project. Thus, the final step in an authorship cycle is the publishing and sharing of the completed book. A list of dissemination activities follows:

1. The tutee gives book talks about their book to other tutees, family members, classmates, or community members.
2. Authors are interviewed by tutors on a digital talk show on TikTok or YouTube.
3. Advertising posters are printed up and placed in the tutoring center, senior centers, a school library or cafeteria, or the community's public library.
4. The tutee sends a press release to a community newspaper or the community center newsletter.
5. The tutee gives readings at retirement communities, hospitals, long-term care centers, community centers, childcare centers, or local libraries.
6. Tutees share books during a young author's night, after which the books are placed in the school or local library in a young author's section.
7. Books are placed in the waiting rooms of local doctors' and dentists' offices.
8. Books can be distributed or shared at local hospitals by volunteers.
9. The tutee takes books to a local preschool to promote early reading readiness as well as to instill a desire to read and write in the young children.
10. Books are shared with teachers in training at local colleges or with in-service teachers at professional conferences and professional development sessions.

If we want a tutee to become a more competent reader and writer, we must provide opportunities for practice, model good writing, and develop authentic purposes for both reading and writing. The authorship cycle incorporates these aspects in an easily managed, learner-centered approach. While training tutees in the cycle initially involves some extra effort by the tutor, continuous use of the process can become somewhat automatic. A desirable outcome of the authorship cycle is that while the steps in the cycle become routine, the content remains fresh and alive with each new authentic experience.

Language Experience Approach

Across the decades, the Language Experience Approach (LEA) (Allen, 1976) has been a staple for the tutor's bag of tricks as it can be used across age groups and tutee backgrounds. While it is often used for teaching beginning reading, the LEA is an extremely flexible approach and is adaptable to virtually any philosophy of reading instruction. It often fills a void left open in the classroom that follows a highly structured approach to reading instruction. More so from the perspective of the tutorial experience, it starts instruction with the tutee's personal interests. The young tutee might express an interest in a neighborhood vegetable plot, a middle school-aged tutee may have an interest in the new skateboard park, and a secondary school-aged tutee might be interested in fixing up a 1984 Buick Regal. These are only examples, but virtually all interests or events can serve as the catalyst for a language experience story. Such is why as a tutor you should encourage the tutee to talk about his or her interests, hobbies, and life events. These have great value as they regularly evolve from a tutee's funds of knowledge (Moll, 1994) and may not receive adequate attention in the formal school setting.

What then are the procedures for implementing a LEA tutorial program for your tutee? The LEA as adapted from Carrillo (1972) can basically be outlined in four steps as described herein.

Step 1: Experiential-Based Learning

The first essential step is to provide your tutee with an experience or to identify a past experience that includes enough sufficient inherent interest to lead to a discussion between the two of you. This experience may vary from the events of a day in the community to describing and evaluating experiences that were undertaken in a trip to a concert, sporting event, family vacation, favorite movie or video game, or any number of activities of high interest to the tutee. By reviewing the interest inventory completed during the first tutorial session, you are likely to discover a number of interests that can serve as a focus for the experience step of the LEA.

Step 2: Building Awareness

In the second step, the tutor and tutee engage in a discussion about the experience identified in step one. Tell the tutee that the outcome of the discussion will be the writing of a story or an account of the event or activity. Begin by asking your tutee to give you a title for the experience story. Then as the discussion continues, with a younger tutee you will likely simply transcribe the tutee's complete story as authored in the tutee's own language. With an older tutee, you can simply record phrases and key sentences used by the tutee. (We will explain more about these two options in a moment.)

Remember that the key for this step is to build upon and then draw out the tutee's experience in detail as promoted by honest and interested questioning on your part. These bits of the tutee's text can be written down by hand, but in an age of more advanced technology and the availability of AI tools, we suggest that you make use of a laptop or tablet with a speech-to-text function as having a digital rendition of the text will make later steps of the LEA a bit easier. Before undertaking the next step, reproduce several copies of the text you have generated. You may also want to cut up a copy of this document into individual pieces of text at the phrase or sentence level to isolate the tutee's attention on segments of text.

Step 3: Composition

Let us begin this step in a manner you might approach the LEA with a younger child, yet please give consideration on how you might adapt the steps for use with an older tutee. The first step requires that as the tutor you read the entire document to the tutee while moving your hand along each line so that the tutee always knows exactly where the two of you are in the text at all times. Be sure to employ your natural voice and pause at appropriate points during the reading. Next, the tutee should attempt to read the story orally along with you. Of course, clues are provided as necessary as the tutee moves through the story. As the tutor, you will carefully record any problems the tutee demonstrates for just-in-time instruction that should follow.

With an older tutee, you might lay out each of the sentences and phrases you transcribed during the discussion, and together you might reorganize these strips of text in sequential order to draft a story or narrative. If the tutee identifies holes in the story or missing details, an additional sentence can be drafted and then slotted into the draft as appropriate. Once the strips are ordered and the story draft is complete, the tutee should again read the text in the manner described above.

Step 4: Permanence

As a tutor, you will want to promote a sense of permanence with the product of the instruction. This step converts the tutee's effort into a published book form or digital text so that it can be archived and easily shared. Stories across time can be bound together, particularly if there is a unifying theme, to share with family, friends, and others. Younger tutees will enjoy illustrating each story with artwork, while older tutees can find images using the Internet. In some cases, tutees may even use photography to capture images that highlight the locations, personalities, or events in the story. With advanced technology available today, it is possible for the tutees to share their stories widely with family members and friends, or even publish their writing on a blog or other web-based platform.

Response Journals

Individuals have been keeping journals or diaries for centuries. For the past five decades, the journaling process has been central to a great many literacy classrooms all the way up through the college years and across content domains as well. Types of journals include dialogue journals, learning logs, science field journals, thought books, dual-entry notebooks, and reader response journals, among others. For the tutoring process, the reader response journal provides the greatest opportunities to promote a tutee's growth with comprehension. Furthermore, the process allows the tutor to become an active participant in the tutee's attempt to make a more sophisticated understanding of the reading process as it is integrated with other areas of the language arts.

The premise of the reader response journal is that to become a reader, the tutee must read on a regular basis to the degree the act becomes a habit. Keeping a response journal not only assists the tutee to develop and practice more advanced reading competencies, but with the tutor's guidance and mentorship across time, the tutee can master competencies that include retelling, summarizing, paraphrasing, integrating prior knowledge and experiences, predicting, evaluating, questioning, synthesizing, and speculating, among others.

One of the strengths of the reader response approach to journaling in the community-based tutorial program is that the tutee can respond to a range of textual sources that might not be an option in the traditional classroom. Let's assume that your tutee is a gnarly skateboarder who is never without his board. Nothing is stopping the tutee from reading *Thrasher* magazine and responding to a skatepark review or article about a personality via an entry in the journal. From there the process of branching might lead to responding to a narrative such as *The Trouble with Skateboarding* or *Matt Christopher: Skateboard Renegade*, to an exposition such as *Skateboarding and the City*, to one of many biographies of Tony Hawk, or to *The Journal of a Skateboarder*, which provides a new focus of storytelling through photography. The topic is of little importance, but the tutee's interest level about a topic is paramount to maintain interest.

So, why does the journaling process promote the reading/writing relationship for the tutee and for the tutor? From our example, it is clear that it builds upon the tutee's interest and provides for individualization of content. Through journaling, the tutee builds fluency in both reading and writing in a non-threatening manner by exploring a topic of high interest. Furthermore, a tutor can provide feedback within a short period of time in a non-judgmental manner, either in writing or verbally. This, of course, requires the tutor to be a sincere and encouraging respondent to the tutee's work. It should be clear that one should try to find something positive in each entry. The nature of feedback will be covered shortly, but now let's focus on getting the journaling process underway.

First and foremost, the tutee's journal writing should become a regular part of your interactions together. There are advantages if both tutor and tutee undertake and share in the journaling process. Next, the tutee will need a notebook or something similar in which to undertake their journaling. Older tutees often find that a traditional composition book, which can be easily customized, serves the purpose well. Then, particularly during summer or vacation time tutoring experiences, the tutee will select a text that holds high personal interest. As the tutee reads a selection, whether it be an article, a chapter, or a defined section of a text, the reader response process begins. Responses may come from key points of interest at the sentence level, a section of text, or the entire selection.

Unlike with the "Every Tutee an Author" plan, the writing within journaling does not strive for writing that employs the conventions of standard English. The tutee is apt to use informal punctuation, grammar, colloquial language from the tutee's peer group, and first-person positioning. Such is appropriate as the desire is to get the tutee to think about and write about texts. Are there formal features? Yes, the tutor should promote the tutee writing longer and longer entries across longer and longer periods of time. Furthermore, it is of importance that the tutee engage in the journaling process on a frequent basis. At the very least, this would take place as the last ten minutes of each tutoring session…if not more often.

At this time simply request in an open-ended manner that the tutee write about what was read, which might be one's thoughts, feelings, likes, or dislikes about the reading. You might also encourage the tutee to make connections to prior experiences, which may include text-to-text, text-to-self, and text-to-world connections (Keene & Zimmerman, 1997). What you as the tutor are trying to promote is a shared experience between the tutee and the text. As the process evolves, the plan should be to move the tutee beyond a literal interpretation of the text. This act requires the tutee to integrate one's prior knowledge and past experiences with the text and any direct and vicarious experiences that might be provided at the same time. Journal writing serves as the bridge between the two.

Twenty High-Interest Reading and Writing Activities for Tutoring

Up to this point, we have presented pedagogical methods that can each serve as a tutorial model, which can be followed across a lengthy time period (i.e., semester, summer vacation). We now share twenty high-interest, community-oriented activities that can be integrated into one or more lessons as tutorial goals might require.

1. The tutee reads the transcript of the verses of favorite songs followed by writing a song. While this may focus on any genre of music, it is important that the words within the song be age-appropriate. Focus on keywords; many will be found on sight word lists. Follow-up by writing critiques or descriptive essays in a music log. Focus on discourse styles such as description and analysis of the work as well as comparison to other songs. The tutee might do background research by reading about the musical artist or group. The respective section of the log might contain a music bibliography or historical narrative about the artist(s).
2. The tutee serves as a weather reporter by keeping a daily weather log. This activity combines reading, writing, and science while improving observation skills. The tutee will use words to describe the weather that are found in a self-designed glossary (e.g., wind speed, humidity, temperature, heat index, precipitation). As a follow-up to build one's research skills on the internet, determine the weather pattern 25 years ago, in another locale, or in the year the tutee was born.
3. Develop secret codes to be used with preexisting text or a passage written by the tutee. Researching the nature of codes and the designs of such would be part of the process. Share the coded message with friends of the tutee or other tutees. The tutee might be introduced to Morse Code or binary code depending on their interests.
4. Read a favorite book and write a book review. Use the critique as the basis for a presentation to a book club at the community center or local bookstore or post the review on Amazon or Google Books.
5. The tutor reads to the tutee from a high-interest book or article. The tutee follows along with a second copy of the text. At strategic points in the

passage, the tutee explains or analyzes the content, makes connections, or checks for understanding.

6. Develop a "This is Me" book that describes the tutee. Facts might include the tutee's height, weight, eye color, foot length (size), hair color, etc. Additional content would include favorite things such as foods, beverages, clothes, friends, etc. The tutee might even use a mirror to draw a self-portrait or use a cell phone to take one or more selfies to be included.
7. The tutee might undertake the role of a community reporter by interviewing individuals within the local area on predetermined topics. After writing up the interview with the help of the tutor, the final product might be printed in the community center newsletter. In a similar vein, the tutee might interview family or community members as part of an oral history project.
8. The tutee develops a comic or manga book based on a story that was read by the tutee or viewed as a movie or digital clip. While the initial work will likely be based upon narrative sources, across time the sources can be based on history, science, biography, etc.
9. After a session in which the tutee and tutor discuss the macrostructure of several advertisements found in magazines (particularly film, television, or book focused), the tutee designs an advertisement for a favorite book, website, television show, etc. The tutee explains why a particular media source is appropriate for the design. Using descriptive language would be a focus of the work. The advertisement could be displayed at a local library, or bookstore or even uploaded to a community-based Facebook page.
10. Following a discussion about the structure of a good story, the tutee orally tells a story to the tutor. It can be a simple narrative or a full-blown whopper (tall tale) about a single character or a cast of characters. The story can be dictated to the tutor or voiced into a digital recorder for later transcription (or use a voice-to-text software program). Once the tutor has developed a printed text, the tutee will reread the text and make additions, corrections, etc. to the work. These changes are incorporated for a final proofread. The tutee might add drawings, photographs, or other visuals to the work. Should this process be repeated several times, the stories can be bound together for sharing as a book with family, friends, and younger tutees.
11. Write a booklet or compose a scrapbook about a friend, sibling or relative, member of the community, etc. This activity begins with identification of the source, followed by interviewing the individual, developing a transcript, proofing the work, sharing it with the informant, and making additions and corrections. There may also be a need to review primary

sources provided by the interviewee as well as secondary sources that provide background information about the world within which that individual has lived.

12. After reading an autobiography of an individual of high interest, the tutee undertakes the process of writing one's own autobiography. Each section would initially be short in length (only a sentence or two) with multiple opportunities across the tutorial experience to return to each section to integrate additional recollections or points of view. The overall document can be kept in a composition book or to promote recursive endeavors across time as a file on a computer. The tutee would read additional autobiographical or even biographical works that may serve as additional models for the tutee's work.

13. Develop a community atlas. The tutee will draw out a set of maps. The first map would be as simple as the room in which the community tutoring activities take place; next, the learner would develop a map/diagram of the community center itself. As the center is fully mapped, the project would lead to mapping the block(s) comprising the center's service area, local parks, shopping areas, etc. Labeling map locations would be of importance, and these can be supplemented with photographs. Brief descriptions of important sites could be written based on interviews or by reviewing written and digital sources. The tutee might draw multiple maps that cross the decades to have an historical perspective. The final project could be shared with a local chamber of commerce or community service organization.

14. The tutee keeps a record book on a subject of interest. This activity can focus on a local or professional sports team, a favorite athlete, or one's own performance in sports. Other options might focus on science projects and experiments, gardening logs, or other hobbies. On a regular basis, the tutee will be asked to evaluate the data and summarize it both orally and in writing.

15. The tutee authors "how to" booklets in which the student describes how to undertake an activity for which the tutee is considered an expert. This booklet could focus on cooking tamales, caring for a cat, building a Pinewood Derby race car, etc. The possible topics are endless, and every tutee is an expert on something. The tutor would guide the tutee through the design and formatting of the work.

16. The tutee goes through the process of producing a short video, which includes developing a storyboard, writing a script, shooting the video, editing the work, and showing it to an audience. Stop motion filming in

which photos are taken of objects that are moved in small increments is another enjoyable activity that leverages a tutee's creativity. There are free Apps (e.g., Stop Motion Studio) available that make these movies easy to develop.

17. The tutee uses a camera (smartphone) to take photographs on a specific topic that can be organized together into a photo essay that is annotated by the tutee. The tutor and tutee might visit the library to review "a year in photographs" type books for ideas of layout for the photo essay. The final project might be the design of a "coffee table" type book or digital slide presentation.
18. The tutee writes a menu for a restaurant serving all their favorite foods. First, the tutee reviews menus from several established restaurants in the area. Then creates a menu, which includes descriptions and photos. An alternative would be to create their own cookbook of favorite recipes. Either of these could be presented as a gift to a friend or family member.
19. The tutee undertakes an oral history of a person of positive influence by interviewing them. The tutee later transcribes the interview with the assistance of the tutor and creates a mini biography. The biography can be illustrated and presented to the interviewee.
20. The tutee prepares a scrapbook about topics and things that are of particular interest (e.g., musicians, cars, television programs, skateboards, pets, etc.). Photos may come from magazines, newspapers, digital images, etc. The tutee will write a brief narrative/caption about each image included in the scrapbook.

These activities should allow the tutee to develop authorship and editorial skills by leveraging technology. However, a tutee might find interest in approaching a task by going old school using an electric or manual typewriter. In undertaking each of these activities, the tutor should assist the tutee in developing a personal word bank that is comprised of high-interest words that can be used as the tutee completes the writing activities associated with the project. The word bank would be revisited on a regular basis and used for additional projects.

Out of School Vacation Time

Community tutorial programs that function during periods in which the tutees are on summer vacation from formal school attendance can play an important role in the education of a tutee. This is a time in which community tutoring programs can build upon the traditional literacy instruction delivered during the school year and can also introduce the tutee to high-interest, real-world reading and writing activities that can teach new competencies and promote positive attitudes about literacy.

Still, tutees may not be available for the duration of a community center's programming, as the learner will often step out to participate in family vacations. These activities should be considered wonderful opportunities that enrich the tutee's funds of knowledge as well as allow for alternative literacy experiences.

One valuable endeavor that involves both reading and writing would be for the tutee to keep a Trip Log (diary) as the process leads to the practice with and perhaps mastery of a range of skills foundational to a literate life, including observation, selection, categorization, evaluation, etc. (for an example see *The Poor Scholar's Soliloquy* in Appendix G). The completed log can then serve as the data bank and reference source that can be the basis for drafting more formal texts upon return to the tutorial experience.

More advanced learners might simply be asked to keep a daily log or journal of the activities undertaken and events encountered after receiving a lesson on how to summarize and then depict each one from across a day. Still, for many tutees, approaching the keeping of a log after such instruction may lead to a "hit or miss" situation. For many tutees, the first step is to provide the tutee a log with printed templates highlighting the possible events of a day on a vacation trip. An example of such a template for a road trip might include details about meals, overnight stays, and main activities.

My Trip Log to:
Date:
Location on this day:

Meals:
Breakfast:
   Time:
   Place (restaurant, relative's house, park, etc.):
   Food:
   Town:
Lunch:
   Time:
   Place:
   Food:
   Town:

Dinner:
    Time:
    Place:
    Food:
    Town:
Sleeping:
    Location (hotel, family's home, campsite, etc.):
    Town:
    Amenities (swimming pool, hot tub, café): _____
Gas Station:
    Town:
    Brand of Gas:
    Car mileage:
    Cost of gas:
    Gallons: _____
Diary:
    The people with whom I traveled or visited:
    The best thing that happened today:
    The most interesting thing we saw today:
    The most important thing I learned today:

This template is only an example, and the logbook will need a page for each day of the planned trip. The tutor will need to design the template to mirror the tutee's upcoming trip as the trip may include air travel, a bus or train trip, or even a cruise. Upon the tutee's return, the log can be used as a resource for reporting on the time away, writing a travel narrative, or reading passages to other tutees.

Benefits of Naturalistic Tutoring

Growth in literacy competency with any of the approaches covered in this chapter is not likely to directly parallel the assessment models found in public and private school classrooms as more formal assessment tends to be more closely tied to sequential and structured instructional processes. These tutee-centered approaches are more apt to provide growth that is cumulative in nature where much of the instruction is formulated on a just-in-time approach. Furthermore, as we adapt and add to Frost's (1967) list of benefits promoted by the naturalistic tutorial orientation to reading and writing instruction with its opportunity for both great breadth and associated depth in the community tutorial experience, we find that tutoring allows for coverage of important reading and writing competencies often overlooked or passed by in the more formal educational environs. By offering tutorial instruction via the approaches presented in this chapter, the tutor promotes the tutee's:

- Ability to express and clarify personal ideas both orally and in writing in an ongoing and reflective manner.
- Development of a positive attitude toward reading and/or writing texts of varied genre and subject matter.
- Self-confidence in the ability to communicate one's ideas and find value in the ideas of others.
- Competency in selecting reading for information, for recreation, and for self-improvement whether for skills or knowledge.
- Comprehension of text whether at the literal, inferential, critical, or applied levels.
- Ability to employ word recognition skills for oral and silent reading of the prepared texts.
- Mastery of vocabulary in a meaningful and developmental manner.

Conclusion

It is important to clarify that such approaches in the tutoring situation are designed to improve the tutee's total literacy persona, and as such, the activities may not parallel the work undertaken in the classroom under the direction of a teacher, reading specialist, or special educator. These approaches support a value-added perspective with the understanding that such activities are unlikely to be undertaken in the highly structured developmental or remedial reading programs of the third decade of the twenty-first century. Instead, these approaches build upon the tutee's interests and draw heavily from the tutee's funds of knowledge (Moll et al, 1992), something the formal education arena may not be able to accomplish (see also Chapter 5).

Chapter 5

Culturally Intentional Tutoring with Multilingual Learners

Laurie A. Henry and Norman A. Stahl

Multilingual learners (MLs) regularly live in an environment that is rich in cultural knowledge, family heritages, and dynamic intergenerational households that interact with the community through lived experiences that can and should be valued and drawn upon as integral to the school-based learning process. Yet the formal education curriculum and instructional approaches delivered across the country do not always value what Moll and colleagues (1992) have described as funds of knowledge, also known as cultural assets, that learners bring to instructional spaces based on their lived experiences.

McIntyre and colleagues (2009) present six principles of effective pedagogy for working with MLs derived from research supported by the Center for Research on Education, Diversity, and Excellence (CREDE). These six principles include:

1. *Joint Productive Activity* (teachers and students work together on joint products),
2. *Language Learning* across the curriculum (teachers help students apply literacy strategies in all areas of the curriculum),

3. *Contextualization* (teachers connect instruction to students' experiences),
4. *Rigorous Curriculum* (teachers design instruction to advance understanding at complex levels),
5. *Instructional Conversation* (teachers provide instruction in small groups using academic dialogue as a tool for learning), and
6. *Family Involvement* (helps students connect their prior experience and knowledge with academic content). (p. x)

While these principles focus on the effective instruction for students learning English in a formal school environment, several of them can be easily modified for a tutorial program that serves multilingual individuals. We believe the most valuable of these principles for tutoring are Language Learning, Contextualization, and Family Involvement, all of which are encapsulated within a funds of knowledge approach to instruction.

Funds of Knowledge

Drawing upon a learner's funds of knowledge counters a deficit philosophy that linguistic, economic, and cultural limitations are the root cause of low school achievement by MLs and other learners identified as minority or non-native learners, those with low socioeconomic status, or first-generation postsecondary students who are the first in their family to attend college. Educators have been urged to link the required school-based curriculum and instructional approaches to the learner's out-of-school social and cultural experiences by leveraging the underlying fundamental skills, cultural customs, and the knowledge and practices embedded in normal familial and community routines (Velez-Ibanez & Greenberg, 1992).

While such an approach to formal teaching has many positive aspects, let us propose that funds of knowledge focused instruction can be a powerful catalyst in promoting the tutorial experience particularly when it is undertaken in and draws upon the community setting for instructional content, not unlike the Foxfire approach that was a Joint Productive Activity (McIntyre et al., 2009) that documented folk culture of the Southern Appalachians (see Wigginton & Students, 1972). Given the freedom tutors often enjoy outside the school's formal instructional plan, we suggest that community-based tutoring permits ample opportunities for a tutor to deliver literacy instruction that draws from a tutee's funds of knowledge and unique worldview experiences. Let us examine how a tutor and a tutorial program might adopt such a pedagogical plan.

Instructional Planning

Fundamental to a funds of knowledge tutorial philosophy is the integration of the tutorial lesson with the varied facets of the tutee's life and environment. In other words, the instructional plan and materials should reflect the ML's cultural background, lived experiences, family customs and traditions, prior knowledge, topics of personal interest, and those drawn from the local community. By doing so, it is more than likely that the tutee will be motivated to fully engage in the literacy activities that comprise the tutorial session. It must be remembered that building a positive attitude (disposition) about the tutorial experience and learning itself is of equal importance to the knowledge learned and literacy competencies mastered.

One thing that should be understood is that the tutorial plan and learning activities selected should lead the tutee to expand both their foundation of knowledge and levels of academic competency. In other words, simply staying within the tutee's comfort zone will not necessarily extend the learner's personal or academic growth. There is a thin line to walk here in promoting the tutee's development while not leading to frustration. Tutoring from a funds of knowledge perspective allows for such scaffolded, individualized learning.

When instruction is provided via a small group tutorial model, collaborative tutoring should include numerous opportunities for shared communication, thus promoting language growth. While individual tutorial instruction is likely to be required in support of each tutee, cooperative activities allow for a tutee to dig deep into one's individual funds of knowledge and then share perspectives with other tutees, all the while learning of the viewpoints that the tutee's peers bring forth from their diverse backgrounds. In addition, there are multiple opportunities for the shared discussion about the content of printed or digital texts (published or learner-authored) as well as the sharing of knowledge and experiences, undertaking collaborative projects, and practicing and expanding upon language competencies.

In promoting a funds of knowledge tutorial philosophy there are motivational and rewarding instructional activities that will prove effective in promoting the tutee's engagement in the learning process. One of the recommendations put forward by advocates of a funds of knowledge approach is that it is necessary to learn as much as possible about the tutee's background and environment. Several of the informal assessment devices found in Chapter 6 will assist the tutor in learning much about a tutee's family background, community ties, personal interests, and attitudes about a range of topics.

Contextualized Language and Literacy Development

All too often, the tutorial process is viewed only as a remedial activity. Yet MLs who participate in tutorial programs are likely to be working to expand both their expressive and receptive English language competencies while learning academic subject matter in a traditional classroom. The logical question then is how a tutor might support the learning of such content matter, whether it evolves from a classroom assignment or it is a freestanding themed lesson designed to promote language learning and content acquisition through the tutorial process.

A starting point would be for the tutor to complete a funds of knowledge Inventory Matrix. Table 5.1 provides an adapted funds of knowledge Inventory Matrix (Washington Office of Superintendent of Public Instruction, 2023). That leads the tutor to record observations about the tutee's funds of knowledge across a variety of areas (e.g., education, geography, agriculture, language, art, cooking, etc.). The matrix has three primary sections:

Table 5.1 Funds of knowledge inventory matrix

Funds of Knowledge	Home/Community Practices	Instructional Application
Educational activities	e.g., going to a museum or library	
Geographic origin	e.g., Guatemala, Mexico	
Agriculture	e.g., coffee plantation, fishing	
Sports	e.g., futbol, baseball	
Technology	e.g., WhatsApp, TikTok	
Home language	e.g., Arabic, Spanish, Navajo	
Health	e.g., homeopathic	
Caregiving	e.g., swaddling baby, co-sleeping	
Art	e.g., quilting, pottery	
Cooking	e.g., tamales, curry, paella	
Entertainment	e.g., video games, movies	
Music	e.g., hip-hop, reggae, drumming	
Dance	e.g., samba, dragon dance	
Holiday traditions	e.g., Dia de los Muertos	
Community	e.g., gardens, library, church	
Friends and family	e.g., barbecues, visiting grandma	
Household chores	e.g., sweeping, dusting, laundry	
Religion	e.g., ancestral worship, Catholicism	
Family values	e.g., work ethic	

(1) Funds of Knowledge topics, (2) Home and Community Practices, and (3) Instructional Applications. In completing the matrix, the tutor would be able to identify funds of knowledge focus areas, connect home and community practices related to the focus area, and then identify corresponding instructional activities that would naturally evolve from an identified theme.

Content Connections

By connecting the tutorial experience to the tutee's funds of knowledge, there is a great range of subject matter that can be drawn upon to promote the integration of literacy activities in lessons that motivate the learning process. While structured and highly systematic tutoring lessons can lead to the mastery of isolated skills that may or may not transfer beyond the lesson itself, a funds of knowledge approach can build across multiple lessons that draw upon meaningful content and promote the expansion of the tutee's knowledge base while mastering literacy competencies through a just-in-time process. The approach thus rests upon a theme such as community gardens, local soccer teams, or a neighborhood art center, so long as it is of interest to the learner.

Themes should be selected to build upon the tutee's background and areas of curiosity. The fundamental purpose of a theme is to motivate the tutee to engage in a set of tutorial lessons that are both meaningful and relevant. Furthermore, by employing reading materials and writing activities that focus upon a theme, the ongoing tutoring leads the tutee to undertake multiple passes across a topic, leading to a deeper understanding of the content and multiple opportunities to master literacy and language competencies. Of course, each tutorial session's inclusive activities must be tailored to meet the diverse needs and competency levels of each individual tutee.

In the school context, focusing on a theme is often associated with the project approach, where classmates develop products built upon topics predetermined by the curriculum or the teacher. In a tutorial setting, the theme for the project approach integrates a tutee's interests and funds of knowledge with a set of appropriate learning objectives. For instance, should a tutee have expressed an interest in riding horses, the project approach would allow for the undertaking of multiple sessions centering on equestrian topics such as the care and housing of horses, types of riding competitions, and large animal veterinary sciences.

In the construction of a final project, whether it be a traditional text, video, photo essay, personal journal, or slide presentation, each of the five pillars of the reading process is promoted along with the other elements of the language arts, such as writing, speaking, listening, viewing, and visual representation. In becoming an expert on a topic, the tutee also extends one's skills with academic inquiry using both traditional print texts and digital sources.

Lesson Example: Multigenerational Family Histories

A powerful value-added component of a funds of knowledge approach to tutoring is the wealth of knowledge the tutee's family or members of the local community can bring to the tutoring process. The funds of knowledge approach supports the tutee seeking out stories, traditions, and cultural knowledge that comprise a unique and valued family and community heritage as initially highlighted in the Foxfire series. While the language used to detail this information may be from the tutee's first language, when the narrative is brought to the tutoring session it becomes the source for printed or audio texts in English. Through this process, tutor and tutee may employ technology to write texts, author blogs, record videos, or create other digital artifacts that can be shared with varied outlets throughout the community.

For decades now teachers have been urged to undertake family visits with parents and caregivers of their ML students to learn about the funds of knowledge the learners bring with them every day to the classroom (Johnson & Johnson, 2016; Sheldon & Jung, 2018). The same suggestion can be made to a tutor, particularly when the tutee is quite young. It is not only the tutor who benefits from learning about the tutee's funds of knowledge as a source for mapping out instructional plans. While the tutor can use informal chats with the tutee about their background, many young learners may not be fully cognizant of family history or cultural norms.

Given such a case, an activity that can lead to a greater depth of knowledge about one's personal funds of knowledge would be to have the tutee undertake interviews of both the immediate family and members of the extended family circle to learn of various individuals' family knowledge, unique skills, experiences across the years, and personal interests as components of a multigenerational family legacy. The tutor and tutee together would develop an interview questionnaire, lay out procedures to be followed in collecting and preserving the information, undertake literature deep dives to develop background information, and finally plan how the collection of information can be crafted into a product.

In many ways this activity builds upon the recommendations put forth by educators interested in having students participate in nearby history projects (Kyvig et al., 2019) by undertaking oral history documentation. The process across multiple steps requires the tutee to engage in a realm of language arts activities. One particularly good resource for undertaking such an interview project in a tutorial environment is the book *The Oral History Workshop: Collect and Celebrate the Life Stories of Your Family and Friends* by Cynthia Hart with Lisa Samson (2009). Not only does it cover the nuts and bolts of undertaking the family interview, but it also provides an extensive set of questions that might be utilized in a well-crafted interview.

Organic Reading

Across the years tutors within our classes and programs have greatly enjoyed and benefited from reading the book *Teacher* by Sylvia Ashton-Warner (1963), as it is considered a reader-friendly, classic book on literacy instruction. Within the text Ashton-Warner described how she employed a literacy scheme known as Organic Reading (also known as the Key Vocabulary Approach). Her students were Māori people from native schools in New Zealand who did not necessarily identify with the standard reading curriculum of the day. As Warner came to understand that the students had a rich cultural background of experiences and interests, she realized that such a context could serve as the basis for developing competencies in the language arts.

Through our experiences with tutors across the land, we observed that the Organic Reading approach is particularly appropriate for use in a community-based tutoring program that is independent from a local educational system. Here there is freedom to employ an approach that builds upon a tutee's funds of knowledge. The system leads the tutee to explore one's personal and community environment. Thus, the tutee will develop new understandings of the world in which one lives, building and expanding upon the tutee's worldview. This approach serves as a foundation for discussion, composing, and reading about an ever-expanding perspective on the tutee's life and place within the community.

The organic approach follows these steps in the tutoring process. First, with the start of the initial tutorial session and at the beginning of each future session, the tutor asks the tutee what word they would like to learn that day. These words are likely to be key words in the tutee's life, and hence, these are high interest, meaningful, and often practical.

The tutor will next print out the daily word on a large index card. The tutee will trace the word with the index finger and say the word while doing so. As the collection grows, the key vocabulary cards will be kept in a word box (e.g., a recipe card box), and at each session the tutor and tutee review each of the words within the collection. If the instruction is part of a small group tutoring session, the tutee will write the word on a whiteboard or chalkboard and share the word and its meaning and importance with the other tutees.

By the point that the tutee has mastered 40 keywords by sight, the next step is for the tutee to write a brief story about a topic of personal interest, all the while drawing from the key words in the vocabulary file. The composition can be either about a real or imaginary experience. The writing activity will take place at each session. The process ends as the tutor and tutee read the work and discuss the content. Across time the varied stories are organized in a book that can be shared with others.

Culturally Intentional Pedagogy

There is a wealth of research that demonstrates the importance of using Culturally Relevant Pedagogy (Brown-Jeffy & Cooper, 2011; Ladson-Billings, 1995) and Culturally Responsive Teaching Practices (Gay, 2002) as a framework for instruction with diverse learners to promote educational equity. A Culturally Relevant Pedagogical approach to teaching aims to connect a student's cultural background and experiences to the curriculum, thus fostering increased academic achievement while making learning more meaningful. Gay (2002) defines Culturally Responsive Teaching as "using the cultural characteristics, experiences, and perspectives of ethnically diverse students as conduits for teaching them more effectively" (p. 106). However, even the most skilled teacher may struggle to make cultural connections for every diverse student sitting in the classroom.

We propose that a tutorial program can enhance this framework to embrace a culturally *intentional* approach to instruction. Since tutoring programs are limited in the number of tutees they serve, the tutor can more easily gain deep knowledge about the cultural background of the student or small group of students being tutored. By leveraging the reading interest inventory presented in Appendix B and the Funds of Knowledge Inventory Matrix shown in Table 5.1, the tutor can develop a rich profile of their tutee(s) that will help connect instruction more deftly to their cultural values and lived experiences.

Diverse Text Selections

One important consideration for *culturally intentional instruction* is the selection of texts. Traditional text materials (both fiction and non-fiction) as well as multimodal sources that are incorporated into the tutorial sessions should build upon the ML's culture, language, and worldview so that the tutee can visualize oneself within the content and context encountered. Here is where the tutor might assist the tutee in selecting materials that focus on one's hopes and aspirations and at times personal struggles. Furthermore, tutorial materials might also spotlight the tutee's locale as well.

During the school year such instructional materials may serve as an individualized supplement to school content, but as an out-of-school educational experience (vacation time, after school) the tutor has free rein to select materials that promote mastery of the learning objectives for each session with a wide variety of text formats. One strategy for text selection is what Flores and Osorio (2021) refer to as *mirror* and *window* books (see also Bishop, 1990). Mirror books reflect the cultural heritage of the reader while window books give the reader a view into a cultural heritage different from their own.

By using mirror text selections, your tutee will come to see main characters, settings, and themes that reflect their own lived experiences. For example, *Felíz New Year Ava Gabriela!* by Alexandra Alessandri highlights the experiences of young Ava visiting family in Colombia, where she participates in family traditions such as making buñuelos (fried dough covered in cinnamon and sugar) and eating 12 grapes at the stroke of midnight for good luck.

Alternatively, window texts will help your tutee establish a new perspective (oftentimes reflective of the cultural norms of their current learning environment) in which you, as the tutor, can help them make connections to their funds of knowledge. Gail Piernas-Davenport's book, *Shanté Keys and the New Year's Peas*, highlights an African American family's New Year's traditions through the eyes of the main character, Shanté. Upon a traditional visit to Grandma's house for lucky New Year black-eyed peas, Grandma discovers she has cooked chitlins, ham, macaroni and cheese, greens, and corn bread, but forgot the lucky peas. Shanté goes into the neighborhood to borrow some peas, where she encounters neighbors from China, Ireland, and other faraway places who share different New Year traditions.

By pairing these two texts, you can leverage your tutee's funds of knowledge focused on the cultural traditions of the New Year holiday. You can make connections to the importance of food and family and other traditions discovered through these texts. You can also extend this activity to look at traditions in other countries (e.g., Chinese New Year) or other unique cultural holidays (e.g., Brazilian Carnival, Día de los Muertos).

In 2016, Gene Luen Yang (National Ambassador for Young People's Literature, Library of Congress) initiated the *Reading Without Walls* platform in which children were encouraged to:

1. Read a book about a **character** who doesn't look like you or live like you.
2. Read a book about a **topic** you don't know much about.
3. Read a book in a **format** you don't normally read for fun. This might be a chapter book, a graphic novel, a picture book, or a hybrid book.

This platform provides a great opportunity to leverage a community-oriented perspective by assisting the tutee in obtaining a public library card, followed by regular excursions to the library to select texts that fit one or more of the descriptions above.

When selecting culturally relevant (mirror) texts that reflect your learner's funds of knowledge, you can refer to the Cultural Relevance Rubric provided on the ReadWriteThink website (NCTE/IRA, 2006) as shown in Figure 5.1.

Another diverse text selection strategy for MLs is to acquire bilingual books that are written in the tutee's home language and English. Bilingual texts help support translanguaging as MLs can leverage their home language as they learn new concepts in English. Bilingual texts can be found in multiple formats. You can locate videos on YouTube that feature books narrated in English and Spanish, like *Marisol McDonald Doesn't Match*, written by Monica Brown and illustrated by Sara Palacios. The English/Spanish/Bilingual Kids Books YouTube Playlist by KidTime StoryTime contains over 80 books read in English and Spanish.

Unite for Literacy (UniteForLiteracy.com, n.d.) is another online platform that celebrates language and culture with a wide range of more than 400 picture books (fiction and non-fiction) with audio narrations in more than 40 languages spoken by native speakers. Leveraging bilingual books and those narrated in the learner's home language can help ML students feel more included in the instructional process and be more motivated to learn new content.

Creating Supportive Learning Environments

Once the instructional planning and selection of materials have been completed, a structured instructional approach can help focus and support the tutorial

Cultural Relevance Rubric

	3	2	1
Characters	The character(s) in the text are very much like me and my family. The character(s) would fit in well.	The character(s) in the text have some similarities to me and my family; but there are also many differences.	The character(s) in the text are not at all like me and my family. The character(s) would not fit in well at all.
Experiences	I have had experiences exactly like the one(s) described in this story. The events matched my experiences well.	I have had some experiences like the one(s) described in this story; but I have had different experiences as well.	I have not had experiences like the one(s) described in this story. The events are unlike my own experiences.
Place (Setting)	I have lived in or visited places just like those in the story. The setting was familiar to me.	I have lived in or visited places that were similar in some ways to those in the stories; but there were definitely differences.	I have never lived in or visited places just like those in the story. The events took place in a location that was not familiar to me.
Time (Setting)	The events in the text could take place this year. They happen in the present.	Some of the events in the text could take place this year, but others either took past in the past or future.	The events in the text could not take place this year. They either take place at some point in the past or the future.
Main Character's Age	The main character(s) in the text are very close to me in age.	Some of the main characters in the text are very close to me in age while others are not.	The main character(s) in the text are not very close in age to me.
Main Character's Gender	The main characters in the text are the same gender as I am.	Some of the main characters in the text are the same gender as I am.	The main characters in the text are not the same gender as I am.
Languages	The characters in the text communicate like me and my family. They talk, read, and write like us.	Some of the characters in the text communicate like me and my family. Others do not talk, read, and write like us.	The characters in the text do not communicate like me and my family. They do not talk, read, or write like us.
Frequency	I read, view, or listen to texts just like this one very often.	I sometimes read, view, or listen to texts just like this one.	I never read, view, or listen to texts just like this one.

read·write·think Copyright 2006 NCTE/IRA. All rights reserved. ReadWriteThink materials may be reproduced for educational purposes.

Figure 5.1 Rubric for evaluating culturally relevant texts from ReadWriteThink.org.

process for MLs. Hence, we suggest that a tutor employ the Sheltered Instruction Observation Protocol (SIOP) Model (Echevarria et al, 2008, 2010a, 2010b). This instructional model is both research-based and has been instructionally validated for promoting the learning of new academic knowledge and language/literacy competencies of MLs. Furthermore, in following the steps of the SIOP model, a structured and supportive learning environment is provided for the learner. SIOP has been used widely in the school setting. Can SIOP be employed in the tutorial process? The answer is clearly in the affirmative, but there are considerations.

Over the years SIOP has been shown to improve academic achievement, lead to greater language proficiency, and promote student engagement in the traditional classroom. If the SIOP model is utilized in the tutee's classroom to promote content learning and language proficiency, the tutor will wish to support this educational model. Yet, given such positive findings, it can be assumed that SIOP may be adapted for the delivery of individualized out-of-school tutoring that focuses on either content knowledge addressed in the class or that is drawn from the tutee's funds of knowledge.

The structured, supportive, and yet highly adaptable nature of SIOP provides the tutor with implementation and delivery guidelines that serve as a step-by-step approach for an individualized session or group of sessions across time that focus upon a thematic topic or project. The seven steps of SIOP are presented in Table 5.2.

By following the structure provided by the SIOP model, we propose that a tutor can effectively support ML tutees (or any tutee, for that matter) as they build language competencies along with academic knowledge,

Table 5.2 Overview of the Sheltered Instruction Observation Protocol for tutoring

Primary Step	Components	Actions
Tutorial lesson preparation	Define content objectives	Develop explicit instructional objectives focusing on academic content or competencies for the tutorial session(s).
	Define language objectives	Determine the language competency objectives (e.g., vocabulary, discourse patterns, sentence structure).
	Utilize supplemental materials	Select visual aids, multimodal materials, technology, and texts that support mastery of lesson objectives.
Building tutee's background	Activate funds of knowledge (prior knowledge and past experiences)	Draw upon the tutee's resources related to academic literacy, language use and conventions, and funds of knowledge through discussion and questioning.
	Pre-teach language of the discipline	Use supplemental materials to pre-teach academic concepts, vocabulary, etc. that are foundational to the content.
Comprehensible input	Use clear language	Speak in clear and understandable language.

(Continued)

Table 5.2 Overview of the Sheltered Instruction Observation Protocol for tutoring (*Continued*)

Primary Step	Components	Actions
	Employ visual aids	Make use of visual aids (diagrams, photos, charts, videos, maps, etc.). Teach how to use and evaluate the content from these sources.
	Explain academic tasks	Thoroughly explain the tasks associated with the tutorial lesson(s), ask the tutee to detail the tasks, and ask for clarifications as needed.
Learning strategies	Teach learning strategies	Directly teach research-based learning strategies appropriate for the respective academic task and subject matter (e.g., predicting, questioning, summarizing, evaluating) and assist in selecting the strategy for content mastery and independent learning.
	Model each strategy	Demonstrate strategic learning approaches for the academic task before expecting the learner to successfully undertake its use.
	Employ scaffolded tutoring	Break down each task into manageable components using guided practice while reducing direct assistance as the learner gains competence.
Interaction	Promote tutee participation	Use Socratic questioning and discussion to lead the tutee to approach, undertake, and assess the learning process in a strategic manner.
	Utilize interactive activities in tutorial sessions	Employ learning games, role-playing, and problem-solving activities to promote the tutee's literacy and language growth.
	Provide wait time as appropriate	Give the learner the necessary time on task to provide responses in English.
Practice/ Application	Utilize active activities	Give the tutee many opportunities to apply what has been learned and use meaningful activities and projects that focus on the tutee's funds of knowledge.
	Build language competency	Stress language use (reading, writing, speaking, and listening) as a reinforcement component of application and practice.

(continued)

Table 5.2 Overview of the Sheltered Instruction Observation Protocol for tutoring (Continued)

Primary Step	Components	Actions
	Provide ongoing feedback	Deliver constructive feedback and praise the mastery of content and the expanding use of the English language (both conversational and academic).
Tutorial lesson delivery	Always check for understanding	Assess the learner's mastery of new content and language competencies as associated with lesson objectives. Reteach the content or skill that has yet to be learned at a satisfactory level.
	Provide pacing throughout the tutoring sessions	Prepare each lesson so the delivery of content reflects the tutee's developmental level and learning abilities. Carefully integrate each component of the SIOP model within and/or across each session.

whether drawn from a school-based curriculum or the tutee's personal funds of knowledge. (For teaching ideas of which many can be adapted for tutoring, see Echevarria & Vogt, 2022.)

We would be remiss if it were not noted that one of the great policy fallacies on designing instruction and hence also tutoring for MLs is that all activities should only lead to mastery of the new language. While it is true that building a tutee's proficiency with all phases of the use of the English language is paramount, the tutor should, whenever possible, support the tutee's development of literacy competencies in their native as well as learned language(s). Doing so facilitates the transfer of literacy skills from their own language(s) to English and acknowledges the value of the tutee's language(s) of origin and cultural heritage.

In closing, let us reinforce the perspective that in utilizing a funds of knowledge approach to tutoring with culturally intentional learning activities, the tutor will honor the tutee's unique background all the while building connections between the tutee, the community, and the school setting. In addition, while this chapter focuses on tutees who are MLs, the fundamental philosophy of a funds of knowledge approach is a powerful pedagogical process that can be used with virtually any learner who might benefit from an individualized tutorial experience. Finally, given the philosophy put forward throughout this guidebook, many of the instructional activities presented within this text fit perfectly in the approach presented in this chapter.

Chapter 6

Assessing Literacy Interests, Attitudes, and Competencies

Laurie A. Henry and Norman A. Stahl

Assessment is one of the cornerstones of good pedagogy. Hence, let us provide a definition that will serve as a foundation for its purpose in a tutorial situation. The Making Sense of Educational Assessment Fact Sheet from the Institute of Education Sciences (IES, 2023) notes, "Educational assessment is a systematic process of documenting and using evidence to improve educational programs and student learning." We contend that this definition encompasses both programming from formal education authorities as well as alternative programs, including community-based tutorial services. The IES Fact Sheet goes on to state, "the evidence or data used for educational assessment can be related to knowledge, skills, practices, beliefs, and attitudes" (see also Allen, 2004).

Given this position, one understands that a tutor needs to be familiar with the concept of assessment but may not be familiar with the three key purposes for assessment, which include assessment for research, evaluation, and instructional purposes. It is quite possible that each function could be at work in a community tutorial program at any given time. A professor could be working alongside the coordinator of a community-based tutorial program, undertaking research to test a hypothesis or collect data, in which the findings might lead to literacy policy changes for a specific population. On the other hand, the coordinator of a program, with support of its advisory board or per the request of a funding agency, may need to conduct an evaluation that measures the effectiveness of the program or one of its components that would lead to program improvements. In either case, the tutor may be required to undertake a range of assessment-guided activities in support of a research or evaluation function.

However, for the tutor and the tutee, the primary goal of assessment pertains to instruction. Initial tutoring sessions will often have the tutor undertaking diagnostic work with the tutee to determine as much as possible about the knowledge, competencies (strengths), interests, beliefs, and attitudes the tutee brings to the tutoring program. These assessments come in a variety of formats, including formative assessments (used frequently to inform instruction) and summative assessments (used to determine mastery of content), as well as more informal questionnaires.

On an interim basis throughout the duration of the tutoring sessions, formative assessment should be used frequently to inform tutoring practices and to measure the growth and achievement demonstrated by the learner. Formative assessments evolve from and then measure the specific objectives for each of the tutoring sessions. A tutorial program that supports an individualized, community-oriented philosophy of instruction will require that the tutor select or design and implement ongoing interim/formative assessment tools.

Summative assessments, much like the standardized testing in public schools, may be required at the end of a specific time period as set by the tutorial center's administration or even by the program's funding agency. The instrumentation that will be selected and employed is generally out of the hands of the individual tutor, as it may be a standardized measure that is benchmarked by age and/or grade level.

In the body of this chapter, several formative or informal assessments that are appropriate for use with tutees receiving services from a community or independent tutorial program are provided. Each is designed to allow the tutor to obtain an understanding of the tutee's literacy competencies, interests, attitudes, etc. The assessments serve a diagnostic purpose, but as most are informal in nature, there is the opportunity to customize an instrument to meet a tutee's background or individual needs.

Tutee Interest Inventory

The first time you meet with your tutee can be a bit awkward. Likely, you are strangers. Perhaps you are from very different backgrounds. Certainly, your relationship to the world of reading and literacy will be different. Hence, an icebreaker for the first session is often in the form of an Interest Inventory. Learning about your tutee sets the stage for further assessment and planning of literacy activities, as well as the selection of instructional materials of high interest to the learner. What follows is an example Tutee Interest Inventory, which can either be presented as an oral prompt or as a fill-in-the-blank activity depending upon the tutee's competency level. It can also be adapted as necessary for the specific age or background of the learner.

Westside Tutorial Program
Tutee Interest Inventory

Directions: I would like to get to know you better. So, I'll ask you some questions. Please share with me the answers to each question below. If there's a question you don't want to answer, that's okay. We can skip it and move to the next one.

- Do you like to watch television?
    - [If yes] What are your favorite shows? Why do you like these shows?
- Do you like to play video games?
    - [If yes] What are your favorite games? What is the best thing about playing this video game?
- What is your favorite movie? What makes it your favorite movie?
- Do you use social media? Which platforms are your favorite?
- What are your favorite things to do on the weekends?
- What are your favorite sports? Do you play a sport? What do you play? Which position?
- Have you ever taken a trip? [If yes] Where did you go? What did you enjoy most?
- What is your favorite food?
- Do you have any pets? [If yes] What name does it have? How do you take care of it?
- What do you want to do when you finish school? Why are you interested in doing this?
- Have you ever had a job? [If yes] What was it?

- If you won a million dollars, what would you do with it?
- If you could meet a famous person, who would that be?
- What school do you attend? What grade are you in?
- What is your favorite subject (and why)? What subject is your least favorite (and why)?
- What do people say you do best?
- What would you like to do better?

After you collect some general information about your tutee's interests, you'll want to learn more about how they feel about reading. This can be accomplished through a series of literacy-focused exploratory activities that help you better understand your tutee as a reader and writer.

The Tutor's Reading Interview

As you begin your service as a tutor, one of the first things you should do is learn about how your tutee views the act of reading (or writing). Certainly, you do not want to put your tutee on the spot with questions that might seem to be a bit too direct and invasive. William Henk, Dean Emeritus of Education at Marquette University, developed a reading interview instrument for future literacy specialists that we have adapted for your use as a tutor.

In using the Tutor's Reading Interview, you would ask your tutee each question in turn. You will want to carefully record your tutee's responses, whether by hand or with an audio recording device. As you review this instrument, pretend that the tutee has identified a classmate named Antonio who is considered a good reader.

Tutor's Reading Interview

When you are reading and come to something you don't know or understand, what do you do? Do you ever do anything else?

- Who is a good reader you know? What makes *Antonio* a good reader?
- Do you think *Antonio* ever comes to something he doesn't know or understand?
- When *Antonio* comes to a word he doesn't know, what do you think he does?
- Suppose that *Antonio* comes to something in his reading he doesn't understand; what do you think he would do?

- If someone was having trouble reading, how would you help that person? What would your teacher do to help that person?
- How did you learn to read?
- What would you like to do better as a reader?
- Do you think you are a good reader? Why or why not?

You will note that these questions are posed in a rather informal manner. Yes, that is the design of the interview. As you get more comfortable in the interview process, you may feel comfortable revising the format to meet your style or even that of the tutee. Still, the key will be to have a good set of notes that will serve in the design of an instructional plan that builds upon the tutee's interests, attitudes, and instructional needs.

The Reading/Writing Autobiography

The reading and writing autobiography is generally used with an older tutee, but with care and some adaptation, the assessment can be employed with younger ones. The device can be used in an interview situation, or it can be used as a reflective writing task about literacy. It is designed to capture a tutee's general interests about reading or writing, their literacy habits, and their attitudes toward reading and writing.

We now share a set of questions that can be used within an interview process where the tutor will either transcribe the tutee's responses or may use an audio device to record the responses for later review and analysis.

Reading/Writing Autobiography

- What are your earliest memories of learning to read?
- What are your earliest memories of learning to write?
- What are your memories of reading to learn in school?
- What are your memories about reading at home or with your family?
- What books/materials do you remember reading when you were younger?
- What topics did you like to read about when you were younger? Is this different today?
- What do you like to read about today? When did you last read about that topic?
- What don't you like to read about now?
- What reading sources do you prefer: books, magazines, online materials, etc.? Can you give some examples?

- How do you feel about reading? How do you feel about writing?
- If English is not your first language, when did you first learn to read or write in English?
- What would you like to achieve from being tutored in reading and writing?

As you engage the tutee in this interview, draw out examples or anecdotes to generate more detailed responses. The questions are designed to identify the tutee's memories, interests, and attitudes as well as to assist in setting the goals for tutoring. As the interviewer, you can easily modify the questions to meet the individual needs of your tutoring situation. The questions provided should get you started with the process. As you gain experience as a tutor, you will likely revise or augment the question sequence to fit your own style and context.

With slight variations, each of the prompts can be revised to meet the age or grade level of the tutee. It is important to remember that a tutee's competency with writing is unlikely to be as strong as the tutee's ability to share responses in a verbal manner. Therefore, using a conversational approach and audio recording the session for future reference is highly recommended.

San Diego Quick Assessment

In some cases, a tutor might receive a diagnostic profile of some sort from the tutee's teacher. This can have useful information to guide your instructional planning. Still, there will be times when such information will not be forthcoming. Therefore, having a straightforward assessment instrument that provides a quick understanding of a tutee's reading level can be rather helpful.

The San Diego Quick Assessment (La Pray & Ross, 1969) has been used successfully by tutors for decades. Its purpose is to first determine a tutee's reading level and then detect gaps in word analysis skills. The test comprises 13 ten-word lists that span the reading levels from PreK through the 11th grade. You can use it with most tutees across the life span for a quick and easy assessment of grade-level reading acumen.

Assessment Administration

The directions for administration of the San Diego Quick Assessment are presented as follows:

- Write out each list of ten words on a set of index cards (or presentation slides if using technology). You will have 13 sets of words when completed.

- Begin with the card that is at least two years below the tutee's current grade level.
- Ask the tutee to read the words on the card aloud to you. If the tutee misreads any words on the list, drop down to an easier list until the tutee can read all ten words with no errors. This will be the base level, and you should make note of it.
- On your copy of the assessment record form (see Appendix H), write down all incorrect responses. As an example, on the Grade 3 word list, *lonely* could be read and thus recorded as *lovely*. *Apparatus* from the Grade 6 word list might be recorded as *per'atus*.
- The tutee should be encouraged to read unknown words so that you might be able to identify the tutee's attempts at phonetic decoding or basic word identification.
- Make note of each word that is missed on each word list. The tutee should read increasingly difficult word lists until three words are read incorrectly from the same list.

Analysis Guidelines

Once the tutee has reached a grade-level word list in which three or more mistakes were made, you have completed the administration of the assessment. Now you can begin your analysis to determine the reading level of your tutee. Use the guidelines outlined below to establish your tutee's independent, instructional, and frustration reading levels.

- The list for which the tutee misses no more than one word is the level at which the tutee can read independently. Texts at this level are relatively easy for the learner to read with minimal errors and good comprehension. Texts at this level are good for independent practice and building fluency.
- The word list in which the tutee missed two words is at the instructional level. Texts at this level require some guidance and scaffolding by the tutor. Texts at the instructional level are often used to introduce new concepts and unfamiliar vocabulary.
- When there are three or more errors on a word list, the tutee will find reading materials at this level to be too difficult, which is referred to as the frustration level. The tutee will struggle with decoding words and making meaning from the text. Texts at this level can be detrimental to the learner's motivation and can impact literacy development.

- An analysis of the errors made by a tutee can inform you of instructional needs. The authors present the following list of common errors followed by an example: reversal (*ton* for *not*), consonant (*now* for *how*), consonant clusters (*state* for *straight*), short vowel (*cane* for *can*), long vowel (*wid* for *wide*), prefix (*inproved* for *improved*), suffix (*improve* for *improved*), and miscellaneous (accent, omission of syllables, etc.).
- Your observation of the tutee's behavior is quite important. A tutor should note the tutee's posture, facial expressions, voice quality, restlessness, lack of assurance, and frustration while reading. Of course, this point should always be followed during every tutorial lesson.

The grade-level word lists are provided on the San Diego Quick Assessment Record Form found in Appendix H. At this point we offer two caveats. First, the San Diego Quick Assessment does not measure either knowledge of vocabulary or comprehension ability. It simply measures the learner's recognition of words out of context. Secondly, while the tutee's performance on this measure may suggest to you the levels of instructional materials that can be used in the tutoring lessons, it is imperative that the tutee's interests and prior knowledge of the textual content be considered in the selection of the instructional materials. Either construct may lead to the tutee being able to handle texts that would be beyond the level suggested by this measure. Keep in mind that this list and any similar assessment measure is but a sample of words at a particular readability level. Hence, the measure should only serve as a rough guide for instructional planning.

The San Diego Quick Assessment does allow for alternative utilization. For instance, each word on a respective grade-level list can be presented on a single index card. The pronunciation guide would be on the reverse side. The word would be "flashed" for the tutee for half a second to determine if there was rapid word recognition (i.e., the word is known by sight). This process would be repeated until there was a word to which the tutee did not respond correctly. That word would then be presented in an untimed manner for the tutee's response. The next word is then presented in the rapid word recognition manner. If that is missed, the untimed protocol is followed, and so on throughout the presentation of the grade list.

It is also possible to check for knowledge of word meaning, as this will provide a rough guide to vocabulary knowledge. In this case, the definition(s) of the word would also be found on the reverse side of the index card. Finally, the procedure can also ask the student to use the word in a sentence.

As the tutee is responding to each specific word, the tutor is keeping a careful record of the responses on a grade-level sheet that contains each word. Common notations for responses include:

- Hesitation: H
- Incorrect response: --
- Correct response: C
- Correct meaning of word: M+
- Incorrect meaning of word: M-
- Correct use in sentence: S+
- Incorrect use in a sentence: S-
- Unknown component of a word: Circle it
- Known component of a word: Underline it

Attitude Toward Reading Scale

The Tutee Attitude Toward Reading Scale shown in Table 6.1 provides an across time judgment by the tutor of the changes in a tutee's attitude about reading. These judgments are made at regular points throughout the tutoring experience. Informal examples of the tutee's progress can be kept in the tutor's daily journal to be used in making periodic evaluations of the tutee's attitudes. The following example can be revised to fit a particular tutoring situation (e.g., tutee's age, focus of the tutoring session). For consistency, it should not be revised throughout the period in which the tutee's attitudes are being monitored.

With this Tutee Attitude Toward Reading Scale, items are listed in the first column. To the right are columns for a variety of time points (Weeks 1, 6, and 12). The evaluation codes to be listed for each item include N for not at all, S for sometimes, and O for often. The codes should be marked for each item at different time points. Growth in attitude toward reading is determined by the total number of N, S, and O responses that are recorded over time. A decrease in the number of N responses and an increase in S and O responses demonstrate positive attitudinal growth.

A more extensive reading attitude scale can provide additional information about a learner's motivation to read. The following directions provide guidance on how you might use the Reading Attitude Scale with a learner (see Appendix I).

- Step #1. Reproduce a scale and distribute it to the tutee.
- Step #2. Provide the tutee with a highlighter.

Assessing Literacy Interests, Attitudes, and Competencies

Table 6.1 Tutee attitude toward reading scale

Item	Week 1	Week 6	Week 12
My tutee brings text materials to our tutoring sessions.			
My tutee borrows books from the public or school library.			
My tutee shares what is read with others.			
My tutee interacts with others about what has been read.			
My tutee talks about having a favorite author.			
My tutee talks about having a favorite genre of text.			
My tutee is interested in reading about favorite topics.			
My tutee reads texts to answer questions.			
My tutee connects content from reading to his/her life.			
My tutee reads for pleasure and recreation.			
My tutee reports reading in the home.			
My tutee's attitude toward reading has improved.			
My tutee believes his/her reading is improving.			
My tutee views himself/herself as a reader.			
My tutee's teacher reports participation in reading in class.			

- Step #3. Inform the tutee that the way they respond to the scale will not have any negative effect on the tutoring experience.
- Step #4. Ask your tutee to read horizontally across the first section of the scale. Ask the tutee to highlight the statement that best fits their attitude about the thought that is presented in the respective section.
- Step #5. After completing the first section, have the tutee move through all 25 sections, highlighting each statement (response) that applies best to them.
- Step #6. Eighteen of the items move from the most positive response to the most negative response. Seven of the items move from the most negative response to the most positive response. Responses to these items will differ in their value.

Item numbers 1, 2, 5, 6, 7, 8, 9, 10, 11, 13, 14, 15, 16, 18, 19, 21, 22, and 23 have a positive directionality. Hence, these are scored in moving left to right for each item as four points, three points, two points, and one point. Item numbers 3, 4, 12, 17, 20, 24, and 25 have a negative directionality. Hence, these are scored in moving left to right for each item as one point, two points, three points, and four points. The tutee's total score (ranging from 25 to 100 points) is a quantitative reflection of the tutee's attitude in reading. A qualitative analysis can focus on specific items and develop a rich reader profile of your tutee.

The Reading Strategy Inventory

The Reading Strategy Inventory has been adapted for the tutorial process. This instrument focuses on mature reading competencies that promote meaning making of text as opposed to skills associated with the basics of learning to read (i.e., phonemic awareness, phonics, and word attack). As such, the Reading Strategy Inventory is a simple checklist of research- and theory-driven actions that might be expected to be in the bag of tricks employed by evolving and mature readers. The tutor can use this checklist to identify specific reading competencies as they develop over time.

Reading Strategy Inventory

Before reading my tutee:

1. Surveys the text to determine the general topic being presented.
2. Hypothesizes what might happen in a story or what is the purpose of the subject matter.
3. Examines the title, pictures, illustrations, photos, charts, summary, etc., to hypothesize the topics/content to be read.
4. Uses the headings and subheadings to generate questions about the content of passages.
5. Thinks about and discusses what can be learned from the text.
6. Poses questions that are likely to be answered in the text passages.
7. Recalls prior knowledge and experiences that are associated with text features.
8. Develops a plan on how to go about reading the passages.
9. Describes what will be the outcomes and possible further actions to be taken when the reading is completed.
10. Explains how the information will be used after reading.

During reading my tutee:

1. Tries to visualize what is being described in the text.
2. Identifies the type of text being read (genre, subject, etc.).
3. Uses knowledge of text type to promote comprehension.
4. Determines the way the author has organized the information in the text.
5. Reads with fluency.
6. Makes predictions based on what has been read.
7. Revises those predictions as appropriate.
8. Is metacognitively aware of what is understood or not understood.
9. Asks questions about the content while reading.
10. Stops regularly to paraphrase the content into one's own words.
11. Employs generative vocabulary strategies to master unknown words.
12. Revises thinking when it does not fit with what has been presented in the text.
13. Rereads the parts of the text that are counter to prior knowledge.
14. Rereads the parts of the text that are not initially understood.
15. Uses text features (including tables, figures, and visuals) when comprehension falters.
16. Employs close reading tactics and word identification skills when needed.
17. Consults alternative sources (printed or digital) when comprehension is diminished.

After reading my tutee:

1. Can summarize/paraphrase the important information from the text.
2. Critically evaluates whether the information is trustworthy.
3. Separates facts from author's opinions.
4. Rereads and studies sections of the text that were not fully understood.
5. Asks questions for clarification and to further research the topic.
6. Can respond to the arguments presented in the text.
7. Analyzes how the author's position (stance) affected their response(s).
8. Decides whether the author's stance makes sense or seeks alternate arguments.
9. Looks for other materials (print or digital) that might assist in developing a deeper understanding of the text's topic.
10. Speculates about the importance of the text's content to a topic, subject field, or aspect of one's life.

These before, during, and after reading strategies are appropriate competencies to be integrated into tutoring sessions. Of course, not every tactic is used for each reading task.

Tutor's Reflective Journal

Within the tutoring environment, one often thinks of journaling as an activity undertaken by the tutee, often with feedback from the tutor. Such is indeed the case, but ongoing journaling by the tutor is a powerful assessment of the effectiveness of the tutorial process and the progress being made by the tutee over time.

Some 50 years ago, Thom Hawkins (1972) published a journal he kept of his nine-month experience in tutoring a 19-year-old African American named Benjamin. This now seminal work in the tutorial literature not only captured Hawkins' thoughts about instructional approaches, selected texts and materials, and the ups and downs of the tutoring interactions, but it also served as a useful evaluation of Benjamin's growth as a literate individual and a consumer and constructor of texts.

Hawkins explained the importance of keeping a tutor's journal as described here:

> This journal of our lessons came about almost accidently. At first, I kept a few rough notes to help guide me along with no intention other than maximizing my efforts with Ben. As luck would have it, a couple of my classes required a term project similar to what I was already doing. I got more deeply involved in my project with Benjamin and soon found that I could not let the journal writing end because it was providing me with valuable feedback on our lessons. By jotting down and evaluating a lesson the day it occurred, I had a much better idea of where we were going than I could have gotten by projecting lesson plans. With the journal's help, our meetings gradually took on distinct characteristics, growing out of my student's interests and his idea of what learning to read was all about.
>
> (x–xi)

The fundamental purpose of keeping a tutor's journal is to promote the process of reflective tutoring. It is through your reflections about each session that you as a tutor undertake a personal dialogue to document those aspects of the recent session that can be viewed as successful or, on the other hand, those events and activities that did not live up to expectations. Through such documentation and then self-critique of the tutorial session you are better able to understand yourself as a tutor and the tutee as a learner. You are also able to then speculate why a particular instructional activity hit the mark or perhaps more importantly why it was not on target. Through this self-reflective analysis, plans can be made for instructional improvements and adjustments for future tutorial sessions.

In committing to the journaling process, you will want to prepare an entry in your log (paper or digital) as soon as possible following the tutoring session. As the first initial step, write down as many details that come to mind. In a sense, you are attempting to capture as many interactions along with your thoughts and opinions so that these will not be lost to you as you move through subsequent happenings in your life. Once you have preserved all these thoughts in the journal, you will turn to the second step that is the analysis of the session, which, of course, includes assessing the tutee's progress in meeting your goals. Through this step, you evaluate the past and plan for the future.

You may ask what basic skills and cognitive strategies your tutee successfully employed in tackling the instructional objectives and what skills or competencies need to be revisited at a future session. You want to consider what accomplishments were demonstrated by the tutee during the instruction that offered proof to you that the objective for the lesson was met and that the skills focused on during past instructional sessions have been incorporated into the tutee's literacy bag of tricks (i.e., competencies). Questions such as these should be carefully spelled out in the journal as they will help to guide the design of the next lesson and serve as the key points for assessment.

The next step simply asks you to develop a reflective statement of evaluation for the essence of the entry. Then, on a regular basis, review your journal entries and write an entry that integrates what might be considered your "findings" from across multiple sessions. As tutoring with a particular student comes to an end, revisit the entire set of entries and compose one last entry that pulls the instructional sequence and learner growth together in a final summative entry.

While the journal process might end here, it is suggested that you share your journal with another tutor or your tutorial supervisor. It is always helpful to learn from others' thoughts and opinions about one's work. Finally, if you are undertaking the tutoring assignment as part of a high school or college class, it is likely that your instructor will have a specific protocol to document your tutoring experiences. The ideas presented here should still be useful in completing such an assignment.

The instruments provided in this chapter are designed to help the tutor get an idea of the tutee's foundational skills and attitudes about the act of reading and/or writing. They are not designed to take the place of formal literacy assessments that might be used in the classroom. Still, the results of these measures can be shared with a tutee's teacher or school literacy specialist as these measures may very well provide additional information about the tutee that may not be found with more formal measures that are part of a school's assessment program.

Chapter 7

Connecting Tutoring to Schoolwork and High-Stakes Assessments

James R. King, with Carson Binder and Denise Perez Binder

Most families have lived through this story. Young children, appearing to be happy, perhaps distracted at times, always moving, it seems. This is every day. But then it happens, out of the blue, your child will need to repeat third grade because of "below level" reading test scores. Before this story plays out, there is some background reading to set the stage.

In 2005, Scott Paris presented an important work of theoretical positioning in literacy, which is specifically important to early literacy intervention. In his writing, literacy competence is represented by both constrained and unconstrained sets of reading skills. And that "some reading skills, such as learning the letters of the alphabet, are constrained to small sets of knowledge that are mastered in relatively brief periods of development" (Paris, 2005, 184). Other skills, such as vocabulary development, are unconstrained and therefore continue to develop across the lifespan. Further thinking suggests that constrained skills, acquired early on and in a relatively short time span, constitute critical periods of learning, or in this case, critical periods for skill acquisition (Robson, 2002; Snow & Hoefnagel, 1978). After the critical period ends, learners who try to acquire these early skills, such as phonics, may face a closed or closing door, after which it may no longer be productive to drill on these skills.

Another way of responding to compromised learning of early skills during a critical period is to make a "work-around." A work-around is a plan or method to circumvent a problem (such as an alternative meaning-making strategy that relies less on graphophonics) without eliminating the problem itself (in this case, *lack of graphophonics*). Work-arounds use extra materials and/or approaches to accomplish (at least partially) what the original early skills enabled (Smillie, 1985). All of which is to beg the following question: What do you do with a struggling reader who is just past the critical period for phonics acquisition? The following is a memoir of my work with my grandnephew, Carson, who found himself on the exit side of that closing door and at risk of failing third grade.

Denise is my husband's niece (a.k.a. niece Da Niece). Her second son is Carson. Carson and his brother Gavin are the closest I will ever come to having grandchildren. They are both dear to me. They matter, and that is why I am telling this story – once for me to remember, once for Carson to be proud, and finally for readers to bear witness.

When Carson was a third grader, his teacher, Ms. Mervis (a pseudonym), summoned Denise to a meeting, and Denise asked me to join her as Carson's concerned uncle. Indeed, I was/I am. What neither she nor I shared with Ms. Mervis was that I was then a professor of literacy studies at the neighborhood university, with three decades of teaching and research in reading education. I do not claim that these credentials made me a superior knower in these or other circumstances. Rather, Denise and I considered that sharing this information would not help Carson's case with Ms. Mervis, his teacher.

Ms. Mervis began our joint meeting after hours, in her classroom, at a kidney-shaped reading table. She began with a short list of what Carson was handling well. But these achievements, presented as positive, soon evaporated. Then she launched into the real reason for the meeting, Carson's impending failure in reading. In Florida, at that time, third-grade reading scores on the Florida Skills Assessment functioned as a "high-stakes" assessment. To progress to fourth grade, Carson needed to pass this upcoming reading test. Ms. Mervis explained the concept of "bubble kids," those who were at a level 2 out of 5, but "high twos," with some chance of rising to a level 3 and thereby passing the assessment and passing into grade four. These were the *lucky* bubble kids.

Ms. Mervis had been coached to concentrate her attention on her bubble students, with a productive goal of increasing her percentage of students who would score at least at level 3, pass the high-stakes reading test, and move on to the fourth grade. They would therefore require no additional administrative resources. Carson was a level 2, but not a relatively lucky bubble kid. Ms. Mervis let us know that she would certainly not ignore Carson, but according to her triaging, he would not receive any extra literacy interventions. The unstated, though very real, purpose of the meeting was to inform Denise (and now me) that we could expect Carson to spend a second year in grade 3. And this was only November of his *first* year in grade 3.

Denise, with a graduate degree and certification in Special Education, was already schooled in what was transpiring during this meeting. She remained calm, asked for any alternatives to the foretold repetition of a grade, which would presumably offer Carson another dose of the same curriculum that had proved ineffective for his engagement with literacy the first time around. Ms. Mervis suggested outside-of-school tutoring, while simultaneously cautioning that any tutoring interventions were unlikely to move Carson's literacy needle. In retrospect, I see the strategic wisdom in this cautionary evaluation of tutoring. After all, if Carson was amenable to tutoring intervention, shouldn't she be offering it as part of a classroom-based approach to Carson's literacy development? Unlike Denise's apparent calm, I was seething. In the moment of the meeting, I managed not to speak from my red face. Instead, I mentally tallied the many remarkable cultural competencies that I knew Carson controlled.

Carson the Narrator

Carson was, and still is, an engaging story weaver. Years earlier, on our way to the Florida State Fair in Tampa, he regaled us with the tales of his friend Zero. Zero had uncommon skills in balance, speed, secrets, flatus, and strength. Husband Richard, who was driving, and I, turning to look back between the two front seats, were both transfixed by these tales of Zero, whom neither of us had yet met. Carson's brother Gavin had not met Zero, either. Older and wiser by three years, Gavin prodded his brother: "Is this real or is this a story?" Apparently accustomed to Gavin's reality checks, Carson's gaze dropped into his lap, and sheepishly, he answered, "It's a story." I am unable to describe the surrender, the slight embarrassment, and the subtextual "caught out, again" conveyed in Carson's "It's a story" reply.

But in the front seats, Richard and I shared a complex glance of pride, some concern, and a loss of control into barely suppressed laughter. Carson's narrative was so compelling that we had just spent a few moments in the palm of his hand. The fact that we had been duped was part of the complexity. Should we be worried that Carson was a fabulist, or should we enjoy the compelling journey that Carson's stories instigated and sustained? You know the answer already. We are not parents. We are actually "grand uncles." What a great spot. We get to enjoy both good and (slightly) not-so-good habits for their pleasurable effects. The fact that I now tell this story about Carson and his imaginary friend Zero is a testament to his narrative force and its lasting impact on us. Finally, it is important to remember that this scenario occurred when he was but five years old, already experiencing a tough time with early literacy instruction, but possessed of a rich vocabulary and narrative technique.

Tutor Reflection on Carson

A question a reading teacher might ask in darker, reflective hours is: "Can you still be a good person if you struggle with how reading is being taught to you?" It is perhaps a silly question on my part, and most teachers of young children would be quick to assure me with "Yes, of course." But after years as an elementary reading teacher and more years developing literacy practice with other prospective and in-service reading teachers, I have been aware of a tendency by some to equate an individual's literacy performance with the overall value or worth of that person. I think I do understand this dilemma and remember my own teaching in similar circumstances with some sense of remorse and guilt when I unconsciously participated in just this kind of teacher transference. If, as a classroom teacher, I am responsible for 30-plus readers achieving their individual literacy potentials (not to mention their achievements in math, science, and social studies), I might resent the extra effort I need to invest in my "lower performing readers," effort that I suspect might not even pay off. If that extra effort is seen as unproductive, and I have been encouraged to focus on students who have the greatest chance of earning a passing mark, then I may teach to the "bubble kids" and pay less attention to the students I figure won't make it to the fourth grade, at least not on the first try. In reflection, I get it, but I cannot forgive it.

Carson the Student

These were the circumstances when Carson and I began our literacy work together, when he was a struggling third grader. Since I was already aware of his humor, intelligence, and formidable work ethic, I thought there might have been a mismatch between the literacy guidance and practice offered by Ms. Mervis and Carson's receptivity to her versions of literacy learning. In my preparation for literacy work with Carson, I did not complete any of the typical "reading diagnoses," not even an informal reading inventory that would try to level him as a reader. Rather, we began by reading interesting picture books together.

In our previous conversations, I had learned of his abiding interests in volcanoes, dinosaurs, and black holes. These are things I like to read about as well. Daily, I would scan the *New York Times* for any mention of these and other similar topics. I did not use readability formulae or Lexile ratings to select his books from my local branch library. What I did look for were interesting pictures with no more than a few lines of text under each picture. I did not exclude books with "hard words," as these became possible teaching points. We always began each new book with a *picture walk* (Clay, 1985). In our discussion of each picture on the successive pages of the target book, I tried to steer our conversation, prompted by the illustration, to the ideas that were present in the related text beneath it, or somewhere in the page vicinity. But steering is perhaps too strong a word. My approach was more like expanding on his tangential mentions, trying to connect his language about the picture with what would also appear in his subsequent reading of the text. This distinction is an important one, as it precludes the direct teaching of teacher-targeted content vocabulary in out-of-context contexts. I have long believed that such teacher-organized targets are misguided. Without instantiating context and authentic engagement, our efforts directed toward vocabulary development miss their target. It is hard to create new *prior knowledge* (Langer, 1981). It is easier and more productive to find *connections between the known and unknown* (Clay, 1985).

As one might suspect with a highly verbal, high-energy kid, engagement on each page of these picture walks was an event that needed to be curtailed with my interruptive "Let's see what's next," and then quickly turning the page. Also mildly problematic is that these expository, informational texts do not depend on a reliable story structure, like the customary narratives used in early reading. The structures for informational descriptive texts are often collections of iterative facts about a topic, sometimes thematically collected into paragraphs. Nonetheless, we talked through the content represented by the illustrations, generating "I wonder" statements about information touched upon, but not detailed enough for his curiosity.

As an aside, I think curiosity must be a prerequisite for avid reading. I was fortunate; Carson was/is innately curious. I know I was wowed by all the things that popped into his head when we engaged with a book. At first, I probed with language like, "What does the picture make you think of?" or, in the middle of a discussion, "What else do you think about the picture?" As we progressed, and as he learned the "picture walk drill with Uncle," we eased into a more conversational approach to new readings but kept to our meaning-based preview.

During our pre-discussion, when I was lucky enough to hear Carson use content vocabulary that was in the text, we cooperatively located its location in the text. It probably went something like this:

ME: You mentioned stegosaurus. Can you find it and frame it in the writing?
C: (tries, but does not find stegosaurus)
ME: What would you expect to see at the beginning of stegosaurus? (exaggerating the sounds/st/in the blend at the beginning of the word) Let's slow down the sounds at the beginning of stegosaurus. Stretch out the first part.
C: (Carson hears and produces the/s/and/t/sounds and then blends them.)
ME: Write those two letters together on the writing pad.
C: Writes s and t.
ME: Ok, now go in and find it.

We co-created several routines like the one described above when a text was too challenging. We borrowed Marie Clay's (1985) "Get your mouth ready." To use GYMR, Carson would have been stuck on an unknown word. In GYMR, he rereads the sentence up to the point of the unknown word. Then he makes the sounds of the first part of the unknown word. If the word is in Carson's speaking vocabulary, it will more than likely pop for him, and he can continue reading. Later in the lesson, during a pause in reading, we can go back to the successful GYMR and review it for strategic implications. Quickly, lightly, reviewing his use of context and graphophonics is undertaken as reinforcement in the moment, or teaching at the point of need.

It is good to teach and reinforce strategy use when it has been deployed successfully. Another similar strategy we used is "write your ear." Write your ear meant write down on the tablet what you hear when you say the unknown word. We used "write your ear" on many occasions, but most productively during a shared writing segment called the "story wrap-up." Like sportscasters who opine after a long (very long for me) sporting event, readers also wrap up the reading action and the textual information. Careful readers of this chapter will notice another nod to Marie Clay. Wrap-up is an extension of Clay's *shared writing of a sentence.* Wrap-ups were usually no more than a sentence or two. Carson and I shared this writing to record author, title, and the important stuff in his reading journal. I kept busy with my own journal that contained observations and jottings about Carson's reading behaviors.

We compared our *reading work journals.* He read my fieldnotes, leading to his questions about my jottings. Though infrequent, his queries about my notes allowed me a second access to possible teaching points and opportunities to reinforce his emerging reading behaviors. When I read his wrap-ups, he graciously allowed me to ask for clarifications and elaborations. *Follow-ups* are where I modeled and probed, based on what I thought he might have written in response to the reading. This part of the intervention is perhaps problematic from student independence and ownership perspectives of the literacy task. It is always a balance between what he did and what I imagine he could have done. So, I carefully appropriate his literacy work to help him expand upon what he already controls. I think this is how successive engagements with whole literacy work must look from an asset perspective (Lin, 2020; Hayslip, 2020). I think allowing him a bigger picture of what he just read and what he just did to read it can be helpful. I still don't know in any way if the modeling and probes made it into his internal cognitive approaches to the wrap-up, or to his literacy practices in general.

We also talked after readings. Of course, I always wanted to know if he liked the books I had curated for the lesson. But I also pushed for more of his thinking. To his "It was good," I asked, "What made it good?" or "Thinking about what you just read, what would you tell Brody?" (Carson's neighborhood friend). Because Brody and Carson are friends in the real world outside of literacy tutoring, there may in fact have been *nothing* worth his and Brody's time spent together. And that would be ok, a tacit evaluation of my text curation proficiency. But occasionally, I got lucky with my text selection and Carson's uptake of it. Much vocabulary work, locating words in the text, and "find it" were deployed to get Carson to review the reading for evidence that supported his wrap-up or to elaborate on his intents to share with Brody. We used Brody as our default authentic audience screen on which to project Carson's attempts to make sense.

Building Reading and Writing Connections

When Carson was assigned a synthesis writing task in fourth grade (yes, he passed the third-grade reading test with a level 3!) about a particular Native

American tribe, he and I started like everyone does. We opened his laptop, accessed a web browser, and typed the tribe's name in the search bar. Several leads popped, and we set about reading across these several texts to gather important facts. We made a handwritten list of "important, must have" and "interesting, might use" facts. We grouped individual facts into categories like food, housing, clothing, and celebrations. Then we started sharing what we knew about each of these categories. We were using an adaptation of Spivey and King's (1989) approach to discourse synthesis or writing from source texts (see also Nelson & King, 2023). The steps in our synthesis writing included:

1. Understand the writing assignment
2. Gather and curate related, reliable sources (text, image, podcasts, videos)
3. Select important ideas from sources
4. Group related important ideas into categories
5. Write a paragraph about each category
6. Organize paragraphs into logical sequence
7. Connect between paragraphs with transitions
8. Write a summary paragraph at the end
9. Write a short introduction that restates the writing assignment

But even with scaffolding, Carson's writing was laborious. His attention toggled between his struggles with hearing and representing the sounds he heard in the words that he needed and with maintaining and referencing meaning creation in his emerging, genre-based writing. The tricks we used for word work here are the same: slow it down, stretch it out, write down the sounds you hear, and see what you need to make it look like a word you have seen. As a reluctant reader, his sight vocabulary remained limited, and this task was heavily weighted by graphophonic analysis.

There is a decided difference and advantage in learning and using phonics at the point of need *during* writing (Nelson, 1991), in contrast with direct teaching of decontextualized phonics drills. As his Mom, Denise, put it, "He knows the sentence he wants to write but skips words when he is writing it down. I've noticed he rereads, asking does it make sense, does it sound right?" Supporting his work at the word and sentence level is his strong oral vocabulary, which has allowed him discursive control over social situations. The trick is getting these social strengths activated during reading and writing tasks.

Carson's disposition toward writing is not positive. I did get Carson's permission to share his writing as follows (with my grammatically challenged addition to his title):

> Writing is so boring! *[but Carson is still good at it!]*
>
> I'm so bored. I would rather watch paint dry.[1] There is no interest in writing because it's just writing words. I would rather do so much more like playing baseball.[2] Writing about baseball would be fun to write about.[3] Writing teaching assignments would find you asleep really fast. The teacher would get angry and disappointed.[4] That is why no one is seeing this.[5]

My comments corresponding to each of his thoughts as numbered above were sent to him at the time. These were meant to help bolster his self-efficacy toward writing. These comments now follow:

1. "Watching paint dry" is good writing. I think it is called figurative language. Whatever it is called, you do it very well. It is like a hook that drags me into your writing.
2. This sentence makes me think about the difference between doing something – really doing it – compared with thinking and writing about doing it. I guess this is what newspaper guys, who write about sports, must feel like when they are covering a really good baseball game. They might think, "Wow, this is such a great game. How can I get the excitement across to someone who will read the paper?"
3. This sentence makes me think that even in just writing, some stuff is better to write about than others. Baseball is certainly better than daffodils. I wonder why in school you can't write about just what you want all the time. Have you thought about this one?
4. I do think that teachers get disappointed sometimes by what their students do. But probably not as much as we think. After all, if you are learning something, anything, shouldn't they be happy about that? What do you think?
5. And my last comment, you are smart to keep some of your writing to yourself. Writing is powerful, and it does cause people to react, sometimes in emotional ways.

In his short essay, Carson had hit upon an understanding that I often ponder. In schools, we spend our time making simulacrum texts about real life. Outside of school, we are more likely to be doing those things in life. Carson realized the oppression schools create by insisting that any shared meaning must be textualized. Things such as speech, performance, and gesture count less than a piece of writing about the same things. To me, this is a bias that especially works against active students, or students who do not kowtow to teachers' appropriation of real life to create their teaching texts.

Ongoing Teaching Points

As time went on, Carson and I both became busier in our respective lives. To keep our connection, we began reading a novel Carson chose, *The Edge of Extinction* (Martin, 2016), an adolescent sci-fi novel centered on the reintroduction of dinosaur species and young protagonists' coping strategies. We set aside a half hour, at least once a week, to take turns reading on FaceTime. It was a happy coincidence that Carson had just received his first iPhone, and the use of that technology seemed to motivate him toward our meetings. When it was his turn to read aloud, I recorded Running Records notes (Clay, 1985) in my copy of *The Edge of Extinction*. These were informal records but detailed enough to guide teaching points.

Teaching points are Clay's focus in choosing the most productive data relative to the teaching goal. There is always so much reading behavior to address. Productive tutors choose a focus supported by data that furthers the lesson goal and may let the rest go by. Fortunately, reading behaviors tend to repeat across lessons. I usually picked one or two reading strategies to discuss after each of his reading turns. We tried to pick the most productive places to talk about his reading. After our discussion of his miscues and strategy uses, I then read aloud long enough to re-establish a meaning-seeking approach to the story. Reading miscue analysis (Goodman, 2015), deployed in real time with active, present readers, is a very productive intervention strategy.

A caveat: I am aware of the underlying resources that we absorbed into Carson's literacy work. He used his own laptop. We could FaceTime with ease on our iPhones. His house, like his school, is bathed in internet connectivity. I depended on the fact that we always had a quiet, low-distraction workspace. His brother Gavin was never around. Gavin was probably *not* very interested in what Carson and I were doing. But I also think Gavin was aware of how his presence might impact Carson. An older brother could be a distracting influence when sibling admiration might have become performance anxiety. I am grateful for our quiet space. Denise (the Niece) was also absent but could be summoned when Carson and I felt the need for a local instantiation of an authentic audience. These contextual resources certainly supported Carson's ability to rework his literacy habits.

My Take on Teaching with Carson – Postscript

In general, teaching and its observation are relational, contingent interactions that resist process/outcomes analyses. Instead, I am being descriptive about the literacy intervention with Carson. And in representing publicly, I implicitly make the claim that our work together has a positive impact on both of us; how Carson approaches and strategizes through his literacy engagements and how I understand intervention instruction as person-centered, we both gained competence while building our whole literacy experiences together. In his junior high years, and now as a sophomore in high school, Carson often brings home report cards comprised of only As. He has made it to the principal's honor roll repeatedly. Now, the discussion about his grades may have shifted to, "What happened in science that you *only* got a B?" Of course, too much is too much, and grade achievement can become its own educational issue. For now, it seems a good time to kvell about all things Carson and claim a little credit for stepping in.

From my professional perspective, there are several lessons I learned that bear labeling for clarity of process and intents. Assets-based pedagogy (Hayslip, 2020; Lin, 2020) operates from the assumption that we all know something about what we intend to learn. Therefore, it makes sense from both ethical and efficiency perspectives to ground any interventions in these strengths. To me, this intent to use assets is much deeper than my catering to Carson's interest areas in my book selection. I tried to honor and bring to the tutoring table as many connections to his life as I could detect and collect. The more I learned about Carson, the better I became at knowing what Vygotsky called his zone of proximal development (Wood et al., 1976; Smagorinsky, 2011). This is the most productive place to work.

The literacy tasks themselves must appear to the student to be real, authentic. Purcell-Gates, Duke, and colleagues strongly suggest that school-based literacy tasks must be authentic – to engage, to sustain, and to make sense (Duke et al., 2011; Purcell-Gates et al., 2011). Likewise, out-of-school literacy practices, particularly within the New Literacies Studies (Hull & Schultz, 2001), work within what is real to the participating students. Literacy, in these cases, is a whole thing, a process and set of competencies that, executed effectively, get stuff done. Literacy can be a tool, but a protean tool grounded in the social contexts where it is needed and productively used. We come to these linguistic tasks with different sets of competencies.

Two recent movements in literacy speak to this linguistic and experiential diversity, especially as it occurs in classrooms. The first of these is translanguaging (Garcia & Kleifgen, 2019), which simply means classrooms are linguistic labs where multiple ways of speaking and writing are germane and productive for creating shared meaning. It is a multicultural exchange in terms of the content information and the linguistic forms it may take. As a classroom group, we agree by implicit social contract that all languages are equal in their capacity to represent, and we also agree to work toward mutual comprehensibility on work we may share with others. We all stand to learn multiple ways of making meaning. Simply put, translanguaging is a productive orientation for literacy interventions, and not only in the limited sense of two languages, but in two braiding lives.

The second idea is related to the first. Flores (2020) proposes the metaphor of language architecture to cover this overall multicultural, multilinguistic blending within classroom language and literacy work. The idea is a shared construction of meaning together as a social group. Just like plans for a building, there are content blueprints that guide meaning construction. Because we cannot foresee all of what will be brought to individual tasks, we cannot know the exact nature of the resulting linguistic products (outcomes). But since we share the curriculum blueprint (the things we are trying to learn), multiple representations of the meaning intention can emerge. This is how our differences can be used to develop content knowledge that is new and immediate. I believe our individual differences enrich our teaching and what can be learned about topics that frame classroom projects, and our mutual building of meaning was a way to describe my work with Carson.

My thinking and practices about tutoring and intervention lessons in literacy are productively influenced by the work of Marie Clay (2015). While Clay's important work is based in emergent literacy and young learners, there are many transferable lessons and much wisdom that inform my interaction with older, struggling readers. The Clay-transfer approaches to intervention lessons include whole text, whole process, ZPD, consistent teacher talk related to specific fix-up strategies, the power in readers' independence, readers' monitoring of their own reading performance, readers' searching for needed information on the text page, their use of cueing in word work, making approximations in spelling, and cross-checking the use of cues for word work. These are all practices and beliefs I used when working with Carson. It has been interesting to extend Clay's emergent-level approach and strategies while looking for tasks, intents, and solutions that accommodate older readers using more complex texts enmeshed in content information about the real world.

Reflections of a Caring Uncle: My Take on Carson "the Squirrel"

I can't help but revisit Ms. Mervis and her compacted and reduced view of who Carson was to her. All teachers, all of us, are pushed into limited views of our students, achieving and non-achieving. The special skills and competencies that each of our students bring to us often get overlooked in our fixation on curricular matters.

Another strength that I wish Ms. Mervis had been aware of is Carson's uncommon ability in baseball. Perhaps during these third-grade days, his prowess may have been most palpable in my imagination, fueled by pride, love, and admiration (and very little conceptual knowledge of the finer points of baseball). No matter, it never occurred to Carson that he and I were engaging in a baseball role-reversal in authority and knowledge. He was and is an interesting and careful teacher. He is still patient with two uncles who claim to have TVs that don't get sports. During our endless shared football games, our ignorance is strategically hidden with our pat response, "You know our TV does not get sports. And we know you two don't consider ice dancing a real sport, anyway." After asking, "What is ice dancing?" Carson's predictable eye roll is followed by a concise explanation for the stylish man currently occupying the TV screen, interrupting a football game. In his white and black striped, hip-length jacket, with gathered waistband and cuffs, and with a matching cap, the man's hands are on his hips, probably in frustration as he just dropped his yellow handkerchief. In the moment, Carson taught us the vicissitudes of penalties in football.

In contrast, Ms. Mervis had referenced Carson's ADHD in her third-grade assessment of Carson. Even one of his baseball coaches noted his unique, active style and named him "Squirrel." The name has stuck. Yet, in baseball, his focus was laser-sharp, and yet still considerate of his audience. This is not literacy, or is it? I am becoming aware of the lateral transfer of analogous skills (e.g., predicting a baseball's trajectory in the sky and predicting the plot progression in a romance novel; both are tediously regular and path-bound).

Carson the Contender

Carson is more than *smart* about baseball (and football and WWE); he is *good* at it. Now a sophomore in high school, he has spent his summers traveling to play in invitational baseball tournaments on what are called "traveling teams." These events are formed around teams compiled by the organizers, like fantasy football, only with real, live, young adults. A coach or sponsor scouts and then collects talent to form his team. Then these coaches, as ersatz talent scouts, arrange to play against other similarly conscripted teams, all hoping to attract the attention of college talent scouts.

It makes me proud to say Carson is a perennial favorite. He is a sought-after player and has been so for several years. He plays baseball with the best age-group players in the country. This has meant his mother, Denise, and his father, Scott, spend their weekends and financial resources on Carson's baseball life. Richard and I ("the two Uncles") are in the audience when the play is close enough. But we don't board airplanes for baseball tournaments like he and his parents do. And just when you think it all may be enough, filled up with secondhand joy, we see him and overhear him from his fielding position at first base, congratulating the successful base runner from the opposing team, slapping a "high five" in the air. Yes, we are convinced he is a good person. And not only because he is playing varsity baseball as a sophomore.

Carson the Party Animal

I could not resist telling you all about how well Carson covers at least a small part of the rest of the measured world (perhaps not so much in literacy). Carson is no slouch in the social realm. In eighth grade, his middle school sponsored a dance and encouraged the formation of couples who would attend the school dance together. The expected form of invitation was to make a poster indicating your request. This poster of request was publicly presented to your intended, with an onlooking audience, perhaps to apply social pressure to help your case. Carson had his eyes on a particular young lady. In his recon, he had learned that her favorite singer was country and western star Morgan Wallen. On his invitation poster, he mentioned, in fact, that he was "no Morgan Wallen," but would still like to take her to the dance. I was moved by his humility in this daunting task, a task that was often given to exaggeration by others, even to the extent of false claims. But to pad his chances, to his poster he stapled two packets of Skittles because, as he put it, "Who doesn't like Skittles, right?"

Case A

Home and Community Literacy

Norman A. Stahl

Many years ago, when one of the authors of this tutoring guide was serving as a volunteer tutor in a junior high school, he had been assigned three eighth-grade girls to tutor in math. Initially, the curriculum was to be a watered-down version of the math instruction being presented to "achieving" students across the hall. To be bluntly honest, these tutees hated every minute of this remedial instruction.

When this situation was shared with the "girls' dean" for the school, she thought for a minute and in acknowledging that the current curriculum would unlikely lead to success as well as then indirectly admitting that the school had more or less given up on these tutees, she suggested that the text be dropped and the modus of instruction focus on the Sears Roebuck Catalog (then known as the "wish book"). That made sense as there was a Sears department store in the community, and each of the girls had been there on many occasions.

After several catalogs were sourced, the new approach – an alternative community-oriented approach – was implemented. It had the promise of assisting the tutees to master community-sourced, real-life competencies (sometimes called survival skills) all the while promoting their understanding of how these competencies had real-world value.

Once we all became consumers of ever so many products of high desirability, the tutees took to the instruction like ducks to water. They were reading about various items to be followed with research on each item's use, quality, value, and guarantee (warranty). These learners practiced basic arithmetic in completing their order forms while determining the tax on each item and calculating delivery charges. As they became more sophisticated "shoppers," they came to become critical readers in coming to terms with the art of persuasion as used in advertising and marketing. Financial literacy evolved as a topic of study as well.

As might be suggested from this case study of a tutorial experience that built upon a resource from the local community, we might acknowledge that tutees are often motivated to read materials that are part of their everyday existence. Furthermore, it was supposed that as these learners were to grow and mature to adulthood, the breadth of alternative learning materials would expand as their interests and needs expanded as well. The experience solidified the belief that when the standard curricular fare from a school does not seem to promote the fundamental literacy competencies, alternative community-sourced teaching materials have a place in the educational arena.

Was this tutorial instruction a success for these young women? Perhaps it was. Certainly, a set of real-life competencies requiring both reading and mathematics was mastered. Furthermore, it was clear that these tutees had positive affective-oriented experiences that would not have been extended as they sat lost and bewildered across the hall in the traditional, formalized mathematics class.

With hindsight, the experience of tutoring these learners demonstrated to this tutor that several recommendations voiced by Weinstein and Fantini (1970) for school-based curricular design may be even more apropos for a pedagogical philosophy for the tutorial experience. These tenets as adapted for tutoring are presented here:

1. Tutoring should be flexible and oriented to the specific needs of the tutee rather than as a prepackaged, uniform, and rigid instructional plan.
2. Tutorial instruction should be experience-based rather than an approach that is focused primarily on traditional texts and other symbol-oriented materials.
3. Tutoring should focus upon building tutee successes through individualized, small-step progressions for attaining competencies instead of through a preconceived plan where all instruction is the same for all learners (i.e., learning outcomes, instruction, standards, assessment).

4. Tutorial instruction should be "now" oriented to the tutee's life and environment as opposed to being "past" or even "future" oriented.
5. Tutoring should focus on doing instead of being primarily academic (knowing). Social participation should be undertaken at some stage of the tutorial experience.
6. The tutorial lesson plan should be based on the learner asking "why" (even posing hypotheses) and then finding answers to one's questions rather than simply being directed to master "what" in some predetermined plan.
7. Tutoring should be authentic rather than confined to an academic silo by making connections to the learner's lived experiences.
8. Tutorial instruction should not only emphasize extrinsic content as central to the traditional school-based education models but should equally emphasize the tutee's inner content (the affect) that is often overlooked yet foundational to long-term success.

These eight recommendations can serve as the initial tenets in developing either a tutorial program or a tutor's personal philosophy of community tutoring. A list of print- and digital-formatted materials that will be encountered across the life span, and which can serve as resources for teaching real-life literacy competencies, including sight vocabulary, word attack, comprehension, and practical writing, along with mathematics, citizenship, and financial literacy, follows.

Resources for Literacy Instruction from Home and Community

Advertisements in newspapers, magazines, and circulars
Apartment leases
Application forms (varied)
Bank statements and forms
Bills and invoices
Book jackets
Brochures
Calendars
Catalogs
Classified sections in media
Comic books and manga
Community bulletins
Community college applications

Contracts
Cookbooks (recipes)
Coupons
Credit policies
Directions and instruction manuals
DMV manuals and license application forms
Greeting cards
Grocery goods (cans, boxes, cartons, etc.)
Health forms (history)
Help wanted ads
Insurance policies
Labels (clothes, food, etc.)
Letters and e-mails
Library card application
Magazines
Medical assistance forms
Maps (road atlas)
Membership forms
Menus
Newsletters (community organizations)
Newspapers
Obituaries
Pamphlets
Questionnaires
Schedules of events
Signs from across the locale
Song lyrics
Sports materials (schedules, rosters)
Tax forms
Technical and job manuals
Theater programs and advertisements
Travel brochures and schedules
USPS forms
Voting policies (ballots)
Warranties (guarantees)
Weather reports
Wills
Withholding and W-2 forms

Next, we follow with four prototypic examples of how such materials can be employed in community-based tutorial instruction.

Evaluating Food Labels

The tutor brings several packages, cartons, or even cans of food (labels or cut-up cartons will work equally well) to the tutoring session. The lesson will focus on the words and information found on the food containers. Alternatively, a Google Images search for the learner's favorite snacks and beverages with the keywords "nutrition facts" will return a digital version of a food label.

Cereal boxes work particularly well as reading material when the product is a favorite of the tutee. Examples of questions and activities that might drive a lesson when using a cereal box might include:

- What is the name of the cereal?
- What is the mascot for this brand of cereal?
- What company produces this brand of cereal?
- How many servings can you get from a box?
- How many calories are in a serving?
- What is the weight of the product in the box?
- What are the main ingredients?
- Why is this cereal your favorite?

Should another product be used as a follow-up to the lesson, the questions may be revised to fit the label. A culminating activity would be for the tutee to design, either by hand or with a digital program, an advertisement for the product. Keywords might be added to the tutee's word bank. An older learner can write a letter to the company sharing their opinions about the product.

Advertising Analysis

The tutor collects several newspaper advertising supplements that are issued by stores in the community, such as Wal-Mart, Target, and Kohl's. Specialty stores and outlets such as Dick's Sporting Goods, Michaels, or Ulta Beauty that might draw upon the tutee's special interests are also appropriate to use with this activity. Do not overlook the advertising supplements and flyers distributed by local stores for sales such as Small Business Saturday.

Together, the tutor and tutee will peruse and evaluate the advertisement using a set of questions that were previously drafted by the tutor. These queries might target the brand names of products and the design and cost of specific products. A deep dive into an individual product would look at availability, warranty, variety in models featured, product dimensions, etc. In addition, the tutee would be asked to determine the name of the store, its location, hours of operation, phone number, homepage, and any upcoming sales as noted in the advertisement.

This activity can be expanded to cover two stores that feature similar products, thus allowing for the comparison of products and merchandising practices. A tutee might end the analysis by explaining why a person should procure a specific product at a particular store. Older learners might be introduced to Consumer Reports or a digital site that evaluates products, like Reddit.

Authentic Literacy Contexts

For those tutors working with a tutee who is in the mid-teen years, there is a widely available community resource that is perhaps the most important text in a teenager's life. Of course, this would be the state driver's manual. Most teens dream of the day when they receive their driver's license, allowing them to move behind the steering wheel.

Passing the driver's test is a rite of passage that brings with it perceived status and freedoms. To earn their license, the tutee must read and comprehend the rules of the road and then pass a multiple-choice test on the content, followed by a driving demonstration that shows the potential driver has transferred the content in the manual to varied competencies when sitting behind the wheel.

The state driver's manual has the potential to be of high interest and a solid motivational tool in promoting both reading and learning. As an instructional source, the manual will likely have some sections that are of a difficult readability level, but this should not stop a tutor from employing this resource with the tutee, as manuals can promote the mastery of technical vocabulary, sight words, fluency, basic comprehension, study habits, and reference skills. In addition, visual literacy is promoted, as these texts are rich sources of charts, diagrams, tables, and graphs. Also, practice tests are regularly available to assess a tutee's mastery of the content, helping the tutor to plan instruction accordingly.

For those tutees who might labor over the text's presentation and content, listening exercises can be substituted for guided reading through the use of audio or video renditions of manuals (refer to Dyslexic Advantage on the internet). High-interest, important, or difficult sections can be rewritten as well. The instructional approaches as presented in other sections of this tutoring guide can be adapted easily for use with the tutee mastering the manual (e.g., word searches, flash cards, and vocabulary logs).

As another aid in using the driver's manual, the tutor should determine whether the state of residence provides instructional guides, learning modules, flash cards, etc., such as the Illinois Rules of the Road Workbook. It is also possible to obtain study guides such as *Learn to Drive Smart: Your Guide to Driving Safely* by allied organizations (Insurance Corporation of British Columbia, 2020). Beyond using the standard rules of the road manual, there are alternatives such as the motorcycle operator's manual or the commercial driver's manual. A follow-up document that can serve as an instructional tool might be a car owner's manual for a vehicle that the tutee would like to own.

Leveraging Literacy through Youth Organizations

Tutees, whether in elementary, middle, or secondary school, will often be members of youth organizations such as Scouts BSA, the Girl Scouts of America, or a 4-H Club. These and other organizations publish age-appropriate texts that promote a group's mission and serve as the foundational guides for individuals as they strive to earn both awards (badges, certificates, etc.) and recognition. These organizational handbooks, merit badge pamphlets, and topic-specific books all have potential use as instructional texts for content matter and literacy skill building in the tutorial setting. The topics will likely be of high interest and motivational in nature. Success in the mastery of the content and the demonstration of associated competencies can result in tangible rewards and peer/parent/community recognition.

Tutorial lessons would be formulated along the lines of the other "real-world" lessons mentioned throughout this guidebook, evolving from and revolving around community texts with rich content. For instance, with any of the 100-plus topic-focused merit badge pamphlets from Scouts BSA, a tutor and tutee would have multiple passes over the content and the language as the tutee employs varied levels of comprehension, leading to mastery of the concepts and constructs for the award. Such is also true with the 4-H handbooks and the GSA requirement documents.

While use of these texts would be more closely associated with content field reading, there is one merit badge from Scouts BSA (2022) that promotes an orientation of becoming a literate member of society. Such is a most worthy goal for all tutoring projects, as the nation not only suffers from the plague of illiteracy, but it suffers to a greater degree from what is called aliteracy…a sizable portion of the population can read, but it chooses not to read. The requirements for the reading merit badge support the goal of adopting what has been called a "readerly" life, that of being a lifelong reader.

The requirements focus on what it means to be a reader in both the community and the nation, along with identifying resources available for a reader and what roles a committed reader might play in promoting literacy in the community. In completing these requirements, the tutee would become a master of the local library, learn how to identify books of interest, read and write about books from different genres, read and utilize content from nonfiction books to master a practical skill, learn about the community by reading from a variety of media sources, and engage in a literacy-oriented community service. A careful review of the goals and objectives for this award shows that they can be adopted or adapted for virtually any community-based literacy program.

A valuable resource for designing such a tutorial project (i.e., a summer reading camp, an academic-year partnership with a youth group, or one-to-one instruction focused on attitudes, motivation, and interests) is the Reading Merit Badge Workbook (Scouts BSA, 2022), which is downloadable from the internet. As the tutor and tutee undertake the activities, the pages of the workbook are completed as a record of the objectives that are mastered. This document can be adapted to meet the needs of the goals of any tutorial program. Of course, if the tutee is a Scout, the tutor should contact a reading merit badge counselor so that the tutee might earn the merit badge for their effort.

Final Thoughts

This orientation for community-sourced literacy that grew from tutoring Sherry, Charlette, and Kathleen so many years ago draws from time-honored pedagogical (tutorial) philosophies now often linked to funds of knowledge and the new literacies. Yet, the position that is being advocated here does not in any way suggest that the traditional, structured skills programming found in the K-12 schools of the current era should be abandoned. Rather, it is suggested that in meeting the needs of learners who are not thriving with the school-based curriculum and materials, there are alternative texts/resources that can be sourced from the community, which, with effective tutoring, can promote the mastery of literacy competencies, positive attitudes toward reading and writing, and nearby knowledge development with a community focus.

Case B

The Story of Jake: Who Was "Never Going to Become a Reader"[1]

MaryEllen Vogt

For Christmas in 2022, Jake (age 10 in grade 4) presented his parents with a published (by Blurb.com) chapter book that he authored. He had previously created a shorter book about *Camo Man* for his dad on Father's Day. For a child who was a nonreader entering grade 2 in the autumn of 2020, completing this book of eight chapters, all of which he can now read independently, was a monumental accomplishment. What follows is an excerpt from Jake's book, *Holly Jolly Christmas:*

> It's the day before Christmas and no animals are stirring. It is 5:00 a.m. and we all wake up and have breakfast. We eat pancakes, waffles, French toast, bacon, and sausage, with a lot of whipped cream!!! Next, Dad, Mom, Avery, Jimmy, and I begin to decorate the house with lights and ornaments. We listen to Christmas music. Mom and I make gingerbread cookies. At 7:00, we set out the milk and four cookies for Santa. We are off to bed! Tomorrow is Christmas!

The Story of Jake: Who Was "Never Going to Become a Reader"

Figure B.1 A boy holding his first published book. Photograph by the author.

Figure B.1 shows Jake as a proud author of his first published book. My husband designed it, with much input from the author. We sent his manuscript (all dictated) to Blurb.com to have it published—it even has an ISBN!

At Jake's first lesson with me in September 2020, he was a quiet, reluctant 7-year-old who was trying to learn how to read during the mandated COVID-19 quarantine. Now in grade 5, Jake is in his fourth year of receiving literacy instruction at our Tutoring Center for two lessons totaling 90 minutes/week. He now considers himself a reader, although he still finds grade-level texts difficult.

Advent of the Literacy Intervention & Enrichment Program

During the summer of 2020, due to my concern about local children and youth who were struggling with remote literacy learning, I created the Literacy Intervention & Enrichment (LIE) program, housed at a music and performing arts studio near Sacramento, California. The owner of the music studio, a good friend and colleague, first offered limited academic tutoring in the spring of 2020 when, during the pandemic, local parents expressed a need for such services. However, no reading instruction was offered because there was no one to teach it. So, to fill the void, in September of 2020, I began teaching an after-school intervention program for struggling readers…in a music studio!

Now in its fourth year at a new site, the LIE program's three teachers provide one-on-one reading intervention and instruction for local youth, ages 6–15, who are experiencing difficulties with reading, writing, and spelling. Their assessed needs have varied, from those requiring some extra reading support to those who have significant developmental delays.

Parents learn about the LIE program through social media, the studio's website (tamraloo.com/literacy-intervention-enrichment), referrals from parents of children in the program, and teachers and administrators in our local school district and neighboring communities. Two of our LIE teachers are fully credentialed and experienced; a fourth, who has a BA in English, has considerable experience tutoring older students in English and writing.

As the LIE Director, one of my roles is to administer a comprehensive literacy assessment to each child or adolescent prior to instruction. I assess proficiency in letter identification, phonemic awareness, phonics, word recognition, fluency, vocabulary, comprehension, spelling, and writing. I use the *Basic Reading Inventory* (Johns, Elish-Piper & Johns, 2017) because there are multiple forms available (e.g., A, B, C, D), which enable us to collect pre- and post-data that measure students' reading development. I prepare a detailed Preliminary Assessment Report for parents, who often share the report with school personnel.

Once enrolled in the LIE program, follow-up assessments at the end of the year are administered to each student to determine the rate and nature of growth in the targeted literacy areas. It is important to note that all students set and write personal literacy goals for each semester, and teachers and students refer to these goals periodically during lessons.

Jake's Story

When I first met Jake in the fall of 2020, he was a 7-year-old second grader. His mother attended an informal meeting I convened of local parents of children who were struggling with learning to read during the COVID-19 quarantine. After the meeting, during which I had explained the new LIE program, I saw Jake's mom waiting for me. She went straight to the point: Jake is neurodiverse with a chromosome deletion, which presents as processing and retention problems; he has vision problems and a significant speech impediment. She stated that doctors said Jake would never learn to read. She added that our new LIE program would be "an answer to our prayers." As I began my work with Jake, the bar was set very high.

Like other young children, Jake was having difficulty learning to read during the pandemic. During his initial assessment, I learned that he could read the words *run* and *go*. He knew the letters of the alphabet but was unclear about the sounds letters make. However, his concepts of print were well developed. Jake said he loved books about fishing and hunting—his mother has read to him frequently from the *Lucky Luke* series (by Kevin Lovegreen), which he thoroughly enjoys. However, Jake seriously disliked reading and writing on his own. After our first session, I knew that Jake was not only smart, but he also had a terrific sense of humor.

The Language Experience Approach: Just What Jake Needed

For over 80 years, researchers have investigated the Language Experience Approach (LEA), a proven reading development and intervention method (Dorr, 2006; Hall, 1978; Stauffer, 1976; Vogt, 2021). Within our program, LEA has been among our most important and successful approaches. Originally designed for beginning reading instruction, it is appropriate for individual and small group instruction for students of all ages, including adults and multilingual learners (Nessel & Dixon, 2008). LEA involves students' dictated words, sentences, paragraphs, and stories, incorporating all language processes: reading, writing, listening, and speaking, and it is predicated by the following:

> What I think about, I can talk about. What I can say, I can write, or someone can write it for me. I can learn to read what other people write for me to read, because most of the words are the same.
> (Van Allen, 1970, p. 1)

LEA values the language and ideas of children and youth, irrespective of how divergent they are from standard English. During instruction, students' language and ideas are the basis of materials produced, through the publication of stories, books, magazines, and so forth.

Specific information about the steps for LEA is included elsewhere in this book (see Chapter 4). Here is a brief review of the steps of the LEA (Van Allen, 1970; Vogt, 2021):

1. Shared Experience: Teacher and student(s) have a shared experience (reading together, watching a video, taking a walk, and so forth).
2. Conversation about the Experience: Teacher and student(s) talk about what they did together.
3. Creating the Text: A student or students dictate a story or information about the shared experience. The teacher writes it on paper, chart paper, or a whiteboard.
4. Interactive Writing*: During dictation, the student(s) writes words they know from their dictation into the story.

5. Teacher Read-Aloud: Teacher reads the story aloud.
6. Corrections: Together, corrections, revisions, and additions are made to the text.
7. Choral Reading: Everyone reads the story aloud together.
8. Publishing the Text: The teacher types the text, adding pictures from the Internet.
9. Extension Activities: Student(s) reread stories to build fluency; stories can be made into books; stories can be shared with younger students, and so forth.

*Note that I have added interactive writing to the list of steps of LEA (Roth & Dabrowski, 2013), during which the students print the words they can spell independently.

Using the LEA when a student and tutor jointly produce learner-generated texts results in the following benefits:

- Integrates reading, writing, listening, and speaking.
- Motivates learners with shared experiences that generate ideas for writing and reading (and extension activities).
- Involves language and literacy instruction that is accessible and meaningful to the learner.

Figure B.2 Boy in ball cap writing his first sentence on a whiteboard. Photograph by the author.

The Story of Jake: Who Was "Never Going to Become a Reader"   129

- Creates stories that provide key vocabulary and enhance sight words for a student's personal word bank.
- Learner-generated stories provide effective fluency practice when the stories are reread multiple times by the student author.

In Figure B.2, Jake is seen printing his first sentence ever after making sentences with his word bank words, gathered from his LEA stories. He was in second grade.

The frequency of having a student participate in LEA decreases over time as a student's reading skills develop. The intent is to phase out LEA and replace it with reading published books. Jake dictated 60+ stories before we phased out

Figure B.3 Boy standing with author celebrating his 100th reading lesson. Photograph by the author.

the weekly LEA activity during his third year of lessons. He is currently working on his third chapter book, which he is writing and dictating as needed. Figure B.3 shows Jake's 100th lesson. He gave me a thank-you card with 100 words written on the cover. It hangs in my office/classroom.

Other LIE Program Instructional Methods

Given the diversity of our students' reading levels, we use a variety of approaches and instructional materials in our center. Activities are selected by the teachers based on their lesson plans. I used the following activities with Jake.

Text Selection to Build Reading Interest

Students regularly read silently and/or aloud from a self-selected text, alternating between fiction and nonfiction. Depending on student interest, a variety of donated and purchased books are available in our bookshelf library. We use expository and informational texts from online resources, as well as a variety of donated copies of *Cricket Magazine*. We also have a set of early reading, repetitive, leveled books donated by a publisher, and some decodable books, as needed for beginning readers. Student choice of texts is an integral component of our program. Both boys and girls, grades 3–5, have enjoyed the hilarious *Mercy Watson* series by Kate DiCamillo. These books challenge readers with interesting character and street names (e.g., Leroy Ninker, Francine Poulet, Deckawoo Drive), which, through repetition, become familiar as students enjoy Mercy Watson's crazy exploits as a pet pig who will do most anything for toast with butter.

Word Work

Depending on need, Word Work includes:

- Phonemic Awareness/Phonics: Students practice and apply knowledge first with magnetic letters; then they build words in the pocket chart with cards we've made (e.g., *ea, oa, ie,* and other vowel combinations; blends; digraphs; and affixes).
- Sight Words: Students build towers with known sight words affixed to large Duplo blocks, each of which has a word affixed to it. Printable address labels for the vocabulary words attach easily to the blocks.
- Word Sorts are organized developmentally by assessed stages of spelling development (see Bear, Invernizzi, Templeton & Johnston, 2024).

The Story of Jake: Who Was "Never Going to Become a Reader"

- Word sorting helps students focus on patterns in words, including structure, rhyme, spelling, morphology, and meaning. The Primary, Elementary, and Upper Grade Spelling Assessments with *Words Their Way* provide important data about a student's development in spelling.
- Young children (emerging readers) and those who struggle with phonics can begin with picture sorts. Pictures and word cards are provided in the *Words Their Way* materials.
- Word Ladders for Vocabulary: These are used regularly with all students, and they are an important component for developing vocabulary. We use the books, *Daily Word Ladders* by Dr. Tim Rasinski (2011), available for grades K–1, 1–2, 2–3, and 4–6. Students really enjoy trying to figure out words for their Word Ladders!
- Word Games: Each LIE lesson ends with a motivating game. Examples include:
  o *Bingo*: We've made several versions from online teacher resources.
  o *Blah, Blah, Blah*: A commercial card game with CVC words for younger children and vowel combinations for older students; kids love it!
  o *Splat!* A commercial card game with 75 sight words; also, a favorite.
  o *Splash!* A commercial game with round "chips," each printed with a word, again, a favorite.
  o Assorted board games we have created with file folders—dice are used to move around the boards; ideas and topics have been found online.

Fluency

To develop students' fluency, we include the following activities:

- Repeated readings of short texts (fiction and nonfiction), short poems, and scripts.
- Repeated reading of phrases (e.g., *down the road, write it down*). The Fry Instant Phrases are available, along with helpful resources and articles about fluency, on Dr. Tim Rasinski's website: http://timrasinski.com/
- *Read Like Me* (Young, Lagrone & McCauley, 2020). Especially effective for non-fluent readers. *Read Like Me* models appropriate pacing, expression, and accuracy, key components of reading fluency. The steps to *Read Like Me* instruction include:
  1. Select a text of high interest to the student.
  2. Read a section or paragraph aloud to the student, while the student follows along.

3. Teacher and student, together, read aloud the same section or paragraph.
4. Student orally reads the same section or paragraph independently.
5. Reread at the next lesson. If fluency is lagging, repeat steps 3 and 4.

Comprehension

We use the following reading comprehension strategies depending on whether the learner is reading a narrative or expository text.

Directed Reading-Thinking Activity (DR-TA)

During a DR-TA (Stauffer, 1969; Ruddell, 2007; Echevarria et al., 2024), the teacher and student stop periodically throughout the reading of a story or book to contemplate predictions about what might logically follow in each section of a narrative (fiction) text. Steps for DR-TA include:

- Select a story or picture book that is interesting, exciting, and compelling. Be careful that picture book illustrations do not give away the ending of the story.
- Begin with the title showing. Ask, *With a title of _____, what do you think this story will be about? Why do you think so?*
- Uncover one paragraph or section of text at a time. As each new section is uncovered, students review earlier predictions and make new ones as warranted (*Now what do you think will happen? Why?*).
- Use probes throughout the story, such as:
  - What makes you think that? Tell me more about that.
  - *What do you think is going to happen next? What makes you think so?*
  - Analyze predictions for relevancy and ask questions only about the student's predictions: *You predicted that _____ would happen, but it didn't happen. Why do you think so? What do you think will happen next?*
- Revisit previously made predictions after a section of text is read.

DR-TA can easily be differentiated for students' reading abilities by varying the difficulty level of the text.

Survey, Question, Predict, Read, Respond, and Summarize (SQP2RS)

Often referred to as "Squeepers," SQP2RS is an instructional framework for teaching expository texts for students in grades 3–10 (Echevarria et al., 2024;

Vogt & Echevarria, 2015), but it can easily be used with older learners. Steps to implementing SQP2RS include:

1. **Survey**: Model surveying through a think-aloud: "I see there are bold-print headings, so I know this is key information that will help me know what the big ideas will be." For older students, if a text is too long to survey in a minute, divide it into sections.
2. **Question**: "Based on your survey, think of two or three questions that you think will be answered by reading this text." Record questions on a whiteboard or paper.
3. **Predict**: This step builds upon the questions generated previously by helping students to narrow their focus and write down the most important concepts they think they will learn.
4. **Read:** While reading, students should note places in the text where they have found answers to the questions initially asked—and where predictions were confirmed or disconfirmed. Encourage students to use sticky notes, arrows, tabs, or highlighter tape to mark their texts.
5. **Respond:** During the response stage, discuss answers to the questions posed earlier and the predictions that were confirmed or disconfirmed. Use prompts, such as:
    - *Might we find answers to some of the questions in the next section? In another chapter? How do you know?*
    - *Did the author take us in a different direction than we originally thought? When did you realize that?*
    - *Are there other questions we should be asking before we read more? If so, what are they?*

    The response step is intended to be a time of discussion, reflection, and interaction among the student and teacher.
6. **Summarize:** At this point, the student should be able to summarize the key concepts that were introduced and discussed in the text. If you have students who need modifications, write key vocabulary on the board to help them incorporate the words into their summaries. Model the summarizing process so that you don't receive a "retelling" rather than a summary.

We have found that one of the biggest benefits of "Squeepers" is that struggling readers begin to see themselves as strategic—they have a plan for how to "attack" expository text, even if it is challenging. See MaryEllen Vogt describing Squeepers implementation in a classroom setting: https://tinyurl.com/VogtSqueepers

Update: Jake's Story

After 247 LIE lessons, as well as excellent instruction in his special education class, Jake is now reading at a third- to fourth-grade level, especially when the text's topic is familiar. This is remarkable given his neurological limitations. He regularly self-monitors when he reads (stops and rereads if something does not make sense), and his comprehension while he reads silently and orally is excellent. Likewise, when he listens to another reader reading grade-level text, his comprehension is spot on. Spelling and writing remain difficult processes for Jake. Figure B.4 shows us celebrating Jake's 200th lesson and his reading progress over the years.

At the end of the school year, 2024, I attended Jake's "transitional meeting" (for all fifth graders going into middle school) with his current teachers, principal, and his sixth-grade Special Day Class (SDC) teacher. Jake was in the room as well. The good news was that Jake would be in general education (mainstreamed) for four of his classes next year (PE, science, history, and an

Figure B.4 A boy standing with the author celebrating his reading progress. Photograph by the author.

elective). He would remain in the SDC for math and ELA and would receive special education support for exams and some assignments. According to his plan, he would be able to use spoken text for all grade-level reading texts and assignments, and he would have assistive technology (speech to print) for his written assignments. Among the educators who have worked with Jake, there is agreement that he is one bright and capable boy who, with the help he will receive, will do well in a mainstream setting. After the meeting, outside in front of the school, Jake's mom was crying. I was tearing up, and we were both relieved because we knew he needed to be in general education classes for part of the day. His mom said through her tears, "Thank you. Jake can now just be a kid, with all of this support for next year." Jake's literacy story, which he began as a non-reading 7-year-old, is not over. He is heading to middle school with the assistive technology he needs and with teachers and parents who appreciate his talents, knowledge, and yes, his sense of humor! Jake is on his way!

Note

1 Jake is a pseudonym. Jake's story and writing are used with permission.

Case C

Connecting through Reading: Tutoring Incarcerated Youth

Olivia M. Gore and Mary E. Styslinger

How many of us have heard that third-grade reading scores are used to predict the number of prison beds a state will need? While not technically true, we cannot deny the relationship between literacy, graduation, and incarceration. A student who can't read on grade level by third-grade is four times less likely to graduate by age 19 than a child who does read proficiently at that time. If the student who can't read on grade level lives in poverty, then that same student is 13 times less likely to graduate on time (Hernandez, 2011). Also, consider that about 1 in every 10 young male high school dropouts is in jail or juvenile detention centers, compared to one in 35 young male high school graduates (Sum et al., 2009). Now the connection between a lack of literacy and the nation's growing prison population can be made. The picture is even bleaker for students of color. In 2015, black children were five times more likely than white children to be incarcerated (Olivares, 2017).

The need for expanded literacy instruction in juvenile detention centers has been widely documented and supported (Christle & Yell, 2008; Krezmien & Mulcahy, 2008; Vacca, 2008). However, conventional teaching methods are not always successful for youth who did not have positive experiences with traditional schooling (Jacobi, 2008; Snyder & Sickmund, 2006). Instead, alternative literacy practices (Jacobi, 2008) are encouraged for these youth. Since the national average length of confinement for youth is 106 days in public juvenile detention centers (Sickmund & Puzzanchera, 2014), such alternative literacy instruction also needs to be implemented in a short amount of time.

Inspired by a need for short-term, alternative literacy curriculum and teaching that expands instruction in correctional facilities, we designed (Mary) and supported (Olivia) a tutoring partnership serving incarcerated youth and the larger community through a collaboration between a state university and the Department of Juvenile Justice (DJJ). This tutoring partnership experience is required for prospective high school English teachers enrolled in a summer intensive adolescent literacy course within a graduate teacher certification program. Whereas the teacher candidates possess undergraduate degrees in English, they have no prior experience planning, facilitating, or assessing learning experiences in reading. Participation is optional for students incarcerated through the DJJ. No costs are associated with the tutoring project other than books provided to the students.

Preparing to Tutor

Before meeting with middle and high school students at DJJ, prospective tutors first develop their literacy foundation through reading, talking, and writing with each other. We begin by reflecting on our personal experiences, critically considering the contextual and cultural experiences that have shaped us as readers. Next, we explore definitions of reading and consider different models of reading instruction. We review data published by the National Assessment of Educational Progress (NAEP) and publications from NCTE's Commission on Reading. To gain a window into a reader's processes, we learn how to conduct a miscue analysis and facilitate a retrospective miscue analysis (RMA). We read books (Mueller, 2001; Gallagher, 2009) to gain understanding of why readers may struggle and to learn how to support readers before, during, and after reading (Tovani, 2000; Beers, 2003; Appleman & Graves, 2011).

Tatum (2005, 2009) reminds us of the importance of always being culturally responsive, and we review the tenets of culturally relevant pedagogy (Ladson-Billings, 1995). We read excerpts from *Literacy behind Bars* (Styslinger, Gavigan & Albright, 2017), learning from those who are incarcerated and those who teach them. Along with reading professional texts related to adolescent literacy, we immerse ourselves in young adult literature. We scour the YALSA (www.ala.org/yalsa/booklistsawards/booklistsbook) and In the Margins (inthemarginssite.blog/awards-list/) award sites, knowing we need to select novels to read alongside incarcerated youth.

Once a literacy foundation has been more firmly established, prospective tutors travel behind the fence, and all future meetings are held on a site associated with the DJJ. Tutors are partnered randomly on the first day and meet with the same student over a three-week period (on average), every other day. DJJ students, all male at this facility, range in age from 12 to 18 years with reading levels from fourth grade to college level.

Developing Relationships

At the initial meeting, reading partners come to know each other through a basic interview process. After an initial informal meet and greet conversation, tutors administer and audio record a reading interview (Goodman, Watson & Burke, 2005) adapted for adolescent readers in the DJJ setting. Responses to the interview provide insight into the literacy background, learning environment, and literacy experiences of the students.

1. Why did you decide to be tutored?
2. Describe your daily routine at DJJ. Do you have time to read?
3. Do you like reading? Why or why not?
4. When you are reading and you come to something you don't know, what do you do?
5. Do you ever do anything else?
6. Think about someone who likes to read. Why do you think _____ likes to read?
7. Do you think _____ ever comes to something she/he doesn't know when reading?
8. If the student says Yes to #4: When _____ does come to something she/he doesn't know, what do you think _____ does about it?
9. If the student says No to #4: If _____ came to something she/he didn't know, what would she/he do?
10. If you know someone is having difficulty reading, how would you help that person?
11. What would a teacher do to help that person?
12. How did you learn to read?
13. Describe yourself as a reader: What kind of reader are you?
14. What would you like to do better as a reader?
15. How much do you like to read? Why do you feel that way?

Depending on the amount of time available, tutors might also ask questions about school, sports, music, and the usual likes/dislikes of teenagers to help select books of interest. Tutors have been forewarned not to ask any questions related to why the student is at the DJJ facility. Tutors also share information about their own likes/dislikes to make direct connections to the learner.

After this first meeting, tutors listen to a recording of the interview a few times and take detailed notes, thinking about this reader. What makes them unique? How did they come to language and reading? What are their interests? Instead of deficits, what "funds of knowledge" do they bring to literacy? Tutors use this information to guide their book selections for their students.

At the second meeting, tutors talk with students about what they have learned from the interview, share their notes, and ask follow-up questions. Eventually, they introduce book choices through a pre-reading strategy such as an anticipation guide (Tierney & Readence, 2000). For example, a tutor creates a list of general statements related to key ideas in Angela Johnson's *The First Part Last*, as shown in Table C.1.

Before reading, the reading partners agree or disagree with each statement. Next, they discuss their responses, activating prior knowledge. Tutors introduce a second book using the same pre-reading strategy. Then, the tutor selects the book that they are most interested in reading. Once a text is selected, the reading partners collaboratively establish a reading calendar.

Over the next several meetings, tutors frontload, support, and extend the reading processes of students, planning and facilitating pre-reading,

Table C.1 Anticipation guide example

Before reading			After reading	
Agree	Disagree		Agree	Disagree
		Your choices define who you are.		
		It's okay to ask for help when you need it.		
		It's important to take responsibility for your actions.		
		Only mothers know how to take care of children.		
		The best time for learning is during a struggle.		
		We live by choice not by chance.		
		Personal choices can impact other people's lives.		
		Parenthood can change your life for the better.		

during-reading, and post-reading strategies for the selected text. Planning is influenced by the initial reading conversation. For example, if a student initially revealed they like to draw during the interview, the tutor might incorporate drawing during a strategy lesson.

Once the text is completed, the reading partners return to the anticipation guide shown in Table C.1 and reread the statements, indicating once again whether they agree or disagree with each. This provides an additional richness to the book discussion, especially when their agreement about a statement changed from before to after reading the text.

Miscue Analysis

In addition, tutors administer and record a miscue analysis, including an oral and silent reading and retelling to better understand the cueing systems (i.e., graphophonic, syntactic, and semantic) utilized by their reader. A miscue analysis is a diagnostic tool developed by Goodman (1969) which provides a window into a reader's processes, assessing students' comprehension based on samples of oral reading.

At a meeting following the administration of the miscue analysis, teacher candidates facilitate a retrospective miscue analysis (RMA) designed to foster metacognition. During the RMA, tutors lead students to consider reading miscues through guided questioning. Tutors select miscues for discussion and help students become more reflective about their own reading processes (Goodman & Marek, 1996), asking questions such as: *Does the miscue make sense? Does the miscue sound like language? Was the miscue corrected? Should it have been? Does the miscue look like what was on the page? Does the miscue sound like what was on the page? Why do you think you made this miscue? Did that miscue affect your understanding of the text?*

The reading partnership concludes with breakfast and the presentation of a new book by the tutor to the student. While these details explain the tutor's preparation and procedure, we can best understand the process through Olivia's personal experiences reading with Ty.

Reading with Ty

I began our first meeting with questions I had drafted previously, which incorporated questions from the Burke Interview so I could come to know Ty both as a reader and as a person, his likes and dislikes when it came to music, food, sports, movies, and even video games. I introduced myself, explained how I was a college student, and shared that helping him better understand his reading processes would help me grow as a future teacher.

As I progressed through the questions, I asked Ty what he had read lately, and before I could finish the question, he immediately answered, "R.L. Stine." I asked him to tell me a little about the book, and he replied, "trouble at a party or something like that." I tried to ask more questions about characters and the kinds of "trouble" he was talking about. I wanted to know whether he liked the book or not. But Ty didn't reveal much. He mumbled something else about the party and said he hadn't read enough. I began to wonder if he was struggling to understand what he was reading, but I opted not to press because we were both a bit nervous.

Continuing with the adapted Burke interview, I asked Ty if he chose to read R.L. Stine for school or for fun, and he proudly replied, "for fun." During this time, we discussed how he could check books out from his dorm library, which doesn't have a huge selection but enough to keep him busy. His favorite genres to read are horror and comedy; he reads every day for about an hour amounting to three or four chapters. He knew that he learned to read in school but couldn't recall how he learned to read. When he confronts a word that is unfamiliar, he sounds the word out letter-by-letter and sometimes grabs a dictionary. For the last question, I asked Ty, "Do you think you're a good reader?" to which he replied, "yeah, I think I'm a good reader because I read every day – there ain't nothing else to do here 'cept read."

Through the interview process, I learned that Ty is 18, almost done with his GED, and scheduled for release from DJJ the following month. He likes to read horror novels. He looks up to his teachers and some of the staff at DJJ and wants to be more like his dad. He enjoys eating at Zaxby's, listening to hip-hop music like NBA YoungBoy, and says he wants to be a better reader. One of the most memorable parts of our first meeting was when I asked where he would go if he could travel anywhere in the world. I expected him to say someplace like Hawaii, but he named New Jersey and Philly "cause I got family there."

After the first meeting, I analyzed the recording from the interview. I listened and transcribed Ty's responses to the questions I asked. I reviewed his responses considering three models of reading (e.g., subskills, skills, and holistic). For example, when Ty responded that he sounds out words, I wondered if he was operating from a subskills model with a focus on the pronunciations of words but thought he might also be processing through the skills model of reading as he looks up words and definitions in a dictionary.

Based on Ty's responses, I selected two books that I thought he would enjoy. Of course, I chose an R.L. Stine novel entitled *The Confession* because Ty liked the author. I also chose a book called *Concrete Rose* written by Angie Thomas. This young adult, urban literature novel is a prequel to *The Hate You Give* by Angie Thomas, which focuses on choices and decision making that I thought

Ty could both relate to and learn from. To introduce each of these books, I planned pre-reading strategies.

At our second meeting, we read the back of the books independently and discussed what we thought the novels would entail. Then, I read aloud the first few pages of each novel, modeling reading fluency as well as introducing the characters and the style of each book. Ty selected *Concrete Rose* to read during our sessions. I provided a writing notebook and had him write a few sentences as to why he chose *Concrete Rose*. Tyler wrote, "I like this book because it starts powerful, and it teaches you how to be a man." To close the meeting, we talked through a reading calendar for the next two weeks and agreed to read two chapters each night.

The next day, we met and talked about the chapters we read. To make him feel more comfortable reading during a miscue analysis, I read aloud for five to ten minutes before explaining the directions for the rest of the day. Then I asked Ty to read aloud from *Concrete Rose*, beginning where I left off. He read about two pages from the novel, which took him two minutes and 45 seconds. I asked him to briefly summarize what he read, and he said, "His mama – she went out to go get something to eat then they, they just had a heartfelt moment." His retelling of the few pages wasn't very descriptive, but he did mention that the main character and his mother had a "heartfelt moment" which shows he is making sense of the characters.

Next, he read independently and silently for a few minutes and again summarized his reading, although this time, he was a bit more descriptive: "Dre just found out that Maverick was selling other drugs for money because Maverick been buying his girl all type a stuff and then Maverick try to lie and say it was odd jobs." Tyler was able to recall more details when he read independently and silently versus when he read aloud, and his retelling was accurate. Figure C.1 shows the miscue analysis markup from the first reading session.

Finally, we finished the miscue analysis by reading part of a nonfiction article about the origins of hip-hop music so that Ty could read a variety of genres. I learned from our initial interview that he favored hip-hop and rap music, so I thought this article would pique his interest. As he read for a few minutes and only got through half the page, I realized I should have chosen an article with a lower reading level. When Ty finished reading after about 2 and a half minutes and I asked him to recall what he'd read, he responded with, "I just read how hip-hop was made." Figure C.2 shows the miscue analysis markup from the second reading session.

That evening, I listened to the recording from Ty's read-aloud to ensure I appropriately marked words that Ty skipped, read incorrectly, repeated, changed, or didn't recognize on a copy of the text. After marking the miscues, I transferred the information to a miscue coding sheet and analyzed each miscue as shown in Figure C.3.

Connecting through Reading: Tutoring Incarcerated Youth   143

Figure C.1

"Forget you," I say.
                    (R) (C) keep coming
"I only speak facts. You keeping him overnight or something?"

I sit on the edge of the couch, get Li'l Man situated, and feed him again.
                                       bounce
"I don't know. Iesha and her momma bounced."

Dre lower the bottle I'm holding. "Don't feed him fast. What you mean

they bounced?"

                        (R)
"Shit—shoot." Dre try not to cuss in front of Ma. "Did y'all look for
(C) him
them?"
                                                          (R)
"We went by the house, and nobody was there," Ma says. "I shouldn't

be surprised that Yolanda's trifling behind would pull something like this." "Dang," Dre says.
            you   (R)   the
"Well, hey, if y'all need a crib, we still got Andreanna's old one in storage and her stroller. I can

bring them over later." "That's sweet of you, baby. Thank you." Ma grab her purse off the
                                      for (C)
couch. "I'm gonna go pick up some dinner from Reuben's. Lord knows I
                              (R)
am not in the mood to cook. Y'all behave while I'm gone."

"Yes, ma'am," we both say. Even though Dre twenty-three, he do

whatever Ma tell him.

She leave, and Dre sit beside me on the couch. He watch me feed Li'l

Man.

"Damn, Mav. You really a father."

Figure C.1 Miscue analysis markup from the first reading session.

Most of Ty's miscues were graphically similar, which supported my earlier assumption that he was operating from a subskills model, but I also wondered if he was focused on reading quickly rather than reading for meaning. He tended to change the words by adding -ed or -ing to words that didn't have these endings. For example, he said "bounced" instead of "bounce" and "turning" instead of "turn," which can alter the meaning of the text. These miscues could also be dialectical and indicative of Ty translating the text into how he speaks. He corrected about 50 percent of the words he missed, demonstrating

> "I still can't believe it."
>
> "I get that. Fatherhood is a trip, but I couldn't imagine my life without my baby girl. Even as bad as she is."
>
> I laugh. "She can't be that bad. She only three."
>
> "Shiiid. She think she know everything, and she get into everything. ⓡ People say twos are terrible. Nah, three. Three is next level." [He get quiet for a second. "I'm gon' miss her li'l bad butt after I drop her and Keisha off.
>
> A couple of years ago, Keisha moved outta town to attend Markham State and took Andreanna with her. It's only two hours away, and Dre visit every weekend. He stay in the Garden to help Aunt 'Nita with Uncle Ray after Unc had a stroke last year.
>
> "Hold tight, man," I say. "Before you know it, Keisha will be graduating and y'all will be saying your vows in July."
>
>   the
> "If I can survive all this wedding stuff." He grab the back of my neck. "You good?"
>
> Hell no. My life got thrown into a blender and I'm left with something I don't recognize. On top of that, I'm suddenly somebody's pops and I wish I had my pops.

Retelling from Read-Aloud

"His mama— she went out to go get something to eat. Then, they— they just had a heart-felt moment."

Independent Retelling

"Dre just found out that Maverick was selling other drugs for money because Maverick been buying his girl all type of stuff and then Maverick try to lie and say it was odd jobs."

Figure C.1 Miscue analysis markup from the first reading session.

that he is monitoring the words he's missing, but he also has room for growth since he didn't correct the other 50 percent.

When it comes to semantic accuracy and meaning change, Ty's data was also about 50 percent, meaning half of his miscues had meaning changes and

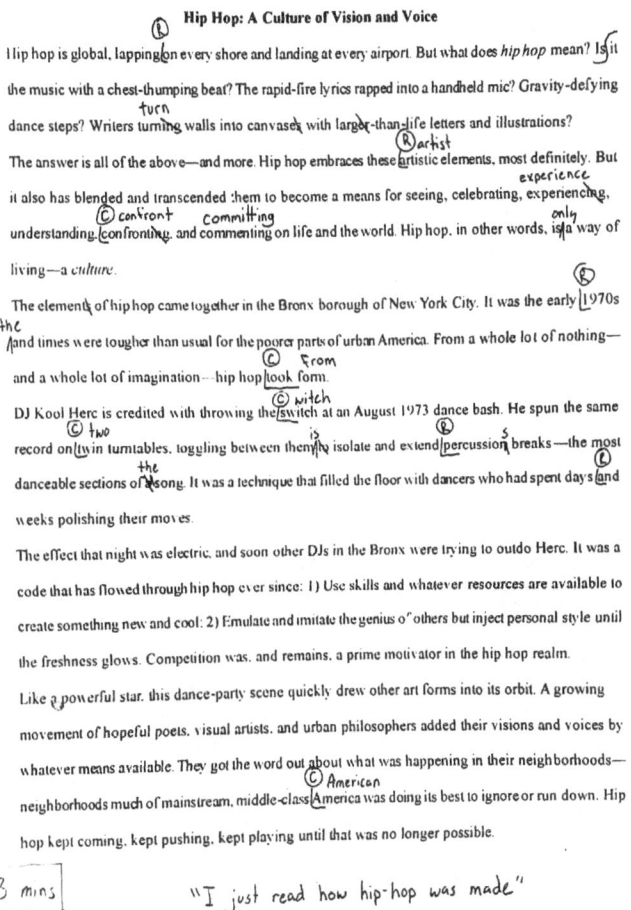

Figure C.2 Miscue analysis markup from the second reading session.

half were syntactic errors. For example, he said "witch" instead of "switch" and "two" instead of "twin." I wanted Ty to understand that reading has nothing to do with speed and everything to do with comprehension. After reviewing his miscues at our next meeting, I planned to reiterate that reading isn't a race – there's no prize for finishing first! What is important is understanding. As I planned for our next meeting, I wanted us to read together, pause, and talk about the novel to enhance his comprehension.

Reader's Name: Ty   Date: Grade:
Teacher: Olivia   School:
Person Doing the Miscue: Olivia   Percentage Accurate:
Title: Hip-Hop: A Culture of Vision and Voice   Publisher:

Miscue #	Reader	Text	1 Graphic Similarity			2 Syntactic Acc			3 Corrected			4 Semantic Acc			5 Meaning Change			3,4,5
			Y	P	N	Y	P	N	Y	P	N	Y	P	N	Y	P	N	COMP
1	keep coming	keeping		✓			✓				✓		✓			✓		loss
2	bounce	bounced	✓			✓					✓	✓					✓	no loss
3	him	them		✓		✓					✓	✓				✓		partial
4	you	ya'll		✓		✓					✓		✓			✓		partial
5	for	from		✓		✓					✓		✓				✓	loss
6	couldn't	can't	✓			✓					✓	✓					✓	no loss
7	got	get	✓			✓					✓	✓					✓	no loss
8	the	this	✓				✓				✓	✓					✓	no loss
9	turn	turning		✓		✓					✓	✓					✓	no loss
10	canvas	canvases		✓		✓					✓	✓					✓	no loss
11	artist	artistic		✓			✓				✓		✓			✓		partial
12	experience	experiencing a	✓				✓				✓	✓					✓	no loss
13	confront	confronting		✓		✓					✓	✓					✓	no loss
14	committing	commenting		✓		✓					✓		✓			✓		loss
15	from	form	✓				✓				✓		✓			✓		loss
16	witch	switch		✓		✓					✓		✓			✓		loss
17	two	twin		✓		✓					✓		✓			✓		loss
18	the	a			✓	✓					✓	✓					✓	loss
19	percussions	percussion	✓			✓					✓	✓					✓	no loss
20	American	America	✓				✓			✓		✓					✓	no loss

8 10 2 6 7 8 9 1 10 9 4 7 3 10

SCRI Research Miscue Coding Sheet
Revised 11 2005 by DS
Y-40% Y-30% Y-45% Y-45% Y-35%
P-50% N-35% N-5%   N-20% N-15%
N-10% P-40% P-50% P-35% P-50%

Figure C.3 Miscue analysis coding sheet with documented miscues from oral readings.

Retrospective Miscue Analysis

We had our next meeting the following week, and I facilitated an RMA. I explained what a miscue was, reiterating that it is not an error and encouraging him to consider what the miscue might reveal about his reading process. We reviewed his phonetic and dialectic miscues from the transcripts and pondered what they meant, why they might occur, and what we could do to address some of them.

Some miscues were dialectical (e.g., saying "gunna" instead of "going"). I explained how these miscues show how smart he is because he is code switching, translating the text to how he talks. With the phonetic miscues, we talked about how he needs to slow down. We also spent time considering his oral and silent retellings. Ty noted that his retelling after reading silently was more detailed than his retelling after reading aloud. When I asked why this was, he explained that reading in his head is easier because he's reading for himself and not for an audience.

Helping Ty reflect on his reading was beneficial because he practiced metacognition and thought about "why" and "how" he is reading. To close our meeting, we read a poem titled "The Rose that Grew from Concrete" by Tupac that connects heavily with our novel *Concrete Rose*. Ty was familiar with the author and explained what he liked about the poem before our meeting time was over.

During-Reading Strategies

During our next meeting, we practiced the Say Something strategy (Beers, 2003). I read the first three pages of Chapter 5 of *Concrete Rose,* and after each page, we paused and said something about what we read. I provided prompts to jumpstart talking about the text:

- *I can't believe they did _____.*
- *I wonder why _____.*
- *I thought it was funny when _____.*
- *I can relate to _____. It reminds of _____.*
- *I think _____ will happen next.*

We practiced this strategy for 25 minutes, taking turns reading a few pages at a time, making predictions about what would happen, connecting the text to our lives, and asking questions about characters and plot. During our reading, a character had to change his son's diaper, and I asked, knowing Ty had younger siblings and cousins, if he had ever had to change a diaper like the protagonist in our novel. Ty told me that he had to change his daughter's diapers all the time and that he missed her as he was in DJJ. This was a huge part of his life to share with me, and I credit the reading strategy for creating a comfortable and respectful environment that encouraged Ty to share personal connections.

In our sixth meeting, we practiced another during-reading strategy and read a short story by Angie Thomas titled "The Black Widows." I read aloud the entire short story, and Ty listened and followed along. When finished, I asked Ty to take out his writing notebook and create three columns on a page while I did the same on a sheet of paper. We labeled one column Khalil, the protagonist in "The Black Widows"; another column labeled Maverick, the protagonist in *Concrete Rose*; and the last column labeled Both. We made a bulleted list, comparing the characters, then discussed why their similarities and differences are crucial parts of each story. Although both characters come from similar backgrounds, they are unique in their experiences and have very different outcomes because of the choices they make. I know Ty engaged with the story and strategy because he asked thoughtful questions about the characters, suggested different outcomes for the endings, and connected elements of the story to his life. To conclude the session, we watched a video on my phone of Tupac performing the poem we read last week, "The Rose that Grew from Concrete." Since technology use is highly regulated at DJJ, he watched closely and listened carefully.

Making Lasting Connections

During our last meeting together, we ate Chick-fil-A for breakfast and engaged in a post-reading strategy called Save the Last Word for Me (Appleman & Graves, 2011). We listened to an audio-recorded excerpt of the novel as we devoured chicken biscuits and minis. When the recording was over, I had Ty choose a quotation or a paragraph that stood out to him. He wrote the quotation and page number in his writer's notebook and explained why the quotation resonated with him. Ty wrote about when the main character's girlfriend told him she was pregnant with his second child. Ty said that their interaction was similar to when his girlfriend told him she was pregnant.

This was a special moment for both of us. I believe we could talk about these experiences because we built a trusting relationship through our time spent together, reading and practicing strategies that helped us connect with the novel and, more importantly, each other. For me as a developing teacher, I learned that the process of tutoring Ty at the DJJ not only revealed the importance of personalized, student-centered reading strategies but also highlighted the transformative power of building genuine connections with others. Through the utilization of the Burke Interview, miscue analysis, teaching reading strategies, and our reflective discussions, it became evident that Ty's reading journey was not just about improving literacy skills and strategies, but it was also about understanding the unique background and experiences he brought to his reading. This tutoring experience underscored the significance of creating a comfortable and respectful environment where students like Ty can share personal connections and find meaning in the texts they read. It reinforces the idea that effective literacy instruction extends beyond books and comprehension – it reaches the heart and soul of the reader, nurturing a love for reading that goes far beyond classroom walls and fences.

Case D

Tutoring Diverse Student Populations

Katherine Marsh and Elizabeth Dinelli

Meet Vedi

Vedi stared back at me with her head tilted and one side of her mouth turned up. My explanation of the word *sauntered* did not seem to make sense to her. Her look contained both confusion and apprehension. Not wanting to lose the teachable moment, I got up and sauntered across the small office room in an exaggerated way that made her smile a little. I hoped that my melodramatic efforts might help her understand not only the vocabulary but also the personality and behavior of the character in the story we were reading.

Vedi is the child of naturalized citizens who were originally from India. When Vedi's parents emigrated from India so that her father could join a medical practice and her mother could obtain her graduate degree in computer science, they expected to raise a small family. Vedi is their second child. She has an older brother, Ishaan, who is two years her senior. Both children were born in the United States. The family lives in a suburban, middle-class neighborhood in the Northeast and is involved in local youth team sports and their church. Vedi's mother has been on the local school board since Ishaan was in kindergarten, and her father volunteers with fundraising efforts to bring cultural activities such as concerts, fairs, and art exhibits to their town.

DOI: 10.4324/9781032688589-11

In preschool, Vedi had difficulty understanding rhymes, mispronounced words, struggled to learn letters, and often applied odd words to explain what she was doing. Vedi's father recalls her asking for "empty" paper when she wanted a blank sheet of paper to draw on. He mentioned that she still called their fluffy, white Persian cat, Igloo, *Ligoo*, no matter how many times he had tried to get her to sequence the sounds correctly.

In the early grades, Vedi was good at memorizing grade-level sight vocabulary, simple open and closed syllable words, and many compound words. Her parents think that she didn't identify as needing specialized help right away because the family supported her with at-home tutoring by both Vedi's parents and her older brother. In fourth grade, Vedi seemed to reach a plateau in reading: struggling with vowel digraphs and diphthongs, mispronouncing r-controlled syllables in multisyllable words, and confusing homophones. Her spelling was extremely poor, which caused discouragement with any writing tasks.

As a rising fifth-grader, Vedi had come to dislike school in general. Her dyslexia-like struggles seemed to make every part of school difficult. She read slowly, taking twice as much time as her peers to read chapter books. She struggled to find the right words when writing. Even math was hard due to the need to recall math facts quickly and follow problems with multiple steps. She loved her fourth-grade science class and enjoyed experiences offered by "specials" (music, art, STEM, gym, nature).

Vedi developed good friendships, had excellent ideas during class discussions, and was seen as sociable, pleasant, and respectful by her teachers. However, if Vedi became frustrated or overwhelmed, she could present with anger and sometimes tears. When discouraged by the hard work, Vedi found some solace in her strengths: building complex scenes with Lego bricks with her brother and younger cousins, and connecting with friends of all ages at her church's community center, where she excelled in music and tap dancing.

Assessments That Guide Intervention

When Vedi's mother first contacted our tutoring center, Vedi had already received informal assessments through their public school that indicated possible dyslexia. While Vedi's school worked to schedule and complete in-depth testing and evaluate whether to develop an individualized education plan (IEP), Vedi's parents wanted to get her started immediately with a tutoring routine that could help rebuild her fading confidence.

Our tutoring center director met with Vedi and her parents in late May and suggested testing Vedi using the CTOPP-2: Comprehensive Test of Phonological Processing, 2nd edition (Wagner et al., 2013), a norm-referenced test that measures phonological abilities and processing skills such as phonological retrieval and memory, and rapid processing of phonological information. The CTOPP-2's game-like approach is engaging for children. The test can be administered in about 40 minutes. The results would be used to identify specific areas of sound processing difficulty and to guide the planned intervention over the summer.

She also recommended giving Vedi the TOWRE 2: Test of Word Reading Efficiency, 2nd edition (Torgesen et al., 2012), which measures the ability to pronounce printed words accurately and fluently. The TOWRE 2 is quick to administer, taking less than five minutes, and would identify Vedi's sight word efficiency as well as her phonetic decoding efficiency. Further reasoning for using the TOWRE 2 was that it could be administered again at the end of the summer to provide evidence of how well Vedi's tutoring intervention had progressed.

Vedi's parents viewed her literacy challenge as twofold: her lack of measurable progress in reading throughout her fourth-grade year and her increasing discouragement with multiple aspects of school, primarily with spelling, writing, and math word problems. Vedi's CTOPP-2 results revealed weak phonological awareness, particularly on the blending words subtest. The blending words subtest measures the ability to blend sounds to form words. For example, a student is asked to listen to each individual sound in a word, such as n/a/p, and then asked to blend the sounds together to say the whole word. On this subtest, Vedi tended to add and omit sounds. Rapid naming was weak, which correlates with Vedi's history of a slow reading rate that negatively impacts reading fluency. Her phonological memory was average, which corresponds to her strong memory. Weaknesses in this area have a negative impact on the decoding of unfamiliar, multisyllable words and the comprehension of complex sentences.

The TOWRE 2 assessment results revealed Vedi's sight word efficiency as above average, which corresponds to her strong sight word vocabulary. But her phonemic decoding efficiency was below average. Most of her miscues were around vowel digraphs and diphthongs, applying the long vowel sound to silent e words, difficulty with r-controlled syllables, as well as adding and omitting sounds.

Our director met again with Vedi's parents to discuss the testing results and propose a tutoring focus and plan. Vedi's parents wondered if the test results indicated a diagnosis of dyslexia. Our director informed them that although these tests indicated the likelihood of dyslexia, a more thorough evaluation, such as that being conducted by Vedi's school, would be the best way to evaluate that diagnosis.

Creating the Tutoring Plan

The primary literacy challenge to overcome would be to provide Vedi with explicit instruction and practice with word decoding to improve her ability to decode unfamiliar words. Vedi's struggle to make progress with reading seemed to stem from her lack of a coherent and efficient strategy to link letter combinations to sounds. Additional challenges for Vedi were spelling and written expression. The pedagogically grounded intervention chosen to support Vedi was the Orton-Gillingham Academy (OG, 2022) approach to language learning. OG is an evidence-based, intensive intervention that is explicit, multisensory, sequential, and systematic. Vedi's parents opted to begin tutoring immediately, committing to twice-per-week sessions from June to August for a total of 12 weeks over a 13-week stretch. Vedi missed one week in July due to family summer vacation plans.

Building Blocks of Language

The OG approach presents students with the sequential building blocks of language, beginning with the most basic information on letter-sound relationships before introducing more complex information. Subsequent OG lessons progress to increasingly more difficult material, with previous concepts systematically reviewed to strengthen recall and automaticity. Students learn individual sounds for letters by hearing the sounds, saying the sounds, and writing the letter(s) representing the sounds. Lessons involve the three associations of visual, auditory, and kinesthetic-tactile brain pathways simultaneously. In practice, OG is flexible and individualized. Each lesson may include writing and spelling as well as reading. Each student moves through the sequence at her own pace. Every OG lesson has three associations or levels of learning incorporated into the session. With all three associations, the goal is automaticity.

- Association I includes the visual-auditory combination, associating the symbol (e.g., A or a) to its name (e.g., a) and its sound (/a/), and the visual-kinesthetic combination, associating the symbol with the feel of the letter when spoken or written. For example, students begin an OG lesson by reviewing a selected set of phonogram cards. The teacher holds up the card, then the student responds with the name of the symbol, the sound of the symbol, and an example word (e.g., "a says /a/ as in apple").

- Association II is the basis of auditory training for spelling and includes the auditory-auditory combination, associating the sound (spoken by the teacher) with the name of the letter that makes that sound (e.g., Teacher: Tell me the name of the letter that has the sound /a/. Student: a, apple, /a/).
- Association III is the basis of written spelling and includes the visual-kinesthetic combination, associating the symbol with the way it feels when the student writes, the kinesthetic-visual combination, associating the feel of the letter with its symbol, and the auditory-kinesthetic combination, associating the sound of the letter with the feel of the letter form. For example, the teacher may model making the letter, followed by the student tracing the letter, copying the letter, and then writing the letter from memory. If the student needs a more strongly kinesthetic memory, the teacher may ask the student to write the letter on a rough surface or in sand. Next, the student will write the letter while looking away from her paper. Finally, the teacher gives the student a sound and asks the student to write the letter that has that sound.

Association I includes the use of phonogram cards, the introduction of the lesson objective, word drills, syllable division (if appropriate), and sentence-level reading. Association II requires that the students practice sounds orally (oral dictation of sounds). Association III involves written dictation of sounds, words, and sentences using the Simultaneous Oral Spelling System recommended by the Orton-Gillingham approach. Reading connected text is always an integral aspect of each lesson. In addition, sight word and vocabulary instruction are added to lessons as needed. The format for each lesson follows a consistent sequence so that decoding and encoding are continuously integrated based on the focus objective.

Orton-Gillingham in Action

As I prepared for Vedi's tutoring session during her third week of tutoring, I gathered a selection of phonogram cards: all consonants (b-z), short and long vowels, vowel teams (ai, ay, oo, ea, ee, and ow), digraphs (sh, ch, th, ck, wh), word lists, word cards for sorting, a page of sentences, chips for segmenting sounds, the boxing words game, highlighters, and dry erase markers.

During our previous session, Vedi struggled with consistently applying the two sounds of the vowel team ow; additionally, she is still adding and omitting sounds with words containing blends. So, our lesson objective was decoding words with the two sounds of ow, as in snow and plow. As I held up each card, Vedi responded by saying the name of the letter, the sound of the letter, and an example keyword. This step went quickly, since Vedi has a strong memory and good recall. After the phonogram drill, Vedi completed a blending drill to target her propensity to add and omit sounds. I said each individual sound in a word with up to five phonemes, pausing between each sound. Vedi needed to blend the sounds together to say the entire word.

Next, Vedi benefited from extra time practicing nonsense words. She tended to be very good at memorizing known words, so blending with nonsense words helped Vedi apply her decoding skills. First, I reviewed the two sounds of *ow*: /o/ as in snow and /ou/ as in plow. Next, I reviewed when to use *ow* for the /ou/ sound as in plow; *ow* is used for the /ou/ sound at the end of words or when the /ou/ sound is followed by a single *l* or *n* or *er* or *el*. Vedi sorted *ow* words according to the sound *ow* makes. She was instructed to read the word before sorting it. Next, Vedi was given a word list with a mixture of nonsense *ow* words. She needed to highlight all *ow* words as a visual reminder to think about which sound of *ow* to use when she decoded the word. Overall, Vedi did a good job decoding the words, committing only two errors. Highlighting the *ow* was a successful strategy for Vedi.

In the next step, Vedi reviewed the VCCV syllable division pattern. Vedi went to the whiteboard that had eight two-syllable words. Vedi needed to underline the vowels or vowel teams and put a v above them. Next, she needed to put a c above each of the consonants between the vowels and then draw a line between the consonants. Vedi read each syllable aloud separately and then blended the syllables together to read the entire word. Vedi was able to read all words correctly.

In order to further emphasize applying the correct sound of *ow*, Vedi and I played boxing words. A 5 × 5 game board with nonsense *ow* words was placed on the table, and we each had a dry erase marker. Vedi was instructed to draw a line, either vertically or horizontally, between two words and to read the word on either side of the line. Then whoever closed a box around a word got to color that box with their color. The winner is the player with the most boxes. This game is skill-based and allowed Vedi another way to apply the lesson objective. Vedi enjoyed the game and said she would like to play it again, especially since she won!

Next, she practiced the two sounds of *ow* by skywriting. We took our time with this (about ten minutes) because this is an area that builds automaticity. Finally, Vedi was asked to read whole sentences and part of a decodable text.

The sentences and text focused on the lesson objective. The text contained only sounds and concepts that Vedi had already learned. After reading the pages of sentences, Vedi was instructed to highlight all words with *ow*. When she was finished, she read all the highlighted words correctly and named the sound the *ow* blend made in the highlighted words.

After reading, Vedi was given some dictation to write. The dictation involved simultaneous oral spelling (SOS), in which the student repeats the dictated word or sentence and segments the sounds by either tapping or using chips while at the same time naming the letters in the word and then naming the letters as she writes. After completing the dictation, error correction was conducted, and with prompting, Vedi was able to self-correct her errors. Lastly, Vedi read the words and sentences aloud.

Reader Self-Efficacy

One challenge that we worked on during tutoring was that Vedi was very hard on herself. If she did not feel she had read quickly enough, she wanted to re-read more than once. Her parents asked if she could take the readings home to practice, which did benefit her fluency. However, I was concerned when Vedi told me that she re-read the texts multiple times each day, timed by a family member, until she could read them fluently within a short time period. Vedi seemed to view this as part of what she needed to do to improve. I advised Vedi and her parents to avoid setting that extra work up as punitive and to provide adequate breaks between readings.

At the end of the summer tutorial period, Vedi was re-tested with the TOWRE-2, and a report was generated for Vedi's parents to share with her school toward evaluating Vedi for special education services or possibly continuing with one-to-one tutoring in OG with the tutoring center. Vedi's TOWRE 2 post-tutoring results showed improvement with phonemic decoding to the low average range. She was able to correctly decode many words with the vowel teams she learned during the summer tutoring sessions. Additionally, her propensity to add and omit sounds diminished. She still did not consistently apply the long vowel sound to silent e words and still needed work with r-controlled vowels. Vedi's decoding was more automatic, indicating that she was internalizing the skills that were imparted to her during the summer tutoring. Overall, she responded well to the interventions.

Oftentimes, it takes learners a significant period of time to overcome self-doubt as a reader. This is especially true for older learners who have experienced years of negative interactions in the literacy classroom.

Providing immediate, specific, and honest feedback about their growth as a reader can help shift a learner's mindset as they begin to believe in their abilities. However, this can only be accomplished if specific learning targets and lesson outcomes are broken down into incremental steps as the OG approach provides. When learners begin to believe in themselves and see themselves as readers, they can begin to build their self-efficacy in the literacy classroom.

Case E

Shifting Ideologies: Teacher as Learner

Gemma Cooper-Novack

Too often, we discuss tutoring as if it is a process that exists solely between teacher and student in a one-to-one relationship. However, in out-of-school-time (OST) spaces, tutoring relationships are often far more expansive. The one-to-one model often defaults to banking education (Freire, 1970), wherein the tutor ostensibly pours from their fount of knowledge into the empty vault of the student—and more, this is often precisely what families seeking private tutoring for their children expect. I, alongside many others who work privately and in small groups with students outside of school classroom spaces, feel it is incumbent upon me as an educator to challenge that expectation. It is, in fact, and should be the province of students to bring their own knowledge to bear to challenge tutors—and, in small learning groups, to challenge each other at the same time.

This tutoring case explores the practices and frameworks I learned from my experiences working with Lys, Kaia, Quinn, and Hart, four white, LGBTQ+ students living in the suburban and rural areas outside a small Rust Belt city, in an OST creative writing program for LGBTQ+ teenagers. Kaia and Quinn were both cisgender and identified as bisexual, while Hart was non-binary and Lys genderfluid, both identifying as queer. The program met once a week, on Saturday afternoons, in one six-week and one ten-week "session" roughly correlated to winter and spring 2021. The meetings took place on Zoom and ran for two hours each session.

Although the program was explicitly teacher-led, with myself as the instructor, I both opened curricular planning to extensive student input between the winter and spring sessions and quickly found that my voice was not, and should not be considered, the primary or even the expert voice in the room. A typical Write It Out session began with a "quick write"—a question prompt designed to illuminate the theme of the day—and then two discussions of readings by queer authors, with a writing prompt designed to follow each. Students could choose to share or not share their work, though in this small group, they elected to share more often than not.

From my time with these students, I found three key practices that helped me to steer our work together into waters both deep and safe, creating spaces of trust and learning wherein my students developed as writers. I was able to learn my students' strengths; I created a clear structure and articulated learning goals that allowed students themselves to steer and shape the content of the curriculum; and I built trust through helping students to know each other and myself. In this chapter, I detail how each of these came to be and why they are significant to the development of tutoring relationships in small groups.

Learn Your Students' Strengths

Taking time to know my students, and to hear what they shared, meant that I could create a space more conducive to both supporting their vulnerabilities (Dutro, 2019) and bolstering their strengths. On the day I brought in a poem A.E. Housman wrote about Oscar Wilde's arrest, I learned that Lys was a fount of deep, intense historical knowledge—when I asked if anyone knew Oscar Wilde, Lys responded as follows:

> Um, Oscar Wilde. First of all, The Picture of Dorian Gray. I love that book. It is a very good book. I have it in German even though I don't speak German—I don't know why I have it in German, actually … but Oscar Wilde was a very outspoken and flamboyant British gay writer in like, what, Queen Victoria's time? Um, and he was known a lot for his kind of being like, "oh yeah, I'm a homosexual, what are you gonna do?'" Um, and he's very like—he dressed in a—in manly clothing but it was very effeminate styled, and he was very himself in a time when people weren't allowed to be … they had to do what everyone else was doing, and to dress how every-

one else was dressed, they had to basically be heterosexual and he's like no, no thank you. Um, and he went to prison for that for—for not like forever, but he went to prison for a time for that, 'cause that was a crime back then, to be gay—to—to do what gay people do. … [A] lot of people who knew Oscar Wilde were afraid that he would like out them as well and that they would go to prison and all of that. E.M. Forster, in his book Maurice—I like that too—talks about things like that and homosexuality and what makes you different during this time period … I think it's really interesting, 'cause it's not just about all like Oscar Wilde and EM Forster and all of that, it's not just about being gay in this time, it's about your class, like in the class system and being gay at this time and what that means, and I just—I don't know, it's Victorian England, like … what can you not like?

(Cooper-Novack, 2022, p. 116)

Given this profundity and depth, I learned that I should often let Lys open or give the first comments in conversations about queer history, knowing their knowledge would invite more connections and questions than any assertion of mine.

Hart, in a similar vein, was a connector—though their knowledge was not so thoroughly researched as Lys, they were always eager to use TikTok and other observations to bridge the gap between the obscure historical and the present moment. They thought about coded language and its roots. "To quickly go back to queer history," they said during a class conversation about coded language in queer historical writing, "[what about], 'hey, are you a friend of Dorothy?' … Everybody knew it was code, nobody could figure out what it was for." From Hart, the students learned to read text with different frameworks and to make connections between their own knowledge and details.

Like Hart, Quinn opened conversations, something she did through personal sharing and vulnerability. Quinn was always immediately ready to share deep and disturbing aspects of experience without monopolizing the conversation. She described harassment she experienced in middle and high school, where boys would notice her interest in girls before she did herself. "I had one friend who was a girl," she explained,

and … we're still really close friends, but like, it always made me so uncomfortable because … there was this like idea that … women-loving women are like predators to their friends and it's just—it was hard for me to … not even understand that about myself at that point and then all these guys who just could not stop with that [vulgar hand gesture] and teasing.

Quinn's clarity and vulnerability created relational transformations in the moment (Ehret, 2018) and allowed our affective connections and, thus, our learning (Immordino-Yang, 2016) to grow.

Kaia, a quiet, careful listener, often saw cohesion and connections among her peers' writings and comments that the rest of us had missed. When I left space for discussion, it was she who would bring our ideas together, giving us a new lens on how we were connected to each other. When Mags, Quinn, and I all alluded to Greek myths in one form or another during a discussion one day, it was Kaia who could make the simple statement, "I always feel Greek mythology revolves around gayness." When Kaia spoke, we often saw, in a new way, what we were talking about.

I, alone, as an instructor, could not have created these connections, plumbed these depths. The students enriched the environment for each other, and because I was attentive to their strengths, I could build further curriculum that served and stretched them ever better.

Students Can Shape Your Curriculum

To leave space for students to learn from each other in small-group lessons isn't to leave the classroom space to educational chaos. Instead, when done with deliberation, it's an opportunity for students to come to the meetings with agency, to create a full-blown partnership with everyone (teachers and learners) invested in the same learning goals.

At the end of our first six-week session, when students had a sense of the pattern of meetings and had had a chance to learn from each other as well as from me, my students were eager to learn about queer cultures that deviated from their own experiences as white teenagers in the United States. This request took me far from the readings I imagined, and I travelled to such sources as Astrud Bowman's "Mourning the Loss of Indigenous Queer Identities," an article about the gender identity of baklá in indigenous Philippine communities and its differences from contemporary non-binary identities in the United States (Bowman, 2021). My teenagers asked for queer histories, and we journeyed from Sylvia Rivera to Tchaikovsky—to my own experience as a queer person several decades older, someone who had been alive (albeit a child) for the AIDS crisis in the United States and an adult at the time of the Pulse nightclub shooting. I found myself doing deep dives on works and ideas I wouldn't have expected or imagined, because my students, knowing the structure, had chosen to push it (and me) in new ways.

It was sometimes a struggle to change midstream to accommodate the needs and desires of my students. On the day we spoke of Pulse, for instance, I hadn't remembered that the date of our class meeting was the anniversary of the massacre until my students told me themselves. When I offered them the option of discussing the planned reading or Pulse, Lys said, "Personally, I just think it would be—I don't wanna say more appropriate, but more ... I personally would want to do the Pulse nightclub one more." Kaia backed them up: "I agree with Pulse because it seems more fitting."

I scrambled to think quickly and then remembered I had published a poem in a special issue of Glass Poetry Journal (2016) relating to the shooting. I found the issue online and, eliminating my own poem from consideration, asked each student to choose a poem in the issue to present to the others. The profundity of their insights demonstrated to me that the last-minute choice, the alteration of my intended trajectory, was well worth it. The students knew that the program, while it taught them to write about and through queer history, was about more than traditional history—it was about sharing memories and experiences with each other in the context of queer fears, knowledge, and experiences. Once I had learned that from them, I found the tools (in the moment) to make a new literary activity that both fit the framework of our classes and met my students' emotional needs.

We Must Know Each Other to Learn from Each Other

The first obligation of a tutor or teacher in creating rich small-group learning, particularly for students from embattled populations, is always to know their students, and indeed to love them (Love, 2019). In working in an affinity space, I might have had some advantages in knowing and loving my students—we shared queerness, an identity that meant we knew similar experiences of fear and marginalization, and thus there were some shortcuts to understanding—but to know them as individuals and as a group working together, I had to provide both the time and space to know them and to allow them to know me.

Affective neuroscience (Immordino-Yang, 2016) confirms that students' trust and desire to learn are essential components of learning and retention. Thus, learning is a vulnerable act; as Dutro (2019) explains, for students and teachers in any learning space to bear "critical witness" to each other, that vulnerability must be mutual. To know my students in their vulnerability, I must let them know me in mine.

When Hart shared a moment of seeing their past crush in Starbucks with great frustration, I told them about my own high school crushes, which all felt dramatically out of reach. When Quinn wrote a poem detailing her first awareness of her own queer desires as a child as an acrostic spelling her crush's name, I revealed that I had written a similar acrostic at the age of 14. When my students shared their memories of seeing the Pulse massacre on the news when they were 10 or 11 years old, they were fiercely eager to know the stories of my adult reactions, comparing and contrasting our experiences. Similarly, Quinn asked about the social status of queer kids in my high school life in the 1990s as part of her struggle to understand her own.

Every one of these literacy-focused interactions deepened our knowledge of each other. I had to be willing to be vulnerable myself to create this atmosphere of trust, leaving room for the students to trust me and each other.

All these key practices are, of course, risky. They mean that a tutor or teacher is losing some elements of classroom control; they render the tutoring session far less predictable. But my experience in Write It Out showed me the value of expanding student learning by opening small groups to deeper dialogue—making sure that they have space and practices that help them learn from each other.

Case F

Upward and Onward: Supporting First-Generation College-Bound Students

Annette Teasdell and Erin Harden Lewis

Upward Bound programs have long played a vital role in supporting the educational aspirations of first-generation college-bound students. Upward Bound aims to provide academic, financial, and social support to students from underrepresented backgrounds to increase their chances of attending and succeeding in college, along with tutorial assistance during the academic year and through a summer enrichment program that can either be in a residential or non-residential college setting (United States Department of Education, 2025).

Designed to motivate and support students from disadvantaged backgrounds, Upward Bound is one of several federally funded TRIO Programs that provide educational opportunity outreach and support. To qualify for Upward Bound, students must meet one of the following criteria: (1) high school student from a low-income family, (2) first-generation college-bound student, or (3) be considered at risk for academic failure (United States Department of Education, 2025). The primary goal of the program is to increase the rate at which participants enroll in and complete postsecondary education programs.

Among the various components of Upward Bound programs, tutoring has emerged as a critical intervention to bolster academic achievement. Tutoring first-generation college-bound students within the Upward Bound context is an important part of student success. The unique challenges faced by these students require effective culturally responsive tutoring strategies to support their academic success (Skelley et al., 2022).

This case addresses culturally responsive tutoring of first-generation college-bound students enrolled in Upward Bound, a federally funded TRIO program under the U.S. Department of Education that aims to increase college access and success for low-income and first-generation college-bound students. These programs offer a range of services, including academic support, college preparation, mentoring, and cultural enrichment activities. Tutoring is a key component of Upward Bound programs, providing personalized academic assistance to students. Through this case, we emphasize the significance of understanding the specific needs of first-generation college-bound students and tailoring tutoring interventions accordingly.

First-Generation College-Bound Students and College Essay Writing

First-generation college-bound students are individuals who will be the first in their families to attend college. These students often encounter several other unique challenges that can impede their academic progress. Challenges faced by this demographic include limited access to resources, lack of familial support, financial constraints, and unfamiliarity with the college application and enrollment process (Tichavakunda & Galan, 2023; Venezia & Jaeger, 2013). Tutoring programs designed specifically for first-generation students within the framework of Upward Bound aim to address these challenges and provide the necessary tools for success. Further, it is important that tutors working with these students are aware of these challenges to provide appropriate support and guidance. Tutors must be aware of these barriers in order to tailor their support and create an inclusive learning environment.

In the case of the Upward Bound students we served through this particular program, it was determined that writing was a significant gap area for our students. Without familial guidance to navigate the college admissions process, students were left to navigate the college admissions essay alone as well. This was an area where the tutors were able to fill in and provide direct support to enhance the academic outcomes of the students. To do so successfully, tutors needed to be culturally responsive to meet the specific needs of the Upward Bound participants.

Culturally Responsive Tutoring Approaches

Cultural responsiveness is crucial when tutoring first-generation college-bound students. Gay (2018) asserts that "when academic knowledge and skills are situated within the lived experiences and frames of reference for students, they are more personally meaningful, have higher interest appeal, and are learned more easily and thoroughly." Tutors should recognize, appreciate, and sustain the cultural backgrounds and experiences of their students, as these factors can significantly influence their academic journey. Culturally responsive tutoring acknowledges and values students' culture and experiences. Tutors adopting this approach should be sensitive to the diversity of students' identities and incorporate culturally relevant examples, materials, and teaching strategies in their tutoring sessions (Ladson-Billings, 1995). This approach helps students feel seen, heard, and understood, enhancing their engagement and learning outcomes.

For the Upward Bound tutors in this program to effectively support the students they were serving, they utilized three culturally responsive tutoring methods: building meaningful relationships, empowerment to foster self-efficacy, and individualized instruction. The following sections address each of these areas and offer guidance on ways to incorporate this tutoring approach.

Building Meaningful Relationships

The foundation of becoming an effective, culturally competent Upward Bound tutor is taking the time to know students as individuals. Each semester, tutors make it a priority to learn about the students' personal stories, family backgrounds, interests, strengths, and goals. Tutors ask questions to learn about family origins, traditions, values, and cultural pride and pressures. When tutors connect with students in a meaningful way, they gain insights into how to best support their learning needs.

Establishing meaningful relationships between tutors and first-generation college-bound students is crucial for effective, culturally responsive tutoring. Tutors should create a safe and supportive environment where students feel comfortable seeking assistance. Tutors should also strive to establish open lines of communication, actively listen to students' concerns, and provide encouragement and guidance throughout their academic journey.

By fostering trust and rapport with their students, tutors can better understand students' individual needs, motivations, and learning goals, thus tailoring their tutoring approaches accordingly. Students really appreciate someone taking the time to understand their individual stories, which is critically important in developing a meaningful relationship. The tutor's goal is to embrace cultural beliefs while nurturing academic success.

Empowerment to Foster Self-Efficacy

First-generation college-bound students may also lack confidence and the self-efficacy needed to display their academic abilities due to a lack of self-belief and limited or no prior exposure to college expectations. Self-efficacy is defined as an individual's belief in their own ability to execute actions necessary to achieve specific goals (Bandura, 1977). Tutors should prioritize fostering self-efficacy by affirming students, supporting students with attainable goal setting, and emphasizing students' strengths and potential. By nurturing self-belief, tutors empower students to overcome challenges and develop a growth mindset.

Since first-generation students often lack affirmation of their capabilities and college potential, intentionally cultivating a warm, empathetic relationship can make students feel valued. When they express self-doubt, reminding them of their strengths and the incredible opportunity before them can foster success. Small gestures and positive affirmations also reinforce encouragement. Creating an environment that represents postsecondary institutions students are considering (e.g., displaying pennants from selected schools) and giving small mementos (e.g., keychains or pens containing a college name and logo) can easily connect them to colleges of interest. To highlight special achievements, giving handwritten cards can emphasize pride in their accomplishments and confidence in their bright future. Upward Bound tutoring also accounts for learning differences by facilitating evaluation and accommodations to clear obstacles on their path to success.

We view the Upward Bound tutor role as so much more than supporting academics. It is directly connected to helping traditionally underrepresented students recognize their potential, guide them to college, and start building the skills to excel once there. It is incredibly fulfilling to plant seeds of empowerment that will allow students to achieve their dreams. Ultimately, effective tutoring requires understanding students' cultures and intentionally bridging academics with tools to retain and leverage cultural assets. This happens by nurturing identity and community while expanding opportunities and providing positive experiences.

Individualized Instruction

Many Upward Bound students will need to navigate cultures drastically different from their own when they transition to college. Understanding the cultural values and norms they were raised with allows tutors to help prepare them for that transition by tailoring instruction and support to validate cultural assets and address cultural barriers. Each student also has a unique set of circumstances that impact their education. For instance, Upward Bound students may be expected to work after school to help provide family income or provide care for younger family members. Often, this presents them with difficult choices, such as continuing to be involved in Upward Bound or other college transitional activities, like attending open houses or participating in a campus tour. This places them at a disadvantage as they may not be aware of tutoring and mentoring services available to them, or other critical information related to financial aid.

Individualized instruction that addresses students' specific needs, setting goals to motivate and guide their progress, developing study skills to enhance their learning strategies, and providing college readiness support can help Upward Bound students navigate the college application, financial aid, and transition from high school to postsecondary education process. Further, collaboratively setting short-term and long-term academic goals helps to motivate and guide students' progress.

In this Upward Bound case, one-on-one and small-group tutoring sessions focused on writing were provided to support the college essay development process. Honing literacy skills to write college admission essays effectively is an important element when tutoring for writing. For instance, using culturally relevant examples and applications meaningful to students' cultural contexts can facilitate personalized essay writing that can be the difference between being admitted and qualifying for scholarships.

In her book, *Write Your Way to a Successful Scholarship Essay*, Chambers (2018) provides proven tips to assist students with composing a scholarship essay. Practicing essay writing skills by drafting the college application personal statement can help them focus on their career goals and college aspirations. Effective tutoring involves guiding them through planning, organizing their story, and revising, while also working on proper grammar and style. This helps improve writing proficiency while creating a polished essay they can proudly submit. Upward Bound tutors utilize these tips to help students improve literacy skills and gain college entry.

Conclusion

Culturally responsive tutoring plays a pivotal role in supporting the academic success of first-generation college-bound students. These programs offer a range of services, including academic support, college preparation, mentoring, and cultural enrichment activities. Tutoring is a key component of Upward Bound programs, providing personalized academic assistance to students. This practitioner perspective on tutoring strategies focused on the importance of building relationships, empowerment to foster self-efficacy, and individualized instruction support culturally responsive approaches to tutoring. By recognizing the unique challenges faced by these students and tailoring tutoring interventions accordingly, practitioners can effectively support their journey toward college success.

The tutoring provided in Upward Bound focused on college essay writing, which allowed participants to leave with products that could be used to meet the desired outcomes of enhancing college admissions for the students. Students were able to leave the program with completed essays that could be modified and adapted for use with applications for different universities. Throughout the tutoring process, students were also exposed to the process of giving and receiving constructive feedback that also supported the successful completion of the essays.

There was, however, some resistance to the feedback provided to enhance students' writing.

Tutors must gently and gracefully approach issues such as this to continue to provide a supportive learning environment and sustain the relationships built with students. To address this challenge, tutors were offered support from Upward Bound staff. This support included the use of affirming approaches to feedback that included the highlight of strengths, as well as areas of opportunity. These affirming approaches kept the feedback constructive and allowed tutors to sustain the trust of the participants.

Metacognitive reflection was also encouraged. Across all subjects, encouraging metacognitive reflection can enhance the learning process (Paris & Winograd, 1990). Identifying and implementing strategies that supported their learning goals fostered self-efficacy. Growth was celebrated and redirection was provided when needed to help students push forward. Overall, the program was successful, and students' needs were met.

The tutoring initiative presented in this case has important implications for all tutors. Adopting a culturally responsive approach to tutoring is beneficial for all. However, further research is needed to explore the long-term impacts of tutoring interventions and to develop evidence-based practices that maximize the academic outcomes of first-generation college-bound students. Future studies can explore the long-term impacts of tutoring interventions on students' college enrollment, persistence, and graduation rates. Additionally, research can focus on developing evidence-based practices that optimize the effectiveness of culturally responsive tutoring programs for this specific student population.

Appendices

Within this section, the reader will find documents and instruments that were described in the preceding chapters as well as a collection of documents that can serve as useful draft tutorial guidelines and administrative forms. These resources may be used exactly as presented in this section or can serve as useful examples (prototypes) that can be customized to meet the immediate needs of a specific community tutoring program. A list of specific documents follows.

- A. Brain Break Resources
- B. Reading Interest Inventory
- C. K-W-L Chart
- D. Alliteration Book List
- E. Tutors Friends: Stategies, Learning Games, and Instructional Books
- F. Tutee Writing Evaluation Checklist
- G. The Poor Scholar's Soliloquy
- H. San Diego Quick Assessment Record Form
- I. Reading Attitude Scale
- J. Teacher Referral Form
- K. Parent Permission Form

L. Tutor Application
M. Tutor Interview Guide
N. Tutor Attendance Record
O. Tutor Self-Evaluation
P. Annual Tutor Evaluation
Q. Tutor Training Course Outline
R. Tutoring Manual and Training Topics
S. Program Administration Resources

Appendix A

Brain Break Resources

Brain Breaks Blog. Energizing Brain Breaks. https://brainbreaks.blogspot.com/

Colorado Education Initiative. Teacher Toolbox: Physical Activity Breaks in the Secondary Classroom. https://www.coloradoedinitiative.org/wp-content/uploads/2014/08/CEI-Take-a-Break-Teacher-Toolbox.pdf

Edutopia. 9 Brain Breaks that Teens Will Love. https://www.edutopia.org/video/9-brain-breaks-teens-will-love-middle-high-school/

GoNoodle. Breathing Exercises. https://www.gonoodle.com/tags/ZwmOzX/breathe

Institute for Arts Integration and STEAM. 45 Creative Brain Breaks for Kids. https://artsintegration.com/brain-breaks-for-kids/

Kiboomers Kids Music Channel. Brain Breaks Kindergarten. [YouTube playlist]. https://www.youtube.com/playlist?list=PL1wrsEJEvZjaQ6UNhtYOU0C6_ThqzDSm_

Minds in Bloom. Brain Breaks – 20 awesome ways to energize your students FAST! https://minds-in-bloom.com/20-three-minute-brain-breaks/

Peninsula Plus. Brainbreaks – they are great for everyone. https://peninsulaplus.com.au/brain-breaks-great-for-everyone/

Teach Starter. 10 Teacher-Tested Brain Break Ideas for the Classroom that Kids Love. https://www.teachstarter.com/au/blog/26-brain-break-ideas-classroom/

WholeHearted School Counseling. Free Brain Breaks for the Classroom in Printable & Digital Formats. https://www.teachstarter.com/au/blog/26-brain-break-ideas-classroom/

Appendix B

Reading Interest Inventory

Adapted from "'But There's Nothing Good to Read' (In the Library Media Center)," by Denice Hildebrandt, Media Spectrum: The Journal for Library Media Specialists in Michigan, Fall 2001, pp. 34–37.

1. Do you like to read?
2. How much time do you spend reading?
3. What are some of the books you have read lately?
4. Do you have a library card? How often do you use it?
5. Do you ever get books from the school library?
6. About how many books do you own?
7. What are some books you would like to own?
8. Put a check mark next to the kind of reading you like best (or topics you might like to read about).

____history	____travel	____plays
____sports	____science fiction	____adventure
____romance	____detective stories	____war stories
____poetry	____cars or motorbikes	____novels
____biography	____supernatural	____astrology
____humor	____folktales	____how to books
____mysteries	____art	____westerns

9. Do you like to read the newspaper?
10. If "yes," place a check next to the part of the newspaper section listed below you like to read.

_____advertisements	_____columns
_____headlines	_____politics
_____local news & events	_____editorials
_____comics	_____obituaries
_____sports	_____celebrities
_____entertainment	_____fashion
_____astrology	_____classifieds

11. What are your favorite television programs?
12. Do you have a hobby? If so, what is it?
13. What are the two best movies you have ever seen?
14. Who are your favorite entertainers and/or movie stars?
15. When you were little, did you enjoy having someone read aloud to you?
16. List topics, subjects, etc., which you might like to read about:
17. What does the word "reading" mean to you?
18. Tell me anything else that you would like me to know about your reading.

Appendix C

K-W-L Chart

What I Already (K)now	What I (W)ant to Know	What I (L)earned

Appendix D

Alliteration Book List

A Light in the Attic by Shel Silverstein
All the Awake Animals Are Almost Asleep by Crescent Dragonwagon
Alligators All Around by Maurice Sendak
Betty's Burgled Bakery by Travis Nichols
Bubble Gum, Bubble Gum by Lisa Wheeler
Chicka Chicka Boom Boom by Bill Martin, Jr.
Click, Clack, Quackity-Quack by Doreen Cronin
Four Famished Foxes and Fosdyke by Pamela Duncan Edwards
In the Tall, Tall Grass by Denise Fleming
Jamberry by Bruce Degen
Lilly's Purple Plastic Purse by Kevin Henkes
Many Marvelous Monsters by Ed Heck
Oh, the Places You'll Go! by Dr. Seuss
Pigs in Pajamas by Maggie Smith
Sheep in a Jeep by Nancy E. Shaw
Silly Sally by Audrey Wood
Some Smug Slug by Pamela Duncan Edwards
SuperHero ABC by Bob McLeod
Too Many Moose by Lisa Bakos
Walter Was Worried by Laura Vaccaro Seeger
Wemberly Worried by Kevin Henkes

Appendix E
Tutors' Friends: Strategies, Learning Games, and Instructional Books

For nearly 100 years, teachers and tutors have turned to books providing strategies, learning games, and instructional activities to supplement tutorial lessons. The following sources are both recently published texts that are readily available from online booksellers (e.g., Barnes & Noble, Amazon) and classic sources that may still be found in libraries or at times for a fraction of the cost of new books at online used book outlets (e.g., ABE Books). The titles were nominated by literacy experts. For tutoring activities, an early edition of a strategy book is likely to be as useful as the most recent edition, and it would be somewhat cheaper to procure.

Anderson, C. (2018). *A teacher's guide to writing conferences K-8*. Heinemann.

Bear, D., Invernizzi, M., Templeton, S., & Johnston, F. R. (2024). *Words their way: Word study for phonics, vocabulary, and spelling instruction* (7th ed.). Pearson.

Beck, I., L., McKeown, M. C., & Kucan, L. (2013). *Bringing words to life: Robust vocabulary instruction* (2nd ed.). Guilford.

Buckner, A., & Fletcher, R. (2005). *Notebook know-how: Strategies for the writer's notebook strategies for the writer's notebook*. Stenhouse.

Buehl, D. (2017). *Classroom strategies for interactive learning* (4th ed.). Routledge.

Burkins, J., & Yates, K. (2024). *Shifting the balance: 6 ways to bring the science of reading into the balanced literacy classroom*. Taylor & Francis. https://doi.org/10.4324/9781032673646

Carlson, R. K. (1970). *Writing aids through the grades: One hundred eighty-six developmental writing activities*. Teachers College Press.

Collom, J., & Noethe, S., (2007). *Poetry everywhere: Teaching poetry writing in school and in the community*. Teachers & Writers Collaborative.

Culham, R. (2005). *6+1 traits of writing: The complete guide for the primary grades*. Scholastic.

Culham, R. (2003). *6 + 1 traits of writing: The complete guide grades 3 and up*. Scholastic.

Cunningham, K. E., Burkins, J., & Yates, K. (2023). *Shifting the balance: 6 ways to bring the science of reading into the upper elementary classroom*. Taylor & Francis. https://doi.org/10.4324/9781032673745

Darrow, H. F., & Allen, V. R. (1961). *Independent activities for creative learning*. Teachers College Press.

Dobler, E., Eagleton, M. B., Leu, D. J. (2015). *Reading the web, Second Edition: Strategies for Internet inquiry strategies for Internet inquiry*. Guilford.

Feriazzo, L., & Hull, K. H. (2018). *The ELL teacher's toolbox: Hundreds of practical ideas to support young students*. Wiley.

Fletcher, R. (2019). *Focus lessons: How photography enhances the teaching of writing how photography enhances the teaching of writing*. Heinemann.

Harrison, D. L., Rasinski, T. V., & French, M. J. (2022). *Partner poems & word ladders for building foundational literacy skills: Grades 1–3*. Scholastic.

Harrison, D. L., Rasinski, T. V., & French, M. J. (2022). *Partner poems & word ladders for building foundational literacy skills: Grades K-2*. Scholastic.

Harvey, S., & Goudvis, A. (2017). *Strategies That Work: Teaching comprehension for engagement, understanding, and building knowledge, grades K-8*. Stenhouse.

Herrell, A., & Jordan, M. (2019). 50 strategies for teaching English language learners. Pearson.

Honig, B., & Gutlohn, L. (2018). *Teaching reading sourcebook* (3rd ed.). Academic Therapy Publications.

Hoyt, Linda. (2008). *Revisit, reflect, retell: Time-tested strategies for teaching reading comprehension*. Heinemann.

Johns, J., & Lenski, S. (2019). *Improving reading: Strategies, resources, and common core connections* (7th ed.). Kendall Hunt.

Kulich, L., Rasinski, T. V., Harrison, D. L. (2024). *The fluency development lesson: Closing the reading gap.* Benchmark.

Lenski, S., Wham, M. A., Johns, J., & Caskey, M. M. (2011). *Reading & learning strategies* (4th ed.). Kendall Hunt.

Petty, W. T., & Bowen, M. E. (1967). *Slithery snakes and other aids to children's writing.* Appleton-Century-Crofts.

Rasinski, T. V., & Cheesman-Smith, M. (2025). *The Megabook of Fluency, 2nd Edition: Strategies and Texts to Engage All Readers.* Scholastic.

Rasinski, T. V., & Zutell, J. (2016*). Essential strategies for word Study: Effective methods for improving decoding, spelling, and vocabulary.* Scholastic.

Russell, D. H., & Karp, E. E. (1951). *Reading aides through the grades: Three hundred developmental reading activities* (2nd ed.). Teachers College Press.

Russell, D. H., & Russell, E. F. (1959). *Listening aids through the grades: One hundred ninety listening activities.* Teachers College Press.

Ryan, A. (2024). *The phonics playbook: How to differentiate instruction so students succeed.* Jossey-Bass.

Serravallo, J. (2023). *The reading strategies book 2.0: Your research-based guide to developing skilled readers.* Heinemann.

Serravallo, J. (2017). *The writing strategies book: Your everything guide to developing skilled writers.* Heinemann.

Shubitz, S. (2016). *Craft moves: lesson sets for teaching writing with mentor texts.* Stenhouse.

Silberman, M. (1996). *Active Learning: 101 Strategies to Teach Any Subject.* Prentice Hall.

Spache, E. B. (1972). *Reading activities for child involvement.* Allyn and Bacon.

Staehr Fenner, D., Snyder, S., & Gregoire-Smith, M. (2024). *Unlocking English learners' potential: Strategies for making content accessible* (2nd ed.). Corwin.

Tierney, R. J., & Readence, J. E. (2005). *Reading strategies and practices: A compendium* (6th ed.). Pearson.

Text Project. https://textproject.org

Tompkins, G. E. (2019). *Teaching Writing: Balancing Process and Product* (7th Edition). Pearson.

Vogt, M. E., & Echevarria, J. (2021). *99 ideas and activities for teaching English language learners with the SIOP model.* Pearson.

Wallen, C. J. (1969). *Word attack skills in reading.* Merrill.

Wilhelm, J. (2013). *Enriching comprehension with visualization strategies: Text elements and ideas to build comprehension, encourage reflective reading, and represent understanding.* Scholastic.

Wilhelm, J. (2013). *Improving comprehension with think-aloud strategies.* Scholastic.

Wright, T. S., & Ray, K. (2020). *A teacher's guide to vocabulary development across the day: The classroom essentials series.* Heinemann.

Zwiers, J. (2004). *Developing academic thinking skills in grades 6-12: A handbook of multiple intelligence activities.* International Literacy Association.

Appendix F

Tutee Writing Evaluation Checklist

Your tutee's writing of stories or essays will improve as they master the skill of self-evaluation of each "manuscript" at the editing stage and again as the work is considered completed. What follows draws from and adds to the evaluation steps advocated in Petty and Bowen's (1967) classic guide: *Slithery Snakes and Other Aids to Children's Writing*.

Story/Essay Evaluation

- [ ] Does my story/essay provide a central focus?
- [ ] Does my story/essay include a beginning that captures the interest of my reader?
- [ ] Do all the parts of my story fit together?
- [ ] Does each paragraph have a topic sentence that relates to my central idea?
- [ ] Does the essay contain important points that are supported by details, facts, and examples?
- [ ] Does the story/essay use interesting words that convey proper meaning?
- [ ] Do my paragraphs transition smoothly from one to another?
- [ ] Does my conclusion restate the essay's primary idea and then clearly summarize the supporting points?

Proofreading

- ☐ Is my story/essay headed correctly?
- ☐ Does each sentence start with a capitalized word?
- ☐ Does each new paragraph begin with an indentation?
- ☐ Have the correct margins been used in the formatting?
- ☐ Has every word been spelled correctly?
- ☐ Does the story/essay contain proper sentences (no run-ons, fragments, etc.)?
- ☐ Has the correct punctuation and grammar been used throughout the story/essay?

Metacognitive Analysis

- ☐ Have I said what I wanted to say?
- ☐ Is my story/essay well organized?
- ☐ Has my writing improved since my last story/essay?
- ☐ Have I used new and interesting vocabulary words in my story/essay?
- ☐ Have I used good sentences?
- ☐ Did I carefully proofread and edit my story/essay?
- ☐ How can I improve my writing for the next assignment?

Appendix G

The Poor Scholar's Soliloquy

One of the important requirements for any tutor is getting to know and value the tutee as a learner. This requires that the tutor understands that the tutee might be classified by any number of terms such as struggling reader, at-risk student, or underachiever among many other terms. Yet every tutee brings to the tutorial experience a set of personal interests, attitudes, and competencies that should serve as the foundation for a positive learning situation. S.M. Corey wrote *The Poor Scholar's Soliloquy Eighty Years Ago* (1944), and in doing so captured the inherent strengths that a young man who was viewed as at-risk within the academic world brought successfully to his lived experience. This work should be read by all potential tutors and used as a foundational activity in discussing all the positive traits a tutee might bring to the tutoring sessions. The Poor Scholar's Soliloquy follows.

The Poor Scholar's Soliloquy

No, I'm not very good in school. This is my second year in the seventh grade, and I'm bigger and taller than the other kids. They like me all right, though, even if I don't say much in the classroom, because outside I can tell them how to do a lot of things. They tag me around and that sort of makes up for what goes on in school.

The Poor Scholar's Soliloquy

I don't know why the teachers don't like me. They never have very much. Seems like they don't think you know anything unless you can name the books it comes out of. I've got a lot of books in my room at home—books like Popular Science Mechanical Encyclopedia, and the Sears & Wards catalogues—but I don't sit down and read them like they make us do in school. I use my books when I want to find something out, like whenever mom buys anything second-hand, I look it up in Sears or Wards first and tell her if she's getting stung or not. I can use the index in a hurry.

In school, though, we've got to learn whatever is in the book and I just can't memorize the stuff. Last year I stayed after school every night for two weeks trying to learn the names of the presidents. Of course, I knew some of them—like Washington and Jefferson and Lincoln, but there must have been 30 altogether, and I never did get them straight. I'm not too sorry though, because the kids who learned the presidents had to turn right around and learn all the vice-presidents. I am taking the seventh grade over, but our teacher this year isn't so interested in the names of the presidents. She has us trying to learn the names of all the great American inventors.

I guess I just can't remember the names in history. Anyway, this year I've been trying to learn about trucks because my uncle owns three, and he says I can drive one when I'm 16. I already know the horsepower and number of forward and backward speeds of 26 American trucks, some of them Diesels, and I can spot each make a long way off. It's funny how that Diesel works. I started to tell my teacher about it last Wednesday in science class when the pump we were using to make a vacuum in a bell jar got hot, but she, didn't see what a Diesel engine had to do with our experiment on air pressure, so I just kept still. The kids seemed interested though. I took four of them around to my uncle's garage after school, and we saw the mechanic, Gus, tear a big truck Diesel down. Boy does he know his stuff!

I'm not very good in geography either. They call it economic geography this year. We've been studying the imports and exports of Chile all week, but I couldn't tell what they are. Maybe the reason is I had to miss school yesterday because my uncle took me and his big truck down and we brought almost ten tons of livestock to the Chicago market.

He had told me where we were going, and I had to figure out the highways to take and also the mileage. He didn't do anything but drive and turn where I told him to, was that fun. I sat with a map in my lap, and told him to turn south, or southeast, or some other direction. We made seven stops and drove over 500 miles round trip. I'm figuring now what his oil cost, and also the wear and tear on the truck—he calls it depreciation—so we'll know how much we made.

I even write out all the bills and send letters to the farmers about what their pigs and beef cattle brought at the stockyards. I only made three mistakes in 17 letters last time, my aunt said, all commas. She's been through high school and reads them over. I wish I could write school themes that way. The last one I had to write was on, "What a Daffodil Thinks of Spring," and I just couldn't get going.

I don't do very well in school in arithmetic either. Seems I just can't keep my mind on the problems. We had one the other day like this:

If a 57-foot telephone pole falls across a cement highway so that 17 3/6 feet extended from one side and 14 9/17 feet from the other how wide is the highway?

That seemed to me like an awfully silly way to get the width of a highway. I didn't even try to answer it because it didn't say whether the pole had fallen straight across or not.

Even in shop I don't get very good grades. All of us kids made a broom holder and bookend this term, and mine were sloppy. I just couldn't get interested. Mom doesn't use a broom anymore with her vacuum cleaner, and all our books are in a bookcase with glass doors in the living room. Anyway, I wanted to make an end gate for my uncle's trailer, but the shop teacher said that meant using metal and wood both, and I'd have to learn how to work with wood first. I didn't see why, but I kept still and made a tie rack at school and the tail gate after school at my uncle's garage. He said I saved him ten dollars.

Civics is hard for me, too. I've been staying after school trying to learn the "Articles of Confederation" for almost a week, because the teacher said we couldn't be a good citizen unless we did. I really tried, though, because I want to be a good citizen. I did hate to stay after school because a bunch of boys from the south end of town have been cleaning up the old lot across from Taylor's Machine Shop to make a playground out of it for the little kids from the Methodist home. I made the jungle gym from old pipe. We raised enough money collecting scrap this month to build a wire fence clear around the lot.

Dad says I can quit school when I am sixteen, and I am sort of anxious because there are a lot of things I want to learn—and as my uncle says, I'm not getting any younger.

Corey, S.M. (1944). The poor scholar's soliloquy. *Childhood Education, 20*(5), 219–220.

Appendix H

San Diego Quick Assessment Record Form

Name_____Grade_____
Date_____

Directions: Begin with a list that is at least two or three sets below the student's grade level. Have the student read each word aloud on that list. Continue until the student makes three or more errors in a list.

Reading Levels: One error – independent level; two errors – instructional level; three errors – frustration level. When testing is completed, record the highest level in each of these categories in the spaces below.

INDEPENDENT_____INSTRUCTIONAL_____
FRUSTRATION_____

Preprimer	Primer	Grade 1	Grade 2	Grade 3
see	you	road	our	city
play	come	live	please	middle
me	not	thank	myself	moment
at	with	when	town	frightened
run	jump	bigger	early	exclaimed
go	help	how	send	several
and	is	always	wide	lonely
look	work	night	believe	drew
can	are	spring	quietly	since
here	this	today	carefully	straight

Grade 4	Grade 5	Grade 6	Grade 7
decided	scanty	bridge	amber
served	business	commercial	dominion
amazed	develop	abolish	sundry
silent	considered	trucker	capillary
wrecked	discussed	apparatus	impetuous
improved	behaved	elementary	blight
certainly	splendid	comment	wrest
entered	acquainted	necessity	enumerate
realized	escaped	gallery	daunted
interrupted	grim	relativity	condescend

Grade 8	Grade 9	Grade 10	Grade 11
capacious	conscientious	zany	galore
limitation	isolation	jerkin	rotunda
pretext	molecule	nausea	capitalism
intrigue	ritual	gratuitous	prevaricate
delusion	momentous	linear	visible
immaculate	vulnerable	inept	exonerate
ascent	kinship	legality	superannuate
acrid	conservatism	aspen	luxuriate
binocular	jaunty	amnesty	piebald
embankment	inventive	barometer	crunch

Copyright© 1999 CORE, *The Graded Word List: Quick Gauge of Reading Ability.*

Appendix I

Reading Attitude Scale

1	I always enjoy reading a book.	I often enjoy reading a book.	I rarely enjoy reading a book.	I never enjoy reading a book.
2	When I get a book for a gift, I am very happy.	When I get a book for a gift, I feel somewhat happy.	When I get a book for a gift, I feel disappointed.	When I get a book for a gift, I am upset.
3	When an adult reads to me, it is a waste of time.	When an adult reads to me, it is rarely enjoyable.	When an adult reads to me, it can be enjoyable.	When an adult reads to me, it is very enjoyable.
4	My best friend thinks reading is no fun at all.	My best friend thinks reading is occasionally fun.	My best friend thinks reading is usually fun.	My best friend thinks reading is always fun.
5	I really like to read books my friends have read.	Sometimes I like to read books my friends read.	I rarely read the books my friends have read.	I never read the books my friends have read.
6	I often read about a movie, television series, or video I've seen.	I sometimes read about a movie, television series, or video I've seen.	I rarely read about a movie, television series, or video I've seen.	I never read about a movie, television series, or video I've seen.
7	I am a very good reader.	I am a good reader.	I am a poor reader.	I am a very poor reader.

8	I always tell my family about things I have read.	I sometimes tell my family about things I have read.	I usually do not tell my family about things I have read.	I never tell my family about things I have read.
9	I always tell my friends about the things I have read recently.	I sometimes tell my friends about the things I have read recently.	I do not usually tell my friends about the things I have read recently.	I never tell my friends about the things I have read recently.
10	I like to read my books from school.	Sometimes I like to read my books from school.	I rarely like to read my books from school.	I do not like to read my books from school.
11	I always like using books to find information for school assignments.	Sometimes I like using books to find information for school assignments.	I rarely like using books to find information for school assignments.	I do not like using books to find information for school assignments.
12	I never read what the teacher assigns to read about school subjects.	I rarely read what the teacher assigns to read about school subjects.	I only read exactly what the teacher assigns to read about school subjects.	I often read extra books or information about the assigned school subjects.
13	I read to find answers to questions somebody might ask me.	Sometimes I will read to find answers to questions somebody might ask me.	I rarely read to find the answers to questions somebody might ask me.	I would rather ask someone else to answer a question than read about it myself.
14	Maps, charts, and tables help me better understand what I am reading.	Maps, charts, and tables sometimes help me to better understand what I am reading.	Maps, charts, and tables rarely help me to better understand what I am reading.	Maps, charts, and tables always make it more difficult to understand what I am reading.
15	I like to give book reports in school.	Giving a book report in school is OK.	I would rather not give a book report in school.	I hate having to give book reports in school.
16	It's fun to read out loud in class.	There are times when I like to read out loud in class.	Most of the time, I do not like to read out loud.	I really dislike reading out loud in class.
17	I think we spend too much time reading in school.	We should spend less time reading in school.	We spend the right amount of time reading in school.	I would like to spend more time reading in school.
18	I like finding new words in stories I am reading.	Sometimes I like finding new words in stories.	I rarely like finding new words in stories.	I do not like finding new words in stories.

19	I often read the books my teacher suggests I read.	Sometimes I read books my teacher suggests I read.	I rarely read the books my teacher suggests I read.	I never read the books my teacher suggests I read.
20	I almost always need help when I find a new word while reading.	Sometimes I need help when I find a new word while reading.	I rarely need help when I find a new word while reading.	I can always figure out new words I find while reading.
21	I am always happy when I get to go to the library.	Sometimes I am happy when I go to the library.	I am usually not happy about going to the library.	I am always unhappy if I must go to the library.
22	I always like reading articles or stories on the internet.	I sometimes like reading articles or stories on the internet.	I usually do not like reading articles or stories on the internet.	I do not like having to read articles or stories on the internet.
23	I can read much better now than I could a month ago.	I can read better now than I could a month ago.	I can read a little better now than I could a month ago.	I read the same as I did a month ago.
24	I really do not like people who read many books.	I do not like to spend time with people who read many books.	It is OK to spend time with people who read many books.	I really like to be around people who read many books.
25	When I grow up, I want to have a job where I never have to read.	When I grow up, I want to have a job where I do not have to read very often.	When I grow up, I want a job where I have to read.	When I grow up, I want to have a job where I have to read all the time.

Appendix J

Teacher Referral Form

Westside Tutorial Program, Sunny View Community Center

Date: _____

To the teacher:
Please complete this form for each student you wish to refer to the Westside Tutoring Program for individual or small group out of school tutoring services. The information will be of assistance in pairing the student with a tutor who is best qualified to meet the tutee's particular needs.

Name of Teacher: _____

School: _____ Grade Level: _____

Phone: _____ E-mail: _____

Student's Name: _____ Grade: _____

Parent or guardian's name: _____

Address: _____

Phone: _____ E-mail: _____

Teacher Referral Form

Have you spoken with the child's parent or guardian about this referral?
Yes _____ No _____

In what subjects or abilities does the child demonstrate strengths?

_____
_____

In what subjects or skills do you believe tutoring will help benefit the child?

_____
_____

Please describe the student's competencies or areas of growth for which this referral is being submitted to the tutoring program (reading, writing, math, other):

_____
_____

Is the student a native English speaker? Yes _____ No _____

If no, what language is primarily spoken in the student's home?

_____

What are the student's attitudes toward school? How does this relate to the student's classroom behavior?

_____
_____

Does the student regularly complete homework assignments? Yes ___ No ___

May the tutor contact you throughout the school year to share tutee progress reports and seek information about how the tutoring is supporting the tutee's class performance? Yes _____ No _____

Please provide any additional information that might be useful in matching a tutor with the student and for instructional planning purposes.

_____
_____

Appendix K

Parent Permission Form

Westside Tutorial Program, Sunny View Community Center

I hereby give my permission for my child _____ to attend tutoring sessions provided by the Westside Tutorial Program at the Sunny View Community Center on _____ (days) at _____ (time) during the 20___ – 20___ academic year.

I understand that the tutorial sessions will be supervised by the Tutoring Program Coordinator _____, who will take due care to provide for my child's safety and well-being.

Signature of parent or guardian: _____

Phone number: _____ Date: _____

I give permission for the following individual(s) to transport my child to/from the Sunny View Community Center on my behalf upon presentation of appropriate identification:

_____

Appendix L

Tutor Application

Westside Tutorial Program, Sunny View Community Center

Date:
Interviewed by:
Program Coordinator:
Reviewed by:

_____
(Last Name)   (First Name)   (Middle)

Street Address: _____

City: _____ State: _____ Zip Code: _____

Phone: _____ (home) _____ (cell)

E-mail: _____

Education:

Institution/School	Course of Study	Dates Attended	Degree/Certificate

Tutor Application

Occupation: _____

Interests, skills, hobbies: _____

Please list any language(s) you speak other than English: _____

Technology skills (please list):
_____
_____

Have you ever served as a tutor? If so, where, when, and for how long?
_____
_____

Why are you interested in serving as a tutor?
_____
_____

<u>Choice of Assignment:</u> Grade level of tutee preferred (check all that apply)

preK/KDGN _____   Grades 1-3_____   Grades 4-5_____   Grades 6-8_____

High school_____   Adults _____

Subject area(s): Reading _____ Writing _____ Math _____
Other
_____

Availability for tutoring (select all that apply):

Day of Week	Morning (9–12)	Afternoon (1–4)	Evening (5–8)
Monday			
Tuesday			
Wednesday			
Thursday			
Friday			
Saturday			

Tutor Application

Please list three individuals we may contact to obtain a personal reference for you:

Name:_____ Phone:_____ Relationship:_____

Name:_____ Phone:_____ Relationship:_____

Name:_____ Phone:_____ Relationship:_____

Emergency Contact Information:

In case of emergency please notify (Name, address, and phone number):

_____
_____

Appendix M

Tutor Interview Guide

Before the formal interview is undertaken, the applicant should be given a brief description of the program and its goals. The interviewer should record the information from the Tutor Application in the top portion of this form prior to the interview session.

Westside Tutorial Program, Sunnyside Community Center

Applicant's name: _____

Address: _____

Telephone numbers: (home)_____(cell)_____

E-mail address: _____

Applicant's availability (days/hours): _____

Interviewer Name:_____ Date of Interview:_____

Interview Questions:

Why are you interested in tutoring for the Westside Tutoring Program?

_____
_____

Why do you think you would be helpful as a tutor?
_____
_____

In what subjects would you like to tutor?
_____
_____

In what subjects would you <u>not</u> want to tutor?
_____
_____

What age of tutee would you feel comfortable tutoring?
_____

Are you proficient in a language other than English?
_____

Would you feel comfortable tutoring a Multilngual Learner who is developing English proficiency?
_____
_____

What competencies with technology would you bring to the tutoring experience?
_____
_____

Are you willing to undergo the program's initial training workshop as well as occasional professional development sessions? What training do you desire at this time?
_____
_____

Interviewer's comments and observations:
_____
_____

Do you recommend this person to serve as a tutor? Yes _____ No _____
Maybe _____

Please explain:
_____
_____

Appendix N

Tutee Attendance Record

Westside Tutorial Program, Sunnyside Community Center

Name of tutee: _____

Name of parent or guardian: _____

Address: _____

Telephone #: (home)_____(work)_____(cell)_____

E-mail: _____

Name of tutor: _____

Tutee Attendance Record

Session Date/Time	Present	Absent	Method Used to Notify Parent/Guardian of Absence	Message Conveyed to Parent/Guardian

Appendix O

Tutor Self-Evaluation

Westside Tutoring Program, Sunny View Community Center

Tutor's name: _____ Date: _____

Tutee's name: _____

Focus of tutoring session: _____

Place a check mark on the line for each item you successfully completed.

Session Preparation

___ My objective(s) for the session clearly stated what was to be taught to the tutee.
___ I had the necessary materials and/or technology on hand to teach the lesson.

Instructional Process

___ I had a clear plan for the steps that would be followed in teaching the lesson.
___ I began the lesson with a review of competencies covered in previous tutoring sessions.
___ I explained to the tutee the objective and rationale for the lesson.

___ I provided for the tutee's motivation by building interest and eliciting prior knowledge.
___ I covered each step in my plan successfully during the session.
___ I used multiple activities to teach the objective of the tutorial session.
___ I reinforced learning with opportunities to practice the skill associated with the objective.
___ I assessed the tutee's mastery of the lesson objective.
___ I promoted the tutee's self-evaluation (metacognition) of meeting the lesson objective.

Evaluation/Reactions

___ I thoughtfully evaluated whether I met the goal for the lesson.
___ I thoughtfully evaluated what went well with this tutoring session.
___ I thoughtfully considered how I might improve my tutoring.

General Actions

___ I encouraged my tutee and offered praise throughout the tutoring session.
___ My tutee clearly saw that I was enthusiastic about tutoring.
___ I made notes about the tutee's successes and needs to be used in planning future sessions.
___ I provided positive feedback to the tutee as necessary.

Next Steps

I will use the information gained from this self-evaluation to prepare for my next tutoring session in the following ways:

1._____

2._____

3._____

Appendix P

Annual Tutor Evaluation

(Adapted from Youth for Service, San Francisco instrument)

Westside Tutorial Program, Sunny View Community Center

Name of tutor: _____ Date: _____

Program coordinator (evaluator): _____

Instructions for Evaluation

The tutor is to be evaluated on the 20 criteria that follow. Indicate the degree to which you *agree* or *disagree* with each criterion by marking the corresponding number as follows: 1-Strongly Agree, 2-Agree, 3-Neither Agree nor Disagree, 4-Disagree, and 5-Strongly Disagree.

Items	1	2	3	4	5
The tutor has great knowledge of the subject matter.					
The tutor presents materials clearly.					
The tutor contributes significantly to the tutee's knowledge.					
The tutor stimulated the tutee's intellectual curiosity.					
The tutor uses appropriate methods to achieve lesson objectives.					
The tutor is enthusiastic about tutoring.					
The tutor can cope with unforeseen situations.					
The tutor displays a sense of humor.					
The tutor is interested in the tutee as an individual.					
The tutor respects the tutee.					
The tutor is fair and impartial in working with the tutee.					
The tutee benefited from working with this tutor.					
The tutor was reliable.					
The tutor asks for assistance when necessary.					
The tutor is punctual.					
The tutor motivates and promotes the tutee's interest in the subject.					
The tutor spends sufficient time with the tutee.					
The tutor is always prepared for a tutorial session.					
The tutor has a positive work relationship with staff members.					
The tutor should be retained for the future.					

Please comment on any positive attributes demonstrated by this tutor.

How might this tutor improve his/her tutoring in the future?

Other comments:

Appendix Q

Tutor Training Course Outline

The following course outline is adapted from a tutoring course offered by a postsecondary institution. It can be easily revised to fit the training agenda of any program, whether it be at a community center, postsecondary institution, or pK-12 volunteer program.

Course Title

Techniques of Literacy Tutoring

Catalog Description

Methods and techniques for literacy tutoring. Development of tutorial resource materials.

Course Objectives

The student will:

1. Identify and explain selected terms in relation to tutoring students (e.g., tutor, tutee, cross-age tutoring, peer tutoring, and reading strategies).
2. Identify the basic purposes and components of literacy tutoring programs.

3. Examine techniques for establishing rapport between the tutor and tutee.
4. Examine issues of diversity, language learning, and literacy as impacting the tutoring process and experience.
5. Identify and develop strategies for supporting the tutee in a tutoring situation.
6. Facilitate the learning processes and goals of a tutee in a tutorial format.
7. Document progress of a struggling learner by using objectives, logs, and informal assessment measures.
8. Develop and review tutorial resource materials, including technology tools.
9. Engage in self-evaluation of tutoring effectiveness by completing a tutoring log, setting and monitoring goals, and conferencing with peers, supervisors, and other educators.

Subject Matter Content

1. Definitions and concepts of tutoring and tutorial programs (Objective 1).
2. The role of the tutor and supervisor in the tutoring program (Objective 1).
3. Ethical issues relating to tutoring, including confidentiality, dependability, commitment, trustworthiness, professionalism, role modeling, and personal interactions (Objectives 2, 3).
4. Establishing rapport between tutor and tutee (Objective 3).
5. Aspects of diversity and how these connect with literacy (Objective 4).
6. Elements of effective tutoring for diverse learners (Objectives 4, 5, 6).
7. Characteristics of struggling learners and Multilingual Learners in the tutorial situation (Objectives 5, 6).
8. Formats for tutoring sessions to support diverse learners (Objectives 5, 6, 7).
9. Methods for documenting a struggling learner's performance (Objective 7).
10. Procedures for evaluating the effectiveness of tutoring sessions (Objectives 7, 9).
11. Selecting, planning, and implementing tutoring techniques (Objectives 8, 9).
12. Preparing instructional materials that support diverse learners (Objectives 8, 9).
13. Self-evaluation and goal setting for tutors (Objective 9).

Appendix R

Tutoring Manual and Training Topics

This is a list of potential topics to include in the development of a tutoring manual or to provide professional learning focus areas for your community-based tutoring program...in no particular order.

- Tutoring with a structured phonics approach
- Using the Language Experience Approach as a tutor
- Informal assessment procedures for the tutor
- A tutor's guide to understanding formal and informal assessment data
- Designing and implementing a peer or cross-age tutoring program
- The writing road to reading as a tutorial process
- Content reading and tutoring
- Promoting literacy enrichment through the tutoring process
- Using children's literature in tutoring
- Using youth adolescent literature in tutoring
- Parents as tutors
- Twenty-five literacy techniques for all tutors
- Programmatic philosophies
- When all else fails
- Supplemental instruction models for secondary students

Appendix S

Program Administration Resources

Additional documents that can serve as draft administrative resources and guidelines for a community tutorial program can be found in *A Field Guide to Community Literacy: Case Studies and Tools for Praxis. Evaluation, and Research* (Henry & Stahl, 2022). The text may be ordered through the Routledge website at https://www.routledge.com/search?sale=bestsellingeducation.

A list of these documents includes:

1. Planning for a Community Literacy Program Audit
2. Checklist for Planning and Implementing a Community-Based Literacy Program
3. Procedural Policies Manual – Community Literacy Program Outline
4. Program Logic Model Example
5. Community Awareness Plan
6. Grant Readiness Assessment
7. Key Steps to Grant Funding
8. Rights and Responsibilities of Community-Based Literacy Volunteers
9. Responsibilities of Literacy Volunteers
10. Job Description: Literacy Program Coordinator
11. Job Description: Adult Literacy Tutor

References for Tutoring Program Administrators and Coordinators

The references that follow should be useful to program coordinators and administrators who are delving into the theory, research, and best practices associated with tutoring. Many of the works are considered seminal in nature, but all will be found to be practical. Furthermore, by reviewing the reference lists in each work, a world of resources will be provided.

Cohen, P. A., Kulik, J., & Kulik, C. L. C. (1982). Educational outcomes of tutoring: A meta-analysis of findings. *American Educational Research Journal, 19*(2), 237–248. https://doi.org/10.3102/00028312019002237

Cornelli Sanderson, R., & Richards, M. H. (2010). The after-school needs and resources of a low-income urban community: Surveying youth and parents for community change. *American Journal of Community Psychology, 45*(3/4), 430–440. https://doi.org/10.1007/s10464-010-9309-x

Devin-Sheehan, L., Feldman, R. S., & Allen, V. L. (1976). Research on children tutoring children: A critical review. *Review of Educational Research, 46*(3), 355–385. https://doi.org/10.3102/00346543046003355

Elbaum, B., Vaughn, S., Tejero Hughes, M., & Watson Moody, S. (2000). How effective are one-to-one tutoring programs in reading for elementary students at risk for reading failure? A meta-analysis of the intervention research. *Journal of Educational Psychology, 92*(4), 605. https://doi.org/10.1037/0022-0663.92.4.605

Fitzgerald, J. (2001). Can minimally trained college student volunteers help young at-risk children read better? *Reading Research Quarterly, 36*(1), 28–46. https://doi.org/10.1598/RRQ.36.1.2

Fitz-Gibbon, C. T. (1977). *An analysis of the literature of cross-age tutoring.* National Institute of Education (ERIC Document Reproduction Service No. ED 148 807).

Good, A. G., Burch, P. E., Stewart, M. S., Acosta, R., & Heinrich, C. (2014). Instruction matters: Lessons from a mixed-method evaluation of out-of-school time tutoring under No Child Left Behind. *Teachers College Record, 116*(3), 1–34. https://doi.org/10.1177/016146811411600301

Gordon, E., & Gordon, E. (1990). *Centuries of tutoring: A history of alternative education in America and Western Europe.* University Press of America.

Gordon, E., Morgan, R. R., O'Malley, C. J., & Ponticell, J. (2007). *The tutoring revolution.* Rowman & Littlefield.

Haverback, H. R., & Parault, S. J. (2008). Pre-service reading teacher efficacy and tutoring: A review. *Educational Psychology Review, 20*(3), 237–255. https://doi.org/10.1007/s10648-008-9077-4

Heinrich, C. J., Burch, P., Good, A., Acosta, R., Cheng, H., Dillender, M., Kirshbaum, C., Nisar, H., & Stewart, M. (2014). Improving the implementation and effectiveness of out of-school-time tutoring. *Journal of Policy Analysis and Management, 33*(2), 471–494. https://doi.org/10.1002/pam.21745

Henry, L. A., & Stahl, N. A. (Eds.). (2021). *Literacy across the community: Research, praxis, and trends.* Routledge. https://doi.org/10.4324/9781003031550

Henry, L. A., & Stahl, N. A. (Eds.). (2022). *A field guide to community literacy: Case studies and tools for praxis, evaluation, and research.* Routledge. https://doi.org/10.4324/9781003228042

Hock, M. F., Pulvers, K. A., Deshler, D. D., & Schumaker, J. B. (2001). The effects of an after-school tutoring program on the academic performance of at-risk students and students with LD. *Remedial and Special Education, 22*(3), 172–186. https://doi.org/10.1177/074193250102200305

Hull, G., & Schultz, K. (Eds.). (2001). *School's out: Bridging out-of-school literacies with classroom practice.* Teachers College Press.

Invernizzi, M., Juel, C., & Rosemary, C. A. (1996). A community volunteer tutorial that works. *The Reading Teacher, 50*(4), 304–311.

Jacob, R., Armstrong, C., & Willard, J. (2015). *Mobilizing volunteer tutors to improve student literacy: Implementation, impacts, and costs of the Reading Partners program*. MDRC. https://papers.ssrn.com/sol3/papers.cfm?abstract_id=2574434

Jones, B. D., Stallings, D. T., & Malone, D. (2004). Prospective teachers as tutors: Measuring the impact of a service-learning program on upper elementary students. *Teacher Education Quarterly, 31*(3), 99–118. https://www.jstor.org/stable/23478886

Juel, C. (1996). What makes literacy tutoring effective? *Reading Research Quarterly, 31*(3), 268–289. https://doi.org/10.1598/RRQ.31.3.3

Lauer, P. A., Akiba, M., Wilkerson, S. B., Apthorp, H. S., Snow, D., & Martin-Glenn, M. L. (2006). Out-of-school-time programs: A meta-analysis of effects for at-risk students. *Review of Educational Research, 76*(2), 275–313. https://doi.org/10.3102/00346543076002275

Nickow, A. J., Oreopoulos, P., & Quan, V. (2020). *The impressive effects of tutoring K-12 learning: A systematic review and meta-analysis of experimental evidence*. (EdWorkingPaper: 20–267). Retrieved from Annenberg Institute at Brown University. https://doi.org/10.26300/eh0c-pc52

Ritter, G. W., Barnett, J. H., Denny, G. S., & Albin, G. R. (2009). The effectiveness of volunteer tutoring programs for elementary and middle school students: A meta-analysis. *Review of Educational Research, 79*(1), 3–38. https://doi.org/10.3102/0034654308325690

Rosenshine, B., & Furst, N. (1969). *The effects of tutoring upon pupil achievement: A research review*. United States Office of Education. (ERIC Document Reproduction Service No. ED 064 462).

Villiger, C., Hauri, S., Tettenborn, A., Hartmann, E., Näpflin, C., Hugener, I., & Niggli, A. (2019). Effectiveness of an extracurricular program for struggling readers: A comparative study with parent tutors and volunteer tutors. *Learning and Instruction, 60*, 54–65. https://doi.org/10.1016/j.learninstruc.2018.11.004

Wasik, B. A. (1997). Volunteer tutoring programs. *Phi Delta Kappan, 79*(4), 282–287.

Wasik, B. A. (1998). Volunteer tutoring programs in reading: A review. *Reading Research Quarterly, 33*(3), 266–291. https://doi.org/10.1598/RRQ.33.3.2

White, S., Groom-Thomas, L., & Loeb, S. (2023). *A systematic review of research on tutoring implementation: Considerations when undertaking complex instructional supports for students* (EdWorkingPaper: 22-652). Retrieved from Annenberg Institute at Brown University: https://doi.org/10.26300/wztf-wj14

Worthy, J., Prater, K., & Pennington, J. (2003). "It's a program that looks great on paper": The challenge of America Reads. *Journal of Literacy Research, 35*(3), 879–910. https://doi.org/10.1207/s15548430jlr3503_4

Zimmer, R., Hamilton, L., & Christina, R. (2010). After-school tutoring in the context of No Child Left Behind: Effectiveness of two programs in the Pittsburgh public schools. *Economics of Education Review, 29*(1), 18–28. https://doi.org/10.1016/j.econedurev.2009.02.005

References

Allen, M. J. (2004). *Assessing academic programs in higher education*. Jossey-Bass.

Appleman, D., & Graves, M. F. (2011). *Reading better, reading smarter: Designing literature lessons for adolescents*. Heinemann.

Arendale, D. (2010). *Access at the crossroads: Learning assistance in higher education*. ASHE Higher Education Report, Volume 35 Number 6. Wiley.

Aston-Warner, S. (1963). *Teacher*. Bantam.

Bandura, A. (1977). Self-efficacy: Toward a unifying theory of behavioral change. *Psychological Review, 84*(2), 191–215. https://doi.org/10.1037/0033-295X.84.2.191

Bartlett, J. (2022, August). *Pronoun usage*. Center for the Advancement of Teaching Excellence, University of Illinois Chicago.

Barton, D., Hamilton, M., & Ivanic, R. (2000). *Situated literacies: Reading and writing in context*. Routledge.

Bear, D., Invernizzi, M., Templeton, S., & Johnston, F. (2024). *Words their way: Word Study for phonics, vocabulary, and spelling instruction* (7th ed.). Pearson.

Beers, K. (2003). *When kids can't read, what teachers can do*. Heinemann.

Bird, C., & Bird, D. M. (1945). *Learning more by effective study*. D. Appleton-Century.

Bishop, R. S. (1990). Mirrors, windows, and sliding glass doors. *Perspectives: Choosing and Using Books for the Classroom, 6*(3), ix–xi.

Bowman, A. (2021, May 24). *Mourning the loss of indigenous queer identities*. Autostraddle. Retrieved April 17, 2022, from https://www.autostraddle.com/mourning-the-loss-of-indigenous-queer-identities/

Brown-Jeffy, S., & Cooper, J. E. (2011). Toward a conceptual framework of culturally relevant pedagogy: An overview of the conceptual and theoretical literature. *Teacher Education Quarterly, 38*(1), 65–84.

Cacicio, S., Cote, P., & Bigger, K. (2023, June). *Investing in multiple literacies for individual and collective empowerment*. [White Paper]. The Adult Literacy & Learning Impact Network. https://allinliteracy.org/wp-content/uploads/2023/06/Investing-in-Multiple-Literacies-for-Individual-and-Collective-Empowerment.pdf

Carrillo, L. W. (1972). Language experience approach to reading. In J. Duggins (Ed.) *Teaching reading for human values in high school* (pp. 257–283). Merrill.

Chambers, C. (2018). *Write your way to a successful scholarship essay*. Create Space Independent Publishing Platform.

Christle, C. A., & Yell, M. L. (2008). Preventing youth incarceration through reading remediation: Issues and solutions. *Reading & Writing Quarterly, 24*(2), 148–176. https://doi.org/10.1080/10573560701808437

Clay, M. (1985). *The early detection of reading difficulties*. Heinemann.

Clay, M. (2015). *Becoming literate*. Heinemann.

Colorín Colorado. (2023). *A bilingual site for educators and families of English language learners*. WETA Public Broadcasting. https://www.colorincolorado.org/

Cooper-Novack, G. (2022). *"A sense of safe connection": An affective narrative exploration with queer teenage writers in an out-of-school time program*. [Unpublished doctoral dissertation]. Syracuse University.

Day, J. D. (1980). *Training summarization skills: A comparison of teaching methods*. [Unpublished doctoral dissertation]. University of Illinois, Urbana-Champaign.

Deans for Impact. (2021). *The PATHS to Tutor Act: Mobilizing future teachers as tutors for vulnerable students*. https://www.deansforimpact.org/about/news-and-blog/2021/02/25/the-paths-to-tutor-act-mobilizing-future-teachers-as-tutors-for-vulnerable-students

DeJulio, S., Massey, D. D., Stahl, N., & King, J. (2023). Terminologically speaking, the reading wars. *Reading Psychology, 45*(4), 386–412. https://doi.org/10.1080/02702711.2024.2309342

Dewey, J. (1997). *Experience & education*. Free Press.

Dorr, R. E. (2006). Something old is new again: Revisiting language experience. *The Reading Teacher, 60*(2), 138–146. https://doi.org/10.1598/RT.60.2.4

Duke, N., Purcell-Gates, V., Hall, L., & Towers, C. (2011). Authentic literacy activities for developing comprehension and writing. *The Reading Teacher, 60*(4), 344–355. https://doi.org/10.1598/RT.60.4.4

Dutro, E. (2019). *The vulnerable heart of literacy*. Teachers College Press.

Echevarria, J., & Vogt, M. E. (2022). *99 ideas and activities for teaching English learners* (2nd ed.). Pearson.

Echevarria, J., Vogt, M. E., & Short, D. (2008). *Making content comprehensible for English learners: The SIOP model*. Allyn & Bacon.

Echevarria, J., Vogt, M. E., & Short, D. (2010a). *Making content comprehensible for elementary English learners: The SIOP model*. Allyn & Bacon. https://doi.org/10.18848/1447-9494/CGP/v14i11/45514

Echevarria, J., Vogt, M. E., & Short, D. (2010b). *Making content comprehensible for secondary English learners: The SIOP model*. Allyn & Bacon.

Echevarria, J., Vogt, M. E., Short, D. J., & Toppel, K. (2024). *Making content comprehensible for multilingual learners*. (6th ed.). Pearson.

Edmentum. (2021). *Fast phonics sounds: Alphabet and phonemes flash cards*. Blake Publishing. https://info.edmentum.com/rs/780-NRC-339/images/Sounds%20Flash%20Cards.pdf

EdReports.org. (2021). *State of the market 2020: The use of aligned materials*. https://storage.googleapis.com/edreports-dev.appspot.com/media/2021/03/EdReports-2020-State-of-the-Market-Use-of-Aligned-Materials_FINAL_2-1.pdf

Ehret, C. (2018). Propositions from affect theory for feeling literacy through the event. In D. E. Alvermann, N. J. Unrau, M. Sailors, & R. B. Ruddell (Eds.) *Theoretical models and processes of literacy* (7th ed., pp. 563–581). Routledge. https://doi.org/10.4324/9781315110592-34

Flores, N. (2020). From academic language to language architecture: Challenging raciolinguistic ideologies in research and practice. *Theory into Practice, 59*(1), 22–31. https://doi.org/10.1080/00405841.2019.1665411

Flores, T., & Osorio, S. (2021). *Windows and mirrors: Latinx experiences in children's literature*. https://www.colorincolorado.org/article/windows-and-mirrors-latinx-experiences-childrens-literature

Fountas, I., & Pinnell, S. U. (2016). *Guided reading*. (2nd ed.). Heinemann.

Frakes, G. F., & Adams, W. R. (1976). *From columbus to aquarius: An interpretive history*. Dryden.

Freire, P. (1970). *Pedagogy of the oppressed*. The Seabury Press.

Friedland, E. S., & Truscott, D. M. (2005). Building awareness and commitment of middle school students through literacy tutoring. *Journal of Adolescent & Adult Literacy, 48*(7), 550–562. https://doi.org/10.1598/JAAL.48.7.2

Frost, J. (1967). *Issues and innovations in the teaching of reading*. Scott Foresman.

Gallagher, K. (2009). *Readicide: How schools are killing reading and what you can do about it*. Stenhouse.

Garcia, O., & Kleifgen, J. A. (2019). Translanguaging and literacy. *Reading Research Quarterly, 55*(4), 553–571. https://doi.org/10.1002/rrq.286

Gay, G. (2002). Preparing for culturally responsive teaching. *Journal of Teacher Education, 53*(2), 106–116. https://doi.org/10.1177/0022487102053002003

Gay, G. (2018). *Culturally responsive teaching: Theory, research, and practice.* Teachers College Press.

Gersten, R., Baker, S. K., Shanahan, T., Linan-Thompson, S., Collins, P., & Scarcella, R. (2007). *Effective literacy and English language instruction for English learners in the elementary grades.* IES Practice Guide. NCEE 2007-4011. What Works Clearinghouse.

Gickling, E. E., & Armstrong, D. L. (1978). Levels of instructional difficulty as related to on-task behavior, task completion, and comprehension. *Journal of Learning Disabilities, 11*(9), 559–566.

González, N., Moll, L., & Amanti, C. (Eds.). (2005). *Funds of knowledge: Theorizing practices in households, communities, and classrooms.* Erlbaum.

Goodman, K. (1969). Analysis of oral reading miscues: Applied psycholinguistics. In F. Gollasch (Ed.) *Language and literacy: The selected writings of Kenneth Goodman* (pp. 123–134). Routledge & Kegan Paul. https://doi.org/10.2307/747158

Goodman, Y. (2015). Miscue analysis: A transformative tool for researcher, teacher, and readers. *Literacy Research: Theory, Method and Practice, 64*(1), 92–111. https://doi.org/10.1177/2381336915617619

Goodman, Y., & Marek, A. (1996). *Retrospective miscue analysis.* Richard C. Owen.

Goodman, Y., Watson, D., & Burke, C. (2005). *Reading miscue inventory: Alternative procedures.* Richard C. Owen.

Gordon, E., & Gordon, E. (1990). *Centuries of tutoring: A history of alternative education in America and Western Europe.* University Press of America.

Gordon, E., Morgan, R. R., O'Malley, C. J., & Ponticell, J. (2007). *The tutoring revolution.* Rowman & Littlefield.

Hall, M. A. (1978). *The language experience approach for teaching reading: A research perspective.* (2nd ed.). International Reading Association.

Hart, C., & Samson, L. (2009). *The oral history workshop: Collect and celebrate the life stories of your family and friends.* Workman.

Hawkins, T. (1972). *Benjamin: Reading and beyond.* Merrill.

Hayslip, A. (2020). Combating bias through asset-based teaching. *Research and Teaching in Developmental Education, 9*(Fall), 12–16. https://www.nyclsa.org/policy.html

Heckelman, R. G. (1969). A neurological-impress method of remedial-reading instruction. *Academic Therapy, 4*(4), 277–282. https://doi.org/10.1177/105345126900400406

Henry, L. A., & Stahl, N. A. (Eds.). (2021). *Literacy across the community: Research, praxis, and trends*. Routledge. https://doi.org/10.4324/9781003031550

Henry, L. A., & Stahl, N. A. (Eds.). (2022). *A field guide to community, literacy: Case studies and tools for praxis, evaluation, and research*. Routledge. https://doi.org/10.4324/9781003228042

Hernandez, D. J. (2011). *Double jeopardy: How third grade reading skills and poverty influence high school graduation*. The Annie E. Casey Foundation. https://files.eric.ed.gov/fulltext/ED518818.pdf

Herschbach, E. (2018). *Expansion of our nation: Slavery and the Missouri compromise*. Focus.

Hershberger, K., Zembal-Saul, C., & Starr, M. L. (2006). Evidence helps the KWL get a KLEW. *Science & Children, 43*(5), 50–53.

Hill, B. C., Ruptic, C., & Norwick, L. (1998). *Classroom based assessment*. Christopher-Gordon.

Hull, G., & Schultz, K. (2001). Literacy and learning out of school: A review of theory and research. *Review of Educational Research, 71*(4), 575–611. https://doi.org/10.3102/00346543071004575

Immordino-Yang, M. H. (2016). *Emotions, learning, and the brain: Exploring the educational implications of affective neuroscience*. Norton.

Indiana Department of Education. (2021). *Phonological Awareness*. https://www.in.gov/doe/files/2024-HQCM-Evaluation-Rubric_-K-5-Reading.docx

INFOhio. (2022, June). *Instructional Materials Rubric*. Ohio's PreK-12 Digital Library. https://www.infohio.org/images/ZOO_DOCS/oer/InstructionalMaterialsRubric.pdf

Institute of Educational Sciences. (2023). *Fact sheet: Making sense of educational assessment*. Regional Educational Laboratory Northeast & Islands. https://ies.ed.gov/ncee/rel/regions/northeast/pdf/RELNEI_FactsheetME.pdf

Insurance Corporation of British Columbia. (2020). *Learn to drive smart: Your guide to driving safely by allied organizations*. Insurance Corporation of British Columbia.

International Literacy Association. (2019). *Children's rights to excellent literacy instruction* [Position statement]. Author.

Jacobi, T. (2008). Writing for change: Engaging juveniles through alternative literacy education. *Journal of Correctional Education, 59*(2), 71–93. https://www.ncjrs.gov/pdffiles1/ojjdp/grants/251118.pdf

Johns, J. L., Elish-Piper, L., & Johns, B. (2017). *Basic reading inventory: Kindergarten through grade twelve and early literacy assessments* (12th ed.). Kendall Hunt.

Johnson, E. J., & Johnson, A. B. (2016). Enhancing academic investment through home-school connections and building ELL students' scholastic funds of knowledge. *Journal of Language and Literacy Education, 12*(1), 104–121. Jolle.coe.uga.edu/wpcontent/uploads/2016/04/E.Johnson3.8.16pdf

Junger, S. (1997). *The perfect storm: A true story of men against the sea.* WW Norton & Company.

Keene, E., & Zimmermann, S. (1997). *Mosaic of thought: Teaching comprehension in a reader's workshop.* Heineman.

Krezmien, M. P., & Mulcahy, C. A. (2008). Literacy and delinquency: Current status of reading interventions with detained and incarcerated youth. *Reading & Writing Quarterly, 24*(2), 219–238. https://doi.org/10.1080/10573560701808601

Kyvig, D., Marty, M. A., & Cebula, L. (2019). *Nearby history: Exploring the past around you.* (4th ed.). Rowman & Littlefield.

Ladson-Billings, G. (1995). Toward a theory of culturally relevant pedagogy. *American Educational Research Journal, 32*(3), 465–491. https://doi.org/10.2307/1163320

Ladson-Billings, G. (2009). *The dreamkeepers: Successful teachers of African American children.* Jossey-Bass.

Lakeshore Learning. (n.d.). *300 Most Common Sight Words.* https://www.lakeshorelearning.com/assets/media/images/pdfs/SightWord_List_1-300.pdf

Langer, J. (1981). From theory to practice: A prereading plan. *Journal of Reading, 25*(2), 152–156. https://www.jstor.org/stable/40030271

LaPray, M., & Ross, R. (1969). The graded word list: Quick gauge of reading ability. *Journal of Reading, 12*(4), 305–307.

Lee, J., & Shute, V. J. (2010). Personal and social-contextual factors in K–12 academic performance: An integrative perspective on student learning. *Educational Psychologist, 45*(3), 185–202. https://doi.org/10.1080/00461520.2010.493471

Lewis, K., & Kuhfeld, M. (2023). *Education's long COVID: 2022–23 achievement data reveal stalled progress toward pandemic recovery.* NWEA. https://files.eric.ed.gov/fulltext/ED630208.pdf

Lin, A. (2020). From deficit-based to asset-based teaching in higher education in BANA countries: Cutting through the binaries with a heteroglossic plurilingual lens. *Language, Culture, and Curriculum, 33*(2), 203–212. https://doi.org/10.1080/07908318.2020.1723927

Love, B. L. (2019). *We want to do more than survive: Abolitionist teaching and the pursuit of educational freedom.* Beacon Press.

Martin, J. (2016). *The edge of extinction: The ark plan.* Harper-Collins.

McIntyre, E., Kyle, D. W., Chen, C. T., Kraemer, J., & Parr, J. (2009). *6 principles for teaching English language learners in all classrooms.* Corwin.

Moll, L. C. (1994). Literacy research in community and classrooms: A sociocultural approach. In R. B. Ruddell, M. R. Ruddell, & H. Singer (Eds.) *Theoretical models and processes of reading* (4th ed., pp. 179–207). International Reading Association.

Moll, L. C., & Arnot-Hopffer, E. (2005). Sociocultural competence in teacher education. *Journal of Teacher Education, 56*(3), 242–247. https://doi.org/10.1177/0022487105275919

Moll, L. C., Amanti, C., Neff, D., & Gonzalez, N. (1992). Funds of knowledge for teaching: Using a qualitative approach to connect homes and classrooms. *Theory Into Practice, 31*(2), 132–141. https://doi.org/10.1080/00405849209543534

Morgan, D. N., Valerio, M., & Evans, K. I. (2024). A 20 year guided reading research synthesis: Examining student data. *Literacy Research and Instruction, 63*(3), 193-216.

Mueller, P. N. (2001). *Lifers: Learning from at-risk adolescent readers.* Heinemann.

National Center for Education Statistics. (2023, October 17). *Most public schools face challenges in hiring teachers and other personnel entering the 2023–24 academic year.* https://nces.ed.gov/whatsnew/press_releases/10_17_2023.asp

National Center for Education Statistics. (2023). *NAEP long-term trend assessment results: Reading and mathematics.* The Nation's Report Card. https://www.nationsreportcard.gov/highlights/ltt/2023/#section-performance-trends-by-student-group

National Center for Education Statistics. (2024). National Assessment of Educational Progress, Reading Assessment 2024. The Nation's Report Card. https://www.nationsreportcard.gov/reports/reading/2024/g4_8/?grade=8

National Commission on Excellence in Education. (1983). *A nation at risk: The imperative for educational reform.* National Commission on Excellence in Education.

National Council for Teachers of English and International Reading Association. (2006). *Cultural Relevance Rubric.* https://www.readwritethink.org/sites/default/files/resources/lesson_images/lesson1003/CR-Rubric.pdf

National Reading Panel. (2000). *Report of the National Reading Panel: Teaching children to read: An evidence based assessment of the scientific research literature on reading and its implications for reading instruction.* National Institute of Child Health and Human Development. https://www.nichd.nih.gov/sites/default/files/publications/pubs/nrp/Documents/report.pdf

National Student Support Accelerator. (n.d.). *High impact tutoring: District Playbook.* https://studentsupportaccelerator.org/sites/default/files/High_Impact_Tutoring_District_Playbook.pdf

National Tutoring Association. (2016). *Tutor code of ethics.* https://www.ntatutor.com/code-of-ethics.html

Nelson, M. (1991). *At the point of need: Teaching basic and ESL writers.* Boynton-Cook.

Nelson, N., & King, J. R. (2023). Discourse synthesis: Textual transformations in writing from sources. *Reading and Writing, 36*(4), 769–808. https://doi.org/10.1007/s11145-021-10243-5

Nessel, D. D., & Dixon, C. N. (2008). *Using the language experience approach with English language learners: Strategies for engaging students and developing literacy.* Corwin.

Nguyen, T. D., Lam, C. B., & Bruno, P. (2022). *Is there a national teacher shortage? A systematic examination of reports of teacher shortages in the United States.* (Ed Working Paper: 22–631). Retrieved from Annenberg Institute at Brown University. https://edworkingpapers.com/sites/default/files/ai22-631.pdf

Ogle, D. M. (1986). K-W-L: A teaching model that develops active reading of expository text. *Reading Teacher, 39*(6), 564–570. https://jstor.org/stable/20199156

Olivares, J. (2017). *Fewer youths incarcerated, but gap between blacks and whites worsens.* Retrieved from https://www.npr.org/2017/09/27/551864016/fewer-youths-incarcerated-but-gap-between-blacks-and-whites-worsens

Orton-Gillingham Academy. (2022). *Principles of the OG Approach.* Academy of Orton-Gillingham Practitioners and Educators. Retrieved September 19, 2023 from https://www.ortonacademy.org/resources/og-approach-principles-2/

Paris, S. G. (2005). Reinterpreting the development of reading skills. *Reading Research Quarterly, 40*(2), 184–202. https://doi.org/10.1598/RRQ.40.2.3

Paris, S. G., & Winograd, P. (1990). How metacognition can promote academic learning and instruction. In B. F. Jones & L. Idol (Eds.) *Dimensions of thinking and cognitive instruction* (pp. 15–51). Routledge.

Partnership for Student Success. (2025). *About us.* https://www.partnership-studentsuccess.org/about/

Patel, N. V. (2003). A holistic approach to learning and teaching interaction: Factors in the development of critical learners. *International Journal of Educational Management, 17*(6), 272–284. https://doi.org/10.1108/09513540310487604

Purcell-Gates, V., Duke, N., & Martineau, J. (2011). Learning to read and write genre-specific text: Roles of authentic experience and explicit teaching. *Reading Research Quarterly, 42*(1), 8–45. https://doi.org/10.1598/RRQ.42.1.1

Rasinski, T. V. (2011). *Daily word ladders*. Scholastic Teaching Resources.

Rasinski, T. V., & Padak, N. (2005). *3-minute reading assessment: Word recognition, fluency, & comprehension*. Scholastic.

Robson, A. L. (2002). Critical/sensitive periods. In N. J. Salkind (Ed.) *Child development* (pp. 101–103). Gale Virtual Reference Library. Macmillan.

Robinson, C., Kraft, M., Loeb, S., & Schueler. (2021). *Design principles for accelerating student learning with high-impact tutoring*. EdResearch for action design principles: Brief #16. Annenberg, Brown University. https://annenberg.brown.edu/sites/default/files/EdResearch_for_Recovery_Design_Principles_1.pdf

Roth, K., & Dabrowski, J. (2013). *Extending interactive writing into grades 2–5*. Reading Rockets. https://doi.org/10.1002/trtr.1270

Ruddell, M. R. (2007). *Teaching content reading and writing*. (5th ed.). Wiley.

Scouts, B. S. A. (2022). *Reading merit badge*. Boy Scouts of America. https://www.scouting.org/merit-badges/reading/

Schwartz, S. (2022/2025). *Which states have passed 'Science of Reading' Laws? What's in Them?* https://www.edweek.org/teaching-learning/which-states-have-passed-science-of-reading-laws-whats-in-them/2022/07

Shanahan, T. (2005). *The National Reading Panel report: Practical advice for teachers*. Learning Point Associates. ED489535.

Shanahan, T., Callison, K., Carriere, C., Duke, N. K., Pearson, P. D., Schatscheider, C., & Torgesen, J. (2010). *Improving reading comprehension in kindergarten through 3rd grade*. IES Practice Guide. NCEE 2010-4038. What Works Clearinghouse. https://ies.ed.gov/ncee/WWC/Docs/PracticeGuide/readingcomp_pg_092810.pdf

Sheldon, S. B., & Jung, S. B. (2018). *Students outcomes and parent teacher home visits*. Center on School, Family, & Community Partnerships, Johns Hopkins School of Education. https://www.sfcp.jhucsos.com/wp-content/uploads/2019/11/Student-Outcomes-and-PTHV-Report-FINAL-2018.pdf

Sickmund, M., & Puzzanchera, C. (2014). *Juvenile offenders and victims: 2014 national report*. National Center for Juvenile Justice.

Skelley, D. L., Stevens, M. L., & Bailey-Tarbett, L. K. (2022). Culturally responsive teaching in an afterschool literacy program: Tutor implementation and experiences. *School Community Journal, 32*(1), 63–84.

Smagorinsky, P. (2011). *Vygotsky and literacy research*. Sense Publishers. https://doi.org/10.1007/978-94-6091-696-0

Smillie, R. (1985). Design strategies for job performance aids. In T. Duffy & R. Waller (Eds.) *Designing usable texts* (pp. 213–243). Academic Press. https://doi.org/10.1016/B978-0-12-223260-2.50015-3

Snow, C. E., & Hoefnagel-Höhle, M. (1978). The critical period for language acquisition: Evidence from second-language learning. *Child Development, 49*(4), 1114–1128. https://doi:10.1111/j.1467-8624.1978.tb04080.x

Snyder, H., & Sickmund, M. (2006). *Juvenile offenders and victims: 2006 national report.* U.S. Department of Justice, Office of Justice Programs, Office of Juvenile Justice and Delinquency Prevention.

Spivey, N., & King, J. (1989). Readers as writers composing from sources. *Reading Research Quarterly, 24*(1), 7–26. https://doi.org/10.1598/RRQ.24.1.1

State of Victoria Department of Education and Early Childhood Development. (2012). *Strength-based approach: A guide to writing transition learning and development statements.* Communications Division, Department of Educational and Early Childhood Development.

Stauffer, R. (1976). *Action research in LEA instructional procedures.* University of Delaware.

Stauffer, R. G. (1969). *Teaching reading as a thinking process.* Harper & Row.

Styslinger, M. E., Gavigan, K., & Albright, K. (Eds.). (2017). *Literacy behind bars: Successful reading and writing strategies for use with incarcerated youth and adults.* Rowman & Littlefield.

Sum, A., Khatiwada, I., McLaughlin, J., & Palma, S. (2009). *The consequences of dropping out of high school: Joblessness and jailing for high school dropouts and the high cost for taxpayers.* Retrieved from www.northeastern.edu/clms/wp-content/uploads/The_Consequences_of_Dropping_Out_of_High_School.pdf

Szuba, L. (2020). Tutor and tutoring in the history of education (to the great French revolution). *21st Century Pedagogy, 1*(4), 49–59. https://doi.org/10.2478/ped21-2020-0008

Tatum, A. W. (2005). *Teaching reading to black adolescent males: Closing the achievement gap.* Stenhouse.

Tatum, A. W. (2009). *Reading for their life: (Re)Building the textual lineages of African American adolescent males.* Heinemann.

Tichavakunda, A., & Galan, C. (2023). The summer before college: A case study of first generation, urban high school graduates. *Urban Education, 58*(8), 1658–1686. https://doi.org/10.1177/0042085920914362

Tierney, R. J., & Readence, J. E. (2000). *Reading strategies and practices: A compendium.* (5th ed.). Allyn & Bacon.

Torgesen, J. K., Wagner, R. K., & Rashotte, C. A. (2012). *Test of reading efficiency.* (2nd ed.). Pro-Ed.

Tovani, C. (2000). *I read it, but I don't get it: Comprehension strategies for adolescent readers.* Stenhouse.

TRIO. (n.d.). *U. S. Department of Education Office of Postsecondary Education Programs: TRIO Programs*. https://www2.ed.gov/about/offices/list/ope/trio/index.html

Unite for Literacy. (n.d.). *About Unite for Literacy*. https://www.uniteforliteracy.com/corp/about

United States Congress. (2001). *No child left behind act of 2001: Conference report to accompany H.R. 1*. 107th Congress, 1st session. U.S. Government Printing Office.

United States Congress. (2024, January). *Partnering aspiring teachers with high-need schools to tutor act of 2024*. H.R.7016, 118th Congress. https://www.congress.gov/bill/118th-congress/house-bill/7016

United States Department of Education. (2025). *The national commission on excellence in education*. A Nation at Risk: The Imperative for Educational Reform, Author.

United States, Department of Education. (1997). *America reads challenge*. https://files.eric.ed.gov/fulltext/ED411504.pdf

Vacca, J. S. (2008). Crime can be prevented if schools teach juvenile offenders to read. *Children and Youth Services Review, 30*, 1055–1062. https://doi.org/10.1016/j.childyouth.2008.01.013

Van Allen, R. (1970). *Updating the language experience approach* [Paper presentation]. International Reading Association Annual Conference (pp. 1–8). Anaheim, CA. ERIC Document ED 040 831.

Velez-Ibanez, C., & G., Greenberg, J. B. (1992). Formation and transformation of funds of knowledge among U. S. Mexican households in the context of the borderlands. *Anthropology & Education Quarterly, 23*(4), 313–335.

Venezia, A., & Jaeger, L. (2013). Transitions from high school to college. *The Future of Children, 23*(1), 117–136. https://doi:10.1353/foc.2013.0004

Vogt, M. E. (2021). Developing children's oral language and literacy with the Language Experience Approach (LEA). *The California Reader, 54*(2), 5–9.

Vogt, M. E., & Echevarria, J. (2015). *99 more ideas and activities for teaching English learners with the SIOP Model*. Pearson.

Vygotsky, L. S. (1978). *Mind in society: Development of higher psychological processes*. Harvard University Press.

Wagner, R. K., Torgesen, J. K., Rashotte, C. A., & Pearson, N. A. (2013). *CTOPP-2: Comprehensive Test of Phonological Processing*. Pro-Ed. https://doi.org/10.1037/t52630-000

Washington Office of Superintendent of Public Instruction. (2023). *Funds of knowledge tool kit*. https://ospi.k12.wa.us/sites/default/files/2023-10/funds_of_knowledge_toolkit.pdf

Wasik, B. A. (1998). Volunteer tutoring programs in reading: A review. *Reading Research Quarterly, 33*(3), 266–291. https://doi.org/10.1598/RRQ.33.3.2

Wasik, B. A., & Slavin, R. E. (1993). Preventing early reading failure with one-to-one tutoring: A review of five programs. *Reading Research Quarterly, 28*(2), 178–200. https://doi.org/10.2307/747888

Weinstein, G., & Fantini, M. D. (1970). *Toward humanistic education: A curriculum of affect*. Praeger.

Wigginton, E., & Students. (Eds.). (1972). *The foxfire book*. Anchor Books.

Wood, D., Bruner, J., & Ross, G. (1976). The role of tutoring in problem solving. *Journal of Child Psychology & Psychiatry, 17*(2), 89–100. https://doi.org/10.1111/j.1469-7610.1976.tb00381.x

Yang, G. L. (2016). *Reading without walls*. [Research Guide]. Library of Congress. https://guides.loc.gov/youth-ambassador-gene-luen-yang/reading-without-walls

Young, C., Lagrone, & McCauley, J. (2020). Read like me: An intervention for struggling readers. *Education Sciences, 10*(3), 1–11. https://doi.org/10.3390/educsci10030057

Tutoring References across the Years

The following reference list presents a range of books that have been published over the past five decades on the topic of literacy tutoring. Some sources focus on school-oriented tutoring programs. Some texts are aimed at community-based programs. Yet, all can be useful to the supervisor or trainer of tutors and tutors themselves regardless of where the service is being offered. Books may be found in public or educational libraries or through either used or new bookstores.

Allen, V. L. (Ed.). (1976). *Children as teachers: Theory and research on tutoring.* Academic Press.

Bloom, S. (n.d.). *Peer and cross-age tutoring in the schools: An individualized supplement to group instruction.* Chicago Board of Education.

Brown, S., & Race, P. (2004). *500 tips for tutors.* Routledge.

Carter, B., & Dapper, G. (1972). *School volunteers: What they do – How they do it.* Citation Press.

Chandler-Olcott, K., & Hinchman, K. A. (2005). *Tutoring adolescent literacy learners: A guide for volunteers.* Guilford Press.

Colvin, R. J. (2009). *Tutor: A collaborative, learner-centered approach to literacy instruction for teens and adults.* (8th ed.). New Readers Press.

Ebersole, E. H. (1972). *Teacher's guide to programmed tutoring in reading: Pupil-team procedures for success in reading*. EberSon Enterprises.

Fisher, P. J., Bates, A., & Gurvitz, D. J. (2014). *The complete guide to tutoring struggling readers: Mapping interventions to purpose and CCSS*. Teachers College Press.

Frey, N., Fisher, D., & Almarode, J. T. (2022). *How tutoring works: Six steps to grow motivation & accelerate student learning*. Corwin.

Goodlad, S. (1998). *Mentoring and tutoring by students*. Routledge.

Green, J. (2003). *Basic skills for childcare-Literacy: Tutor pack*. Davis Fulton Publishers.

Herman, B. A. (1994). *The volunteer tutor's toolbox*. International Reading Association.

Hiebert, E. H., & Ganske, K. (2015). *Toolkit for tutoring. Using beginning reads with young readers*. TextProject. Retrieved from https://textproject.org/wp-content/uploads/resources/ToolKit-for-Tutors-BeginningReads.pdf

Invernizzi, M., Lewis-Wagner, D., Johnston, F. R., & Juel, C. (2021). *Book buddies: A tutoring framework for struggling readers*. (3rd ed.). Guilford Press.

Janowitz, G. (1965). *Helping hands: Volunteer work in education*. University of Chicago Press.

Johnson, A. P. (2008). *Teaching reading and writing: A guidebook for tutoring and remediating students*. R&L Education.

Jones, M. (1984). *The tutoring handbook: A complete guide for student tutors*. Rosen.

Koselak, J., & Lyall, B. (2017). *The revitalized tutoring center: A guide to transforming school culture*. Routledge. https://doi.org/10.4324/9781315644738

Koskinen, P. S., & Wilson, R. M. (1982). *Developing a successful tutoring program*. Teachers College Press.

Miller, D. M. (2105). *The neighborhood tutoring program*. WestBow Press.

Morris, D. (2005). *The Howard Street tutoring manual: Teaching at-risk readers in the primary grades*. (2nd ed.). Guilford Press.

Morrow, L. M., & Woo, D. G. (Eds.). (2001). *Tutoring programs for struggling readers: The America Reads challenge*. Guilford Press.

National Student Support Accelerator. (2021). *Toolkit for tutoring programs*. https://doi.org/10.26300/5n7h-mh59

Pippit, M., Davies Samway, K., & Whang, G. (1995). *Buddy reading: Cross-age tutoring in a multicultural school*. Heinemann.

Pope, L. (1976). *Tutor!: A handbook for tutorial programs*. Book Lab, Inc.

Pope, L., Edel, D., & Haklay, A. (1972). *Tutor's sampler*. Book Lab, Inc.

Rabow, J., Chin, T., & Fahimian, N. (1999). *Tutoring matters: Everything you always wanted to know about how to tutor.* Temple University Press.

Rauch, S. J. (Ed.). (1969). *Handbook for the volunteer tutor.* International Reading Association.

Richards, J. C., & Lassonde, C. A. (Eds.). (2009). *Literacy tutoring that works: A look at successful in-school, after-school, and summer programs.* International Reading Association. https://books.google.com/books/about/Literacy_Tutoring_that_Works.html?id=dME5s_DiYzwC

Sanders, J., & Damron, R. L. (2016). *"They're all writers": Teaching peer tutoring in the elementary writing center.* Teachers College Press.

Siljander, R. P., Reina, J., & Siljander, R. A. (2005). *Literacy tutoring handbook: A guide to teaching children and adults to read and write.* Charles C. Thomas.

Sleisenger, L. (1965). *Guidebook for the volunteer reading teacher.* Teachers College Press.

Smith, C. B., & Fay, L. (1973). *Getting people to read: Volunteer programs that work.* Dell.

Strayhorn, J. M. (2009). *Manual for tutors and teachers of reading.* Psychological Skills Press.

Tindall, J. A., & Black, D. R. (2008). *Peer programs: An in-depth look at peer programs: Planning, implementation, and administration.* Routledge.

Topping, K., Duran, D., & Van Keer, H. (2016). *Using peer tutoring to improve reading skills: A practical guide for teachers.* Routledge. https://doi.org/10.4324/9781315731032

Walker, B., Morrow, L. M., & Scherry, R. (1999). *Training the reading team: A guide for supervisors of a volunteer reading program.* International Reading Association.

Author Index

Albright, K. 137
Alessandri, A. 82
Allen, M. J. 88
Allen, R. 63
Amanti, C. 74, 77
Annenberg Institute xvi
Appleman, D. 137, 147
Arendale, D. xv
Armstrong, D. Z. 44
Arnot-Hopffer, E. 3
Ashton-Warner, S. 80

Bailey-Tarbett, L. K. 164
Baker, S. K. 10
Bandura, A. 166
Barlett, J. 23
Bear, D. 130
Beers, K. 137, 146
Bigger, K. 36
Bird, C. 50
Bird, D. M. 50
Bishop, R. S. 33, 82
Bowman, A. 160
Brown-Jeffy, S. 81
Brown, M. 83
Bruno, P. xvi
Burke, C. 138

Cacicio, S. 36
Carrillo, L. W. 63
Cebula, L. 80

Chambers, C. 167
Chen, C. T. 75
Christle, C. A. 136
Clay, M. 18, 106, 107, 111, 113, 114
Collins, P. 10
Colorín Colorado 10
Cooper, J. 81
Cooper-Novack, G. 159
Corey, S. M. 71, 185–187
Cote, P. 36

Dabrowski, J. 128
Day, J. D. 52
DeJulio, S. xviii, 36
Dewey, J. 1
DiCamillo, K. 130
Dixon, C. N. 127
Dorr, R. E. 127
Duke, N. 112
Dutro, E. 158, 161

Echevarria, J. 84, 87, 132, 133
Edmentum 42
Ehert, C. 160
Elish-Piper, L. 126
Evens, K. I. 18

Fantini, M. D. 117
Flores, N. 113
Flores, T. 82
Forster, E. M. 159

232 Author index

Fountas, I. 18
Friedland, E. S. 7
Frost, J. 72

Galan, C. 164
Gallagher, K. 137
Garcia, O. 113
Gavigan, K. 137
Gay, G. 81, 165
Gersten, R. 10
Gickling, E. E. 44
Gonzalez, N. 74, 77
Goodman, K. 111, 169
Goodman, Y. 138, 140
Gordan, E. xvi
Graves, M. F. 137, 147
Greenberg, J. B. 75

Hall, M. A. 127
Hart, C. 80, 157, 159, 162
Hawkins, T. 32, 100
Hayslip, A. 108
Heckelman, R. G. 46
Henk, W. 91
Henry, L. A. xii, xiii, 211
Hernandez, D. J. 136
Herschbach, E. 28
Hershberger, K. 49
Hildebrandt, D. 175
Hill, B. C. 49
Hoefinagel, M. 103
Housman, A. E. 158
Hull, G. 112

Immordino-Yang, M. H. 160, 161
Invernizzi, M. 130

Jacobi, T. 137
Jaeger, L. 164
Johns, B. 126
Johns, J. L. 126
Johnson, A. 139
Johnson, A. B. 79
Johnson, E. J. 79
Johnston, F. R. 130
Junger, S. xvi
Jung, S. B. 79

Keene, E. 66
Khatiwada, I. 136
King, J. xviii, 36, 109
Kleifgen, J. A. 113
Kraemer, J. 75
Kraft, M. 5

Krezmien, M. P. 136
Kuhfeld, M. xvii
Kyle, D. W. 75
Kyvig, D. 80

Ladson-Billings, G. 81, 137, 165
Lagrone, S. 131
Lam, C. B. xvi
Langer, J. 106
Lee, J. 3
Lewis, K. xvii
Linan-Thompson, S. 10
Linn, A. 108
Loeb, S. 5
Love, B. L. 161

Marek, A. 140
Martin, J. 111
Marty, M. A. 80
Massey, D. D. xviii, 36
McCauley, J. 131
McIntyre, E. 74, 75
McLauglin, J. 136
Moll, L. C. 3, 63, 74, 77
Morgan, D. N. 18
Morgan, R. R. xvi
Mueller, P. N. 137
Mulcahy, C. A. 136

Neff, D. 74
Nelson, N. 109
Nessel, D. D. 127
Nguyen, T. D. xvi
Norwick, L. 49

Ogle, D. 9
Olivares, J. 136
O'Malley, C. J. xvi
Osorio, S. 82, 113

Padak, N. 47
Palacios, S. 83
Palma, S. 136
Paris, S. G. 102, 168
Parr, J. 75
Pearson, N. A. 151
Piernas-Davenport, G. 82
Pinnell, S. U. 18
Ponticell, J. xvi
Purcell-Gates, V. 112
Puzzanchera, C. 137

Rashotte, C. A. 151
Rasinski, T. V. 47, 131

Readence, J. E. 139
Robinson, C. 5
Robson, A. L. 103
Roth, K. 128
Ruddell, M. R. 132
Ruptic, C. 49

Samson, L. 80
Scarcella, R. 10
Schueler, B. 5
Schultz, K. 112
Schwartz, S. xviii
Sendak, M. 39
Shanahan, T. 10, 49
Sheldon, S. B. 79
Short, D. 84, 132
Shute, V. J. 3
Sickmund, M. 137
Simille, R. 103
Skelley, D. L. 164
Slavin, R. E. 35, 36
Snow, C. E. 103
Snyder, H. 137
Spivey, N. 109
Stahl, N. xiii, xviii, 36, 211
Stauffer, R. 127, 132
Stevens, M. L. 164
Stine, R. L. 141
Styslinger, M. E. 137
Sum, A. 136
Szuba, L. 3, 7

Tatum, A. W. 137
Templeton, S. 130
Thomas, A. 142, 147
Tichavakunda, A. 164
Tierney, R. J. 139
Toppel, K. 132
Torgesen, J. K. 151
Tovani, C. 137
Truscott, D. M. 7
Tupac. 146, 147

Vacca, J. S. 136
Valerio, M. 18
Van Allen, R. 127
Velez-Ibanez, C. 75
Venezia, A. 164
Vogt, M. E. 84, 87, 127, 132, 133
Vygotsky, L. S. 2, 6, 14, 36, 112, 113

Wagner, R. K. 151
Wallen, M. 115
Wasik, B. A. 6, 35
Watson, D. 138
Weinstein, G. 117
Wigginton, E. 75
Winograd, P. 168

Yang, G. L. 83
Yell, M. C. 136
Young, C. 131

Zimmerman, S. 66

Subject Index

Note: **Bold** page numbers refer to tables and *italic* page numbers refer to figures.

Adult Basic Education programs 19
AIDS crisis, in United States 160
Alessandri, Alexandra 82; *Felíz New Year Ava Gabriela!* 82
Alligators All Around (Sendak) 39
alliteration 38, 39
Alliteration Book List 178
America Reads 17, 20
America Reads Challenge Act xvi, 9
AmeriCorps xvii, 17, 20
Annenberg Institute xvi
Annual Tutor Evaluation (form) 206–207
anticipation guide example **139**
artificial intelligence 26
Ashton-Warner, Sylvia 80; *Teacher* 80
assessment: definition 88; formal 31; formative, 89; informal 31, 89; summative, 89
asset-based approach *see* strength-based approach
attitude toward reading scale 96–98, **97**
authorship cycle 62
autobiography, reading/writing 92–93

Basic Reading Inventory 126
below grade students 9–10
Benjamin: Reading and Beyond 32
Bishop, R. S. 33, 82
Blurb.com 124
bookmaking 56, 61, 62
book sharing 56, 62

Brain Break Resources 173–174
brain breaks 5
brainstorming activity 59
Brown, Monica 83; *Marisol McDonald Doesn't Match* 83
"bubble kids," concept of 103

campus-based America Reads or AmeriCorps program 17
Carson Binder: building reading and writing connections 108–111; the contender 114–115; the narrator 104–105; ongoing teaching points 111–112; the party animal 115; "the Squirrel" 114; the student 105–108; teaching with 112–114; tutor reflection on 105
Center for Research on Education, Diversity, and Excellence (CREDE) 74
Center for School and Student Progress xvii
Chambers, C. 167; *Write Your Way to a Successful Scholarship Essay* 167
Code of Ethics for the National Tutoring Association 23
collaborative learning 12
Colorín Colorado 10
community-based tutoring xv
comprehension 35; identifying key points in text 50; LEA 132–133; reading 49–50
Comprehensive Test of Phonological Processing, 2nd edition (CTOPP-2) 151

consonant-vowel-consonant (CVC): spelling pattern 43; words 43
content mastery 31
contextual factors 3
COVID-19 quarantine 10, 125, 126
Cricket Magazine 130
critical witness 161
cross-age tutoring programs 18
Cultural Relevance Rubric 84
culturally intentional pedagogy 81–82; creating supportive learning environments 83–87; diverse text selections 82–83
Culturally Responsive Teaching 81
culturally responsive tutoring approaches 165; individualized instruction 167–168; meaningful relationships 165–166; self-efficacy 166–167
curricular connections 15
Custom Cars, in Hot Rod Magazine 52–54

Daily Word Ladder 131
Deans for Impact 20
Department of Juvenile Justice (DJJ) 137
DiCamillo, Kate 130; *Mercy Watson* 130
Directed Reading-Thinking Activity (DR-TA) 132
dissemination activities 62
During-Reading Strategies 146–147
dyslexia 150, 151, 152

echo reading 46
editor's workshop *56*, 59–61
Elkonin Boxes 39–40, *40*
English Learners (EL) 8
evaluation 31–32; food labels 120; program 15
Every One Graduates Center xvii
Every Tutee an Author approach: background research 58–59; bookmaking 61; book sharing 62; editor's worshop 59–61; experience stage 56–58; writng 59
experiential-based learning 63

face-to-face tutoring sessions 12
federal work-study program xvii, 20
first-generation college-bound students 164
five-finger method 44, *45*
Flores, T. 82; *mirror* and *window* books 82
fluency: echo reading 46; LEA 131–132; modeling fluent reading 45; neurological impress method 46; repeated reading 46–47, **47**
fluent reading 45
foundational skills, instructional strategies 37–38
Foxfire 75, 79

Fry Instant Phrases 131
Funds of Knowledge: content connections 78–79; contextualized language and literacy development 77–78; definition 3; instructional planning 76; inventory matrix 77, **77**; multigenerational family histories 79–80; naturalistic tutoring 73; relationship to Language Experience Approach 63

G.E.D. preparation programs 19
Gersten, R. 10
Get your mouth ready technique (GYMR) 107
Gickling, E. E. 44
Glass Poetry Journal, issue of 161
Gradepower Learning 20
Guided Reading Framework 18

Hall, M. A. 127
Hart, C. 80, 157, 159, 162; *The Oral History Workshop: Collect and Celebrate the Life Stories of Your Family and Friends* 80
Hawk, Tony 66
Hawkins, T. 32, 100; *Benjamin: Reading and Beyond* 32, 100
Henk, William 91
high-dosage tutoring 5
high-impact practices: building strong relationships 7; group size 6; high-dosage tutoring 5; high-quality instructional materials (HQIM) 8–9; providing structured tutoring sessions 6–7
high-impact tutoring 4, 4–5
high-interest activities 67–70
high-quality instructional materials (HQIM) 8–9, 15
Hip-hop music 141
Hoefnagel, M. 103
Holly Jolly Christmas (Jake) 124–127, *125*
home and community literacy 116–118; advertising analysis 120–121; authentic literacy contexts 121–122; evaluating food labels 120; resources for 118–119; through youth organizations 122–123
Huntington Learning Centers 20

Illinois Rules of the Road Workbook, 122
Immordino-Yang, M. H. 160, 161
Indiana Department of Education 38
individualized education plan (IEP) 150
individualized instruction 167–168
inductive outline 50–52, *51*
INFOhio *8*, 9
Institute of Education Sciences (IES) 88
instructional elements 11, 14

Subject index

instructional texts 32–33
Insurance Corporation of British Columbia: *Learn to Drive Smart: Your Guide to Driving Safely* 122
In the Margins award sites 138

Johnson, Angela 139; *The First Part Last* 139
joint productive activity 75

Key Vocabulary Approach *see* organic reading
KidTime Story 83
KLEW 49
K-12 schools 123
Kumon Centers 20
K-W-L chart 9, 49, 177

LakeshoreLearning.com 44
Language Experience Approach (LEA) *128, 129*; building awareness 63–64; composition 64; experiential-based learning 63; learner-generated texts results 128–129; permanence 64–65; reading development and intervention method 127; steps for 127–128
learning environment 13–14
learning gaps 10–11
learning objective(s) 27–28
learning theories: addressing learning gaps 10–11; below grade level students 9–10; contextual factors 3; high-impact practices 5–9; high-impact tutoring *4*, 4–5; Multilingual Learners 10; programmatic decision making 11–15; programmatic guidelines 15–16; strength-based (or asset-based) approach 2–3; Vygotsky's Zone of Proximal Development 2
letter-sound correspondence 42–43
LGBTQ+ teenagers 157–162
Literacy behind Bars 137
Literacy Intervention & Enrichment (LIE) program: advent of 125–126; comprehension 132; Directed Reading-Thinking Activity (DR-TA) 132; fluency 131–132; Survey, Question, Predict, Read, Respond, and Summarize (SQP2RS) 132–133; text selection to build reading interest 130; Word Work 130–131
literacy skills: fluency 44–47; inductive outline 50–52, **51**; instructional strategies to develop foundational skills 37–38; National Reading Panel Report 35; "Nation at Risk–Round 2" 35; phonemic awareness 39–41; phonics instruction 41–44; phonological awareness 38–39; reading comprehension 49–50; summarization 52–54; vocabulary development 47–49

Making Sense of Educational Assessment Fact Sheet 88
Management Council of the Ohio Education Computer Network 9
Martin, J. 111; *The Edge of Extinction* 111
materials or technology section 28–29
miscue analysis 111, 140, 142–145, 148
miscue analysis coding sheet 145
modeling 2, 14, 36, 37, 45, 54, 60, 108, 142
motivation 3, 7, 11, 26, 29, 36, 76
multilingual learners (MLs) 10; contextualized language and learning 83–87; culturally intentional pedagogy 81–87; Funds of Knowledge 75–80; instructional planning 76; organic reading 80–81; ReadWriteThink. og 30, 83, *84*; SIOP model 84–85, **85–87**; supportive learning environments 83–87; on tutees 87; tutoring for 87

National Assessment of Educational Progress (NAEP) 137
National Center for Educaion Statistics xvii
National Reading Panel Report 35
The National Student Support Accelerator 4
A Nation at Risk xvi
"Nation at Risk–Round 2" 35
naturalistic authoring approaches: benefits of naturalistic tutoring 72–73; Language Experience Approach (LEA) 63–65; out of school vacation time 70–72; response journals 65–67; tutee an author 55–62
nearby history 80
neurological impress method 46
No Child Left Behind xvi

online tutoring 18
on-set/rime with word families 39
The Oral History Workshop: Collect and Celebrate the Life Stories of Your Family and Friends (Hart) 80
oral reading fluency 35
organic reading 80–81
Orton-Gillingham Academy approach (OG) 152–155
Osorio, S. 82, 113; *mirror* and *window* books 82
out-of-school-time (OST) spaces 157

Parent Permission Form 195
partnership 7, 21, 123, 137, 140, 160
Partnership for Student Success xvii
PATHS to Tutor Act 20
peer tutoring 18
Perfect Storm xvi
personal or community photo guide 48

Subject index

phoneme manipulation 40–41
phoneme substitution 40, *41*
phonemic awareness 35; Elkonin Boxes 39–40, *40*; phoneme manipulation 40–41; phoneme substitution 40, *41*; in Word Work 130
phonetic decoding, elements of 41, **41**
phonics continuum 42, *42*, 43
phonics instruction 35; elements of phonetic decoding 41, **41**; letter-sound correspondence 41–42; moving through phonics continuum 43; phonics continuum 42, *42*; sight-word vocabulary 43–44; teaching CVC words 43
phonological awareness: alliteration 39; on-set/rime with word families 39; phonological sensitivity 38; syllabification 39; word level identification 38
phonological sensitivity 38
picture walk technique 106
Piernas-Davenport, Gail 82; *Shanté Keys and the New Year's Peas* 82
pK-12 students 9, 35
The Poor Scholar's Soliloquy 71, 185–187
problem-solving 12, 14
Program Administration Resources, 211
program evaluation 11, 15
programmatic decision making: curricular connections 15; delivery mode 12; dosage 12; group size 12–13; instructional elements 14; learning environment 13–14; location 13; program evaluation 15; tutor selection 13
programmatic guidelines 15–16

reader response approach 65–66
reading: autobiography 92–93; Carson Binder 108–111; comprehension 35; echo 46; modeling fluent 45; oral reading fluency 35; organic 80–81; phonemic awareness 35; phonics 35; pillars of *see* literacy skills; repeated 46–47, **47**; tutor's interview 91–92; twenty high-interest 67–70; with Ty 140–145; vocabulary 35
Reading Attitude Scale 190–192
reading interest inventory 7, 81
Reading Interest Inventory (instrument) 175–176
reading log 33
Reading Merit Badge Workbook 123
Reading Recovery xvi
Reading Strategy Inventory: after reading my tutee 99; before reading my tutee 98; during reading my tutee 99
Reading Wars xviii, 36

Reading Without Walls platform 83
reading work journals 108, reflections 31–32
reading writing connections 108–111
reading-writing-sharing process 56
ReadWriteThink.org 30, 83, *84*
reinforcement stage 30–31
relationships: building strong 7; developing through interview process (instrument) 138–139; meaningful 165–166; tutoring as helping 21–22
repeated reading 46–47, **47**
response journals 65–67
retrospective miscue analysis (RMA) 137, 140, 146
review 26–27

San Diego Quick Assessment: analysis guidelines 94–96; assessment administration 93–94
San Diego Quick Assessment Record Form 188–189
save the last word for me technique 147
savvy shopper 48
Say Something strategy 146
scaffolding 2, 14, 36, 37, 44, 94, 109
Science of Reading xviii, 35
Scouts BSA 122, 123
Sears Roebuck Catalog 116
self-efficacy 155–156, 166–167
shared writing of a sentence 108
Sheltered Instruction Observation Protocol (SIOP) Model 84–85, **85–87**
sight-word vocabulary 43–44, in Word Work 130
simultaneous oral spelling (SOS) 153, 155
Special Day Class (SDC) teacher 134
State of Victoria Department of Education 2
Stine, R.L. 141; *The Confession* 141
strength-based approach 2–3, 108, 112
structured tutoring sessions 6–7
students' strengths 158–160
Success for All xvi
summarization 52–54
Survey, Question, Predict, Read, Respond, and Summarize (SQP2RS) 132–133
syllabification 38, 39
Sylvan Learning 20

Teacher Referral Form 193–194
Techniques of Tutoring course 20
Test of Word Reading Efficiency, 2nd edition (TOWRE 2) 151
Thomas, Angie 142, 147; *Concrete Rose* 142, 147; *The Hate You Give* 142

238 Subject index

TOWRE 2 post-tutoring 155
translanguaging 113
TRIO Programs 163–164
Tupac 146, 147; *The Rose that Grew from Concrete* 146, 147
tutee: background research 56, 58–59; bookmaking 56, 61; book sharing 56, 62; definition 18–19; editor's workshop 56, 59–61; experience stage 56, 56–58; feedback 22; interest inventory 90–91; writing 56, 59
Tutee Attendance Record 202–203
Tutee Writing Evaluation Checklist 183–184
tutor: assessments guiding intervention 150–152; creating tutoring plan 152–155; diverse student populations 149–150; preparing to 137–138; reader self-efficacy 155–156; reading interview 91–92; reflective journal 100–101; selection 13
Tutor Application (form) 196–198
Tutor Interview Form 199–201
Tutor Self-Evauation (form) 204–205
Tutor Training Course Outline 208–209
tutorial lesson 25; content mastery 31; evaluation/reflections 31–32; learning objective(s) 27–28; materials or technology section 28–29; motivation 29; procedure 30; reinforcement stage 30–31; review 26–27; tutorial lesson plan **27**
tutorial program: finding assistance 24; guidelines for tutors 22–24; instructional texts 32–33; locations for tutoring services 19–21; prototypic chart 33, **33**; tutees 18–19; tutorial lesson 25–26; tutoring as helping relationship 21–22; types of tutoring 17–18
Tutoring Manual and Training Topics 210

Tutors' Friends: Strategies, Learning Games, and Instructional Books 54, 179–182
Tutor's reflective journal 100–101

University of Illinois Chicago 23
Upward Bound programs 163–165, 168

vacation time activity 70–72
virtual tutoring 12
vocabulary development 35; personal or community photo guide 48; savvy shopper 48; words where I live 48–49

Washington Office of Superintendent of Public Instruction 77
What's Climate Change?, National Geographic 52, 54
word ladders 131
word level identification 38
word sorts 130–131
Words Their Way 131
Word Work 130–131
work-arounds 103
Write It Out session 158
writing: activities for tutoring 67–70; autobiography 92–93; Carson Binder 108–111; tutee an author 56, 59

YALSA book awards 138
You Are Welcome here: Supporting Newcomer Students in Dearborn, MI 10

Zone of Proximal Development (ZPD) (Vygotsky) 2, 6, 14, 112, 113
Zoom 158

For Product Safety Concerns and Information please contact our EU
representative GPSR@taylorandfrancis.com
Taylor & Francis Verlag GmbH, Kaufingerstraße 24, 80331 München, Germany